THE GARDEN OF MYSTIC LOVE

*The Origin and Formation
of the Great Sufi Orders*

THE GARDEN OF MYSTIC LOVE

Volume I

*The Origin and Formation
of the Great Sufi Orders*

Gregory Blann
Sheikh Muhammad Jamal al-Jerrahi

Foreword by

Robert Frager, Ph.D.
Sheikh Ragip al-Jerrahi

Albion
Andalus
Boulder, Colorado
2022

*"The old shall be renewed,
and the new shall be made holy."*
— Rabbi Avraham Yitzhak Kook

Albion-Andalus, Inc.
P. O. Box 19852
Boulder, CO 80308
www.albionandalus.com

Design and layout by Albion-Andalus Books
Cover design by Sari Wisenthal-Shore
Cover illustration of Yusuf listening to music played by the handmaidens of Zuleika, from a manuscript of Yusuf u Zuleika by Jami, 1540.
Author photo by Nicola D'antona.

ISBN: 978-0692228616 (Paperback)
ISBN: 978-1-953220-16-5 (Hardcover)

This book is dedicated to
all lovers of Truth

CONTENTS

SECTION III

The Middle Period: The Formation of the Great Sufi Orders

* *Indicates sheikhs in the Halveti-Jerrahi silsila.*
** *Indicates founding pirs in the order.*

NOTE ON TRANSLITERATION

As THIS WORK makes extensive use of Arabic and Turkish words, a glossary of foreign terms has been included at the end of the book. Because there is no universally accepted system of transliterating Arabic into English characters, I attempt to employ as many familiar spellings of Arabic words in the text as possible. I use the character ' to represent the Arabic letter *ayn*, as in *'aleikum*, and an apostrophe for the *hamza*, as in the word *Qur'an*. The letter *dhal* (pronounced somewhere between *zhal*, *dhal* and *thal*) is sometimes represented as a *dh,* as in *dhikr* (spelled *zikr* in Turkish), and at other times with a "z" as in *Azim*. Where the spelling of the Arabic preposition *al* (meaning "the" or "of the") takes on the sound of the letter which follows it, instead of the "l" sound, I generally spell the phrase as it sounds; for instance, Nureddin rather than Nur al-Din ("Light of the Faith").

In many cases where the use of the correct Arabic or Turkish plural transforms a relatively familiar word into a less recognizable one, I simplify the spelling by using the letter "*s*" as a suffix on a number of foreign words. I retain the original plural form in certain cases, such as the word *awliya* ("saints"), the plural of *waliyullah* ("saint" or, literally, "friend of Allah"), *hufaz,* the plural of *hafiz* (one who has memorized the entire Qur'an), and *turuq,* the plural of *tariqa* (the mystic path of Islam—a Sufi Order). Conversely, with terms such as *khulafa*, the plural of the Arabic word *khalifa* (Turkish: *halife,* meaning "representative"), and *ilahiler*, the plural of the Turkish word *ilahi* ("divine," or a dervish hymn), I simply form the plural with an *s*. As the spelling "*Caliph*" is widely used to designate the Muslim rulers in a direct line of succession from the Prophet Muhammad, I adopt that familiar spelling where appropriate. I also favor some spellings which more closely approximate their pronunciation, such as *waliyullah* and *Rasulullah* (rather than *wali Allah* and *Rasul Allah*), but have retained the traditional spelling of the word: "sheikh" (pronounced *shaykh*). The Arabic word *masjid* and the anglicized word *mosque* are used interchangeably.

As this volume is part of a larger work on the historical development and teachings of an order based in Turkey and disseminated in Turkish, rather than in Arabic, I occasionally defer to Turkish usage in the spelling of certain terms; or in some cases, I use the Arabic form during the early pre-Turkish period and switch to its Turkish spelling when events became fully centered in the Turkish world. A case in point is the Arabic word *khalwa*, which is *halvet* in Turkish. The word means "spiritual retreat," and is the name from which the Khalwati Order (later called the Halveti Order) is derived. Another significant set of words in this class are the Arabic words for the four levels of Reality: *shar'ia* (*shariah*), *tariqa, haqiqa* and *ma'rifa*. The popular Turkish forms, whose spellings I primarily adopt in this book, are: *shariat, tarikat, hakikat* and *marifat*.

When the characters of the Turkish language were changed, during the 1920's, from Arabic script to Romanized letters, several letters were introduced which differ from English either in appearance or pronunciation. Three of these, c, ç, and ş, are generally replaced in this book with their English equivalents. The Turkish "*c*" is pronounced as an English "*j*"; thus we have used the anglicized spelling, *Jerrahi*, rather than the proper Turkish *Cerrahi*. The Turkish "ç" and "ş" are pronounced in English respectively "*ch*" and "*sh*"; thus the spelling *ashk* (mystic love) rather than *aşk,* except when we are quoting an entire line of Turkish or a Turkish book title. The Turkish letter ğ is pronounced somewhere between a swallowed "y", (place comma before end quote mark)a silent letter and an elongated vowel. For example, the name of the Halveti Pir, Yiğitbaşı Veli, is pronounced closer to "Yee-itbashe Veli" but is sometimes spelled Yighitbashi Wali in English works; I use: Yiğitbashi.

In order to spare the reader any further linguistic details, I will allow the examples above to suffice as general indications of my approach. Otherwise, I ask the reader's forgiveness in advance for any mistakes either in the handling of foreign words or in the general text of the manuscript itself. A glossary of Arabic and other foreign words is provided at the end of the book.

ACKNOWLEDGMENTS

I WOULD LIKE TO EXPRESS my deepest thanks to all those who helped and offered encouragement in the writing of this book, whether in the form of providing information, translations or help with the editing of the manuscript. These include: Safer Dal, Ömer Tuğrul Inançer, Ibrahim Akkökler, Tosun Bayrak, Rabia Terri Harris, Ragip Robert Frager, Reb Zalman Schachter-Shalomi, Salik Schwartz, Nur Lex Hixon, Amina Teslima Ortiz Graham, Fariha Friedrich, and Haydar Friedrich.

To the several persons who provided invaluable help with the translation of Turkish source materials and poems, I wish again to extend my most heartfelt appreciation. These include: Kaan and Ayşegül Erdal (who graciously translated material on the ancient Sufis and Halvetis), Gönül Cengiz (who generously volunteered to translate from several books on the Halveti pirs and Jerrahi khalifas) and Sixtina Friedrich (who skillfully translated a number of Turkish ilahis and allowed the use of her research papers on the Halveti masters). Much of this material has never before appeared in English. Though the author is in most cases responsible for the final English form of these translations, access to the material would not have been possible without their kind help. On occasion, the author has partially re-translated materials drawn from poems or other translated quotations of Sufi masters in published English works, while acknowledging the contribution of the original translators.

A special note in this regard concerns the ilahi translations of Sheikh Nur (Lex Hixon), who passed from the earthly realm on All Saints' Day, November 1, 1995. From 1991 to 1994, the author collaborated with Sheikh Nur on approximately fifty English settings of Turkish mystic hymns or ilahis. Some of these hymns, which are presently sung in a number of Jerrahi dervish circles throughout America, are quoted in the course of this book with Sheikh Nur's full permission and blessings. In a very few cases, where Sheikh Nur's adaptations freely depart from the original text, I provide fresh renderings from the primary Turkish source.

Finally, loving thanks is due my wife, Sylvia, who reviewed the various drafts of the working manuscript, offering suggestions as to editorial and grammatical improvements. Thanks also to Abdul Malik Massie, Abdus Salaam Manakas, Fatih Tatlilioğlü, Sipko den Böer, Habiba al-Jerrahi, Abdul Karim Chisti, Habiba Ashki and Mahmud Kabir for all their help and encouragement. We also very much appreciate Peri Fezier, who made available rare photographs of her relative, Fahreddin Efendi

The majority of the photographs and works of art used in this book are in the public domain. Permission has been sought and credit given in all cases where the photographer or artist was known; any omission in this regard is strictly inadvertent and will be corrected as soon as we are notified.

LIST OF ILLUSTRATIONS

FOREWORD

Robert Frager, Ph.D.
Sheikh Ragip al-Jerrahi

THE SUFI TRADITION has existed for over a thousand years, and Sufism has spread throughout the globe to a wide variety of countries and cultures. Sufism has continued to develop throughout its history, building on the wisdom and experience of generations of Sufi masters. The Sufi tradition has existed for centuries in Arabia, Iran, India, China, Indonesia, Africa, and Eastern Europe. Today Sufism has spread, along with Islam, throughout Europe and in both North and South America.

This book is a product of the growth of Sufism in the West. Sheikh Muhammad Jamal is an American-born Sufi. He has studied, practiced, and taught Sufism for many years. He is a "home-grown," second generation Sufi teacher, who sees Sufism with modern, American eyes and presents the tradition through this perspective. He has presented a wealth of information in this book, much of which has not been available in English until now.

Muhammad Jamal's history of Sufism is a valuable tool for all Westerners who practice Sufism. It is said that every generation must rewrite history, that each era brings its own concerns and perspectives to viewing and assessing the past. This is true of Sufi history as well. Those of us who follow this path are obliged to examine our roots, and explore what is most viable and effective for those of us living in the West today.

Blind imitation of the past is certainly no solution. At one extreme, there are some Westerners who insist on wearing Bedouin clothing and imitating other aspects of Middle Eastern culture. On the other hand there are others who try to ignore the past and who feel free to make up their own Sufi rituals and practices, as though modern "creativity" can somehow substitute for the spiritual wisdom and insight of generations of great Sufi masters.

Muhammad Jamal provides a look at Sufi history, imparting inspiration and information for serious students and practitioners of Sufism. He is an amateur in the best sense of the word, someone who loves his or her field of study. Coincidentally, the Halveti-Jerrahi term for someone formally beginning this path is *muhib*, which also means one who loves the Sufi tradition.

Muhammad Jamal is not a detached scholar with only an intellectual acquaintance with Sufism. He is a practicing Muslim, a dervish, and a Sufi teacher, a man who loves his tradition and who has dedicated himself to exploring deeply its history. This book represents years of study and inquiry.

What is Sufism? In any discussion of Sufism it is important to remember the tremendous breadth and long history of this tradition. There are major exceptions to virtually any general statement one might make about Sufi beliefs or practices. Different teachers have emphasized extremely diverse principles and practices, often to the point of seeming contradiction.

Sufism is generally described as the mystical core of Islam. However, some Sufis also describe Sufism as the universal mystical dimension in all religions. My own teacher, the late Sheikh Muzaffer Ozak, said religion is a tree whose roots are outward religious observances. The branches of the tree are the mystical traditions, and the fruit is Truth.

The conventionally religious tend to focus on the outer modes of practice. They believe in God, live moral and ethical lives, and practice prayer and other forms of worship. For the Sufis this is only the beginning. When I first met Sheikh Muzaffer, he told me, "It is not difficult to learn the outer forms of prayer. But the goal of Sufism is to develop a *heart* that can pray, and that is a real achievement."

When my second Sufi teacher, Safer Efendi, was asked if one had to be a Muslim to be a dervish, he replied, "Yes, but one has to be a 'real Muslim.'" This is not what most people understand to be Muslim. Most people think a Muslim is someone who prays five times a day. A real Muslim is someone who is in constant prayer.

Foreword

The Sufis have explored the depth and breadth of human experience by beginning with the fundamental understanding that we are all underdeveloped. They view human development in an evolutionary perspective. As part of life on this planet, we evolved from mineral to vegetable, animal, and human states. Sufi masters remind us human development can continue to evolve to still higher, spiritual states. However, we are all caught by contradictory forces within ourselves. We all possess a fundamental drive toward further inner evolution, but our spiritual desires are countered by our biological drives and egocentric motives. Most people do not even recognize this inner conflict. They seek to escape through drugs or alcohol, or through television and other entertainments designed to keep themselves distracted and asleep.

My teachers have explained that the goal of Sufism is to become a real Muslim, and the goal of a real Muslim is to become a real human being. A real human being is someone who never forgets God, who knows he or she is in God's presence at every moment, in every activity. A real human being is also someone who is dedicated to honest self-evaluation, to seeing oneself clearly and transforming inner shortcomings.

These two tendencies provide a basic balance in Sufism, like two wings on a bird or the two wheels of a two-wheeled cart. Both are necessary or else we will simply go around in circles and get nowhere. The practice of Sufism serves to cleanse our insides through self-examination and sincere service, and also to open our hearts and foster in ourselves greater compassion, faith, and love of God.

The following are some fundamental Sufi principles:

1. There are as many ways to reach God as there are individuals. And all paths to God involve outer service and inner transformation.

2. Sufi practice is aimed at bringing about the cleansing and awakening of the heart. Truth cannot be understood by the head alone; it requires the intelligence of an awakened heart.

3. The heart is a divine temple, the house of the divine spark which is within each of us. When we truly understand this truth, we will treat everyone with compassion and kindness, and dedicate ourselves to serving God through serving others.

4. A teacher is essential on this path. True inner transformation requires a guide. A Sufi teacher is like a physician, who has the training, knowledge, and remedies to treat our inner illnesses. Those with no medical knowledge who try to treat themselves have a fool for a physician.

5. Love is one of the great qualities developed in Sufi practice. The capacity to love comes from inner work and expresses itself in sincere service. All love is founded on divine love, and love of the beauty of this world is meant to lead to deeper love of God.

INTRODUCTION
TO VOLUME I

SUFISM IS THE MYSTICAL TRADITION of divine love and unity. Whether in subtle or manifest form, it has existed in our world as long as conscious beings have inhabited it. Between the seventh and tenth centuries CE, according to the Western calendar, the historical spiritual movement known to the world as Sufism developed under the aegis of Islam, in light of the deeply self-transcendent, unitive teachings revealed through the Prophet Muhammad (peace and blessings be upon him). Before his time, this same primordial wisdom was the spiritual life-blood and sustenance of the ancient prophets, realized sages, saints and *hanifs* of pre-Islamic times. Its central proclamation is that there exists but One Reality, which lovingly emanates and continually sustains this vast and intelligent universe, a realm of physical existence which is never separate from its Divine Creative Source.

From Arabia, the birthplace of the Prophet Muhammad, the mystical tradition of Islam, known as *tasawwuf* or Sufism, spread to Iraq and its capital, Baghdad. There, the first major Sufi orders arose in the time of Junayd (d. 910 CE). From Baghdad and other centers, Sufism and Islam spread to Central Asia, North Africa, India, Anatolia and Spain. This book offers a history of Islamic mysticism up to the founding of the great Sufi orders, including biographies of many of its major saints, founding pirs, and the trends which have developed out of their teachings.

Sufism has seen a tremendous growth in popularity in the United States in recent years, both in its traditional Islamic context and in its universal, ecumenical form. Before 1970, there were scarcely a few dozen English books on the subject of Sufism. Today, publications number in the thousands, as Western interest in Sufism—the religion of the heart—continues to grow.

Beyond the horizon of biography, this book seeks to unfold the path of mystic love as it passes through various phases in history, each stage timelessly representing a *makam*, or station, on the path of spiritual realization. By "mystic love" we mean to indicate non-dual love, in which the soul awakens from its sense of separation into its own Essential Source, becoming the Beloved which it loves. Thus, mystic love is not fixated on any material object of love, nor a remote deity, but is a subjectless, objectless expression of union within the One All-Pervading Reality. This love comes from God, is for God, transpires through God, and operates within the Oneness of God, or Allah—the Sole Reality.

According to Sufi teachings, all the divine attributes, the stations of love, and the souls of human beings, which co-exist in this one many-splendored Reality, emerge from the celestial realms—from the Garden of Divine Essence. As the Turkish Sufi poet, Niyazi Misri, wrote (referring to the human soul):

This nightingale, stranger to space and time, has come here from the Garden of Pure Essence. That abode is simply the Friend, all Divine Face, gazing, gazing.[1]

The Garden of Mystic Love is a Sufi metaphor which describes this one vast spectrum of existence. From the eternal realms, Allah Most High brings forth the temporal life of the world, replete with conscious souls, who are spiritually nurtured and sustained by divine guidance and the realization of unity. These guiding sacred revelations to humanity are poured out abundantly over the centuries through the hearts and minds of authentic divine messengers and prophets. According to the Qur'an, at least one of them has been sent to every nation on earth.

The Divine Oneness is proclaimed by the Prophet Abraham; the sacred law is revealed to Moses and other noble messengers, known and unknown; the way of divine love, forgiveness, and mystic union is revealed through the Messiah Jesus. Finally, the cycle of divine revelation is brought to its fullest fruition by the Seal of Prophets, Muhammad, upon him be peace. Through the Prophet Muhammad is revealed the quintessential teaching of unity, succinctly formulated in the

---

1 From Nur Lex Hixon's English setting of the Turkish ilahi, *Ey Garip Bülbül.*

Introduction

Arabic words, *La ilaha illallah,* meaning approximately: "there is nothing except Divine Reality." The power of this illuminating principle, the radiant well-spring of the mystic tradition, was spiritually transmitted by the Prophet Muhammad to his son-in-law, Hazrat 'Ali, and indeed flows to all conscious humanity.

After the passing of Muhammad, what can be called the Sufi tradition, in its historical Islamic setting, first assumed the form of rigorous ascetic practice and poverty, an austere attitude of God-fearing repentance and retreat from the ways of the world. This is exemplified in the lives of such early Sufis as Uways al-Qarani and Ibrahim Adham. With Rabi'a al-'Adawiyya, the heart of Sufism begins to further reveal itself as a path of pure love for Allah, divested of all secondary desires, such as the hope of paradise and avoidance of hell. The ecstatic states of union experienced by Bayazid Bistami and other "intoxicated" Sufis mark a further tendency toward divine Self-discovery in the consciousness of the Sufi mystics, a trend sealed by the martyrdom of Mansur al-Hallaj and Shams-i- Tabriz.

In the Sufi understanding, it was not Mansur, but the Divine Source that ecstatically cried out through him: "I am the Absolute Truth!" Nor was it Rabi'a who offered supplications of unconditional love to her Lord; it was pure worship, without one who prays. This passionate pursuit of divine love, beyond all duality, was fervently celebrated by such mystic poets as Mevlana Jalaluddin Rumi and Yunus Emre, and incorporated into the mystic orders in many ways, including the ecstatic ceremonies of Divine Remembrance *(dhikr).*

The path of mystic Self-realization and boundless love is the spiritual high road, the great promise of religion, the soul's open door to union with Truth. Beyond all divisions and creeds, love is our innermost nature, our Divine Essence. As Hazrat Inayat Khan has most beautifully written: "You are love. You come from love; you are made by love; you cannot cease to love."[2]

It was with the intoxication of love for the light that the moth, circling around the candle, sacrificed everything and threw itself

2 Inayat Khan, *The Complete Sayings of Hazrat Inayat Khan,* 214.

into the flames. This same fire of love purifies and illuminates the human heart, cooking that which is raw and radically transforming it. We, too, are invited by the words of the *Mevlud* to draw near and feel its intoxicating power:

> Come close now, true dervishes of love, to the very fire of Divine Love, which burns in the Prophet's noble heart as he ascends through the heavenly spheres to the most intimate Presence of Allah. This same fire of love will now burn within you, for such is the highest mystic teaching of Islam.[3]

---

3 Lex Hixon, *Atom From the Sun of Knowledge,* 71. (adapted from the *Mevlud.*)

SECTION ONE

Mystic Love: The Heart of Islam

Renouncing Paradise for the Sake of Love

FROM THE VERY BEGINNING of human life on earth, the door of wisdom has always been open to humanity. For thousands of years, spiritual guides, seen and unseen, have assisted the citizens of this world in their search for Truth, self-realization and meaningful experience, especially in the beautiful way of unconditional love.

According to the mystical tradition, when our primordial parents, the noble Adam and Eve, first set their feet upon this earth, the profound mystery of love began to unfold. As the Qur'an affirms,[1] Allah Most High originally taught all the divine names to Adam in paradise. There, the eternal souls "in the loins of Adam" each enacted a pledge—in advance of their manifestation as individual souls—to uphold the sovereignty of the Divine Truth on earth.

The immortal soul of Adam dwelt timelessly in the eternal dimension where the essence knows no separation from the One, his spirit immersed in great joy. Eventually, according to the hidden tradition, Adam perceived Allah's creation of Love and asked to be allowed to experience it. But he was told by the Source of Love, "To experience love, you would have to leave the bliss of paradise; to truly know love involves also knowing the pain of separation, longing and tears, as well as the transformation of these into joy. None of these experiences are possible here in the realm of paradise where no sorrow exists, but only the constant joy and beauty of divine intimacy."

Upon hearing these words, the noble Adam (peace be upon him), in accordance with the divine will, yearned to fully experience the mystery of love. He ate of the forbidden tree of knowledge and

---

1 Qur'an 2:31.

abandoned the repose of the Garden, his consciousness flooded with the perspective of duality; and the one archetypal human was now two. Thus, our primordial father and mother, Adam and Eve, emerged from paradise to dwell on earth.

According to the Qur'an,[2] the male and female are twin souls, two halves of one primordial self. Emanated by the Divine Breath, these timeless souls arose on earth, covered with external bodies made of the fabric of the planet, while inwardly they existed as channels of divine creativity, blessed with a cornucopia of possible attunements of consciousness.

Sura Tin (chapter 96 of the Qur'an) states that the human being, in essence, represents the highest of forms coming forth from the Divine Source, but, while living on earth, is disposed toward the very lowest states of consciousness. There is an inevitable condition of spiritual forgetfulness, a drunkenness which affects the soul when it incarnates on earth. The body of flesh and blood is imbued with a dense quality called *khannas*, which tends to pull one into physicality and ego-consciousness, tying the soul to the world and to its desires through the sensual inclinations of the carnal self *(nafs al-ammara)*.

Such was the situation facing the newly incarnated bodily consciousness of Adam and Eve. In the pursuit of love on earth, they merged in sexual union, and found satisfaction in their newly-gained autonomy. In their progeny, they beheld the wondrous expression of their newly manifested procreative abilities. As absorption in the consciousness of the physical world began to predominate the couple's awareness, the glorious inner light of their pristine spiritual natures gradually faded, the clear and expansive perception of Reality clouding over as a fogbank might enshroud an eagle in flight.

As the sense of Divine Nearness gradually receded from their awareness over successive generations, a feeling of isolated individuality took root in humanity, thoroughly displacing the intimate, natural self-identification with the Divine Breath of Life. Eternal awareness gave way to the limited perspective of

2 Qur'an 4:1.

the personal *nafs* (the living, breathing, "separate" self or ego), a condition in which the Divine Essence *(Zat-ullah)* is covered with as many as 70,000 veils of illusion. According to the perennial wisdom of all the world's authentic mystical traditions, beneath the mortal covering of self is none other than pure Divine Essence, a hidden treasure which has willed to express itself in physical form.

Those who are mainly familiar with the biblical account in Genesis may be accustomed to thinking of Adam and Eve simply as culpable agents in the saga which produced humanity's fallen state; however, the Qur'an contains a notable further teaching on this point. It adds that, through divine foresight, Allah taught our primordial parents how to pray and reconnect while they were still in paradise. Then much later, on earth, Adam and Eve realized the extent to which they had become alienated from their own Essential Source. They turned and earnestly prayed with tears of repentance, and again found spiritual access to the divine well-spring at the core of their being.

In this way, Adam became the Father of the Way of Mystic Return and is counted as the first in a vast lineage of noble messengers on the path of divine love and unity. And through Eve was transmitted—along with the reproduction of the physical body and its *nafs*—the holy light of compassionate motherhood, a spiritual quality of being so pregnant with exaltation that the Seal of Prophecy, the beloved Muhammad, was moved to proclaim: "Paradise lies at the feet of the mother."

Thus humanity, the noble earthly representative of the One Essential Reality, who emanates from the light of the Divine Essence, has collectively chosen to dwell absorbed in its *nafs*, in a narrow "man-made" world of its own fashioning. Caught in the repetitious and alienating thought-patterns of its primordial ancestors, most human beings remain only dimly and tenuously aware of their exalted nature and spiritual potentialities. Those who awaken from this self-imposed and conditioned dream of separation are the sages and wise heralds of divine revelation who, in every age and culture, resound the message of unity and give voice to the cry of the Divine Beloved: "Return to your Lord!

Consciously reunite with your own True Source from Whom you have never in reality been separate, and live from that authentic knowledge of Self."

According to the Holy Qur'an, as many as 124,000 prophets, or divine messengers have taught the path of mystic return to unity for as long as this earth has been populated by human beings. Only twenty-eight of these exalted prophets are mentioned by name in the Qur'an, including: Abraham, the father of two great spiritual nations, Moses of Israel, the Messiah Jesus, and Muhammad of Arabia, may divine peace and blessings be upon all of them. The Qur'an specifies[3] that no major world community has been devoid of these worthy bearers of divine revelation. Thus, we must assume that great figures, such as Buddha and other sages of India, China, and the rest of the world are all implicitly included in this vast tradition of perennial divine wisdom and self-transcendence.

According to the Prophet Muhammad, the message of Islam is precisely a continuation and clear summation of the rich legacy of teachings brought by all these holy messengers and mystic saints of the past, who affirmed the oneness of the soul with its Lord. In its pristine doctrine, uncontaminated by sectarian interpretations, historical Islam defines itself in terms of the broadest possible universality, and has done so from the beginning. Sufism, or *tasawwuf,* the mystical inner teaching of Islam, represents both the deepest expression of that Qur'anic wisdom as well as the highest truth *(hakikat)* of all the world's great religious traditions. These two aspects are really inseparable.

Many examples from Qur'an and Hadith can be cited to show the mystical perspective on which the foundations of Islam are laid. The most fundamental principle upon which both exoteric Islam and its interior science of Sufism are built is the declaration of unity: *La ilaha illallah,* which carries the essential meaning that "There exists nothing, except the One Divine Source of Being." ("There is no deity or power but *the One,*" known in Arabic as *Allah.*) This is also the essential meaning of the *Shema Yisrael,* by which Moses, and later Jesus, proclaimed to the people of Israel

---

3 Qur'an 10:47.

that the Divine Source ("the Lord our God") is One, and there is none else beside this One Indivisible Reality—including idols or other deities in the exoteric meaning.

The Qur'an exhorts humanity to practice *dhikr*, the remembrance of Allah, as often as possible—to repeatedly affirm: *"La ilaha illallah,"* losing oneself and finding oneself as that One Reality. To this end, the mystics of Islam have adopted the custom of chanting and repeating the sacred phrase, *La ilaha illallah* and other divine names, such as *Allah* and *Hu*, when they meet together in their assemblies.

In Islam, the affirmation of unity is generally linked with the additional phrase: *Muhammad ar-Rasulullah.* This clarifies an immensely important point: that the full significance of the teaching of divine unity does not lie simply in some rarified goal of transcendence. Rather, it is precisely through the medium of the human being—in this case the God-conscious servant and messenger Muhammad—that Divine Reality can be seen manifesting in the world. Two of the Prophet's sayings can be taken together to illustrate this: "Whoever has seen me has seen the Divine Truth *(Haqq)*." And: "I am a human being just like yourselves." Similar statements were also uttered by Jesus. From the mystic perspective, not only the great prophets and the Messiah, but all humanity participates in this process of divine Self-revelation on earth.

A selection of essential verses from the Qur'an and *Hadith Sherif* (the collected sayings of the Prophet Muhammad) confirm the existence of a strong central core of mystical teachings at the heart of Islam:

Allah is the light of the heavens and the earth. (24:35)

Allah Most Intimate says: "We are nearer to you than your jugular vein." (50:16)

Whether in the East or in the West, there is nothing independent of Divine Reality. Wherever you turn to look, there is the One Essential Face of God. (2:115)

Allah Most Exalted promises humanity: "We will show you
Our signs in the world, and intimately within yourselves."
(41:53)

Not a leaf falls without the All-Knowing conscious
awareness of God. (6:59)

Allah reveals His mystic secret through the Beloved
Prophet Muhammad, peace be upon him: "When you threw,
it was not yourself but Allah who threw." (8:17)

We make no distinctions between any of the messengers of
God, and unto God have we surrendered our entire beings.
(2:285)

Hadith: He who truly knows himself knows his Lord.

Allah reveals in another hadith: "When I love one of My
intimate servants, I become the hearing with which they hear,
and the seeing with which they see, the hands which they
move, and the feet with which they walk."

Again, in a Hadith Qudsi, Allah Most High addresses
humanity, saying: "We have created your light from Our light
and from this light have We created the whole universe."

The noble Messenger of God once said to his companions,
"Shall I reveal to you something which is the greatest of
deeds, and the highest in the eyes of your Lord, which will
elevate your station in the hereafter, and which carries more
merit than charitable acts or fighting on God's behalf, or
even martyrdom? It is the dhikr (remembrance) of Allah
All-Mighty." And again: "You should make it a point to
join the gatherings of those who do dhikr-Allah, and when
you are alone remember as continuously as you can that no
power exists except the One." On still another occasion, the
Prophet advised his closest companions: "When you come
upon the gardens of Paradise, feast freely upon the fruits you
find there." Asked what those gardens were, he replied, "The
circles of the dhikr are the garden of Paradise."

Many more such quotations could be cited, but these few suffice to show the profound level of mystic revelation and unitive consciousness which lies at the heart of Qur'an and hadith. *Surat al-Imran* [4] specifies that some of the verses of the Qur'an are literal and others allegorical. In keeping with the esoteric tradition, the sages of Islam give the further teaching that there are at least seven levels on which each *ayat* of Qur'an can be interpreted.

Just as feathers, when microscopically examined, reveal a structural pattern of progressively finer layers of feathers and sub-feathers, so it is with the deep structure of any authentic revealed scripture. The Qur'an, self-described as an open and clear book of guidance for all humanity, can appeal to even the simplest reader on the literal level, while at the same time pointing advanced souls toward the highest spiritual truths. As such, the most profound mysteries of Qur'an involve states of unity utterly transcending the limits of conventional language.

Like all the prophets before him, it was necessary for the Prophet Muhammad to deliver the message of God to a wide public audience. For a prophet, the very art of successful public preaching depends upon formulating the limitless Truth into living words that can simultaneously speak to souls of every level of understanding, encompassing the whole range from the most fundamental knowledge to the most sublime mysteries.

Thus, with his consciousness open to the divine mind, the Prophet Muhammad brought through the Arabic Qur'an, an earthly version of the heavenly Qur'an, also known as the "Mother of the Book" *(Umm al-Kitab)*. This celestial prototype, which transcends any earthly language or human doctrine, is considered the source from which all the holy books are drawn—Gospel, Torah, Psalms, even the inspiration for the Vedas, Gathas and Buddhist scriptures.

Once the inspired revelations become written scriptures, there is always the danger that shallow or willfully distorted human interpretations of the divine message will arise, perverting and obscuring true religion. If this is not done by enemies of the faith,

---

4 Qur'an 3:7.

it may well occur at the hands of its well-meaning friends or the arm of the government.

A well-known Sufi tale represents the devil as rejoicing to find a document on the side of the road, entitled "Truth." Asked why finding a paper that freely reported the truth should thrill him, he replied, "I intend to *organize* it."

The Age of Spiritual Darkness in Arabia before the revelation of the Qur'an is known as the *Jahiliyyah*. As in other spiritually degenerated periods of human history, the Arabian society of Muhammad's time exhibited a profusion of moral and social ills which the Qur'an would address directly, often with detailed practical advice. Female infanticide, slavery, alcoholism, and idolatry are but a few of these ills. In light of this social imperative, the divine message of the Qur'an could never have penetrated the people's hearts had it been formulated exclusively along mystical lines, or as an overt treatise on divine love. Nevertheless, the mystic sees the entire Qur'an as built on an underlying foundation of divine unity, love and wisdom—from its opening *Bismillah ir-Rahman ir-Rahim* ("In the name of the One Source, Who is All-Loving and All-Compassionate") to its final *ayat* ("I take refuge in the Lord of all humanity..."). Finally, it is this perspective of unity, mystic love and wisdom which has, over the centuries, blossomed forth in the form of numerous Islamic *turuq*,[5] the mystical orders of Islam.

Sufism, or the way of mystic union, existed before the time of historical Islam in sixth century Arabia (first century, Islamic calendar) and was taught by the holy prophets and teachers who preceded Muhammad, including Abraham, Moses and the Messiah Jesus. It is a widespread Sufi intuition that the Prophet Muhammad "opened up the station of *marifat*" to an extent that had not been possible for the prophets of the past, who, vessels of Divine Truth as they were, frequently passed from the physical plane before experiencing the earthly success of their mission. *Marifat* (gnosis) represents a level of intimate divine disclosure in which the highest Truth *(hakikat)* becomes realized and

---

5 *Turuq* (Arabic for Sufi Orders); plural of *tarikat* or *tariqa* (the mystic way).

thoroughly integrated in one's being. As the Seal of Prophets, Muhammad is considered to have manifested this station of embodied spirituality to an extraordinary degree while he lived the fullness of human life as son, orphan, caravan merchant, husband, father, spiritual and military leader, ambassador, dream interpreter and divine messenger. This high level of spiritual integration has become the ideal of the Sufis and is alluded to in the verse of the modern poet, Ashki, who writes: "Hands are at work; heart is with the Friend." In his own time, the Prophet's wife, 'A'isha, characterized him as the "living Qur'an"—the living, breathing manifestation of Allah's divine revelation in human form.

Westerners, raised in an anti-Islamic culture, may be unaccustomed to hearing such exalted characterizations of the Prophet Muhammad; yet for 1,400 years he has won the hearts of millions of Muslims world-wide—venerated as a trustworthy, gentle-hearted sage, capable of showing compassion even to those who persecuted and slew his family and friends. Loving-kindness, self-transcendence, and submission to the One Ultimate Source are the hallmarks of the divine manner which, over the centuries, have drawn mystics to the Prophet Muhammad as a model of full humanity and as a guide to the higher levels of divine knowledge.

To the Prophet's closest spiritual heirs—particularly Hazrat 'Ali, the mystic guide through whom most Sufi turuq trace their lineage—a new level of esoteric wisdom was transmitted, a treasury of interior knowledge and spiritual presence which is the basis of Islamic Sufism. In time, the tradition ripened into a fertile spiritual culture stretching from Spain to India, culminating in Sufism's "golden age" in the thirteenth century. Like a fine wine increasing in subtly with age, the mature Sufism of the high Middle Ages exudes a spiritual sophistication and resonance of mystical love of which adepts of earlier times had scarcely dreamed. The greatest Sufi poets and metaphysicians of the era, from Mevlana Jelaluddin Rumi in the East to Muhyiddin Ibn al-'Arabi in the West, were all firmly grounded in the unitive Qur'anic world-view as well as the *sunna* of the Prophet Muhammad. Their writings, as such, are most cogently comprehended within that context.

Sufism, as a distinct line of Islamic mystical transmission and oral teaching, began with the Sultan of Mystic Lovers, the noble Prophet Muhammad himself. It was the practice of the Prophet to extend his right hand to be grasped in covenant by those who received Islam from him. In doing so, he witnessed their *shahada* (their affirmation of unity and their acceptance of Muhammad as an authentic voice of divine prophecy). He also spiritually initiated them into the fullness of Islam (with its four worlds and seven mystic levels).

Those whom the Prophet initiated received a powerful spiritual transmission, which symbolically re-enacted on earth their pledge to uphold the Truth, a covenant which all souls ratified before the dawn of time.[6] Among the ones who received the true essence and knowledge of Islam were the first four khalifas of the Prophet. Each of these inheritors of the Prophetic transmission were given forms of dhikr and concentration on unity suitable to the expression of their temperament.

The four khalifas of Muhammad

---

6 See Qur'an 7:172.

THE FIRST THREE CALIPHS OF ISLAM

ABU BAKR *AS-SIDDIQ* was the first caliph *(khalif)* of Islam, a noble and generous-hearted man who had great love for Allah's qualities of *Rahman* (divine mercy) and *Rahim* (divine compassion) and for contemplating the divine oneness *(Wahid)*. An intimate companion and father-in-law of the Prophet, it was Abu Bakr "the truthful" who accompanied Muhammad during his dangerous *hijra* from Mecca to Medina. It was during this auspicious journey through the desert that the Messenger of God taught him the art of silent dhikr, the inward remembrance of divine unity, while the two of them kept company in the depths of the mystic cave, hidden from their enemies.

This silent way, taught to Abu Bakr, is called *khafi*. It finds its expression in silent, contemplative dhikr *(dhikr khafi)* as well as the silent noon and afternoon prayers of Islam *(salat khafi)*. In contrast, some of the other daily prayers are done *jahri*, that is, spoken aloud. Many traditional dhikr ceremonies of the Sufis also feature this balance of audible pronouncement of the *tawhid* (repeating the words: *La ilaha illallah),* followed by a silent internal invocation *(fikr),* or "dhikr of the heart" *(dhikr qalbi).*

Abu Bakr as-Saddiq

Since Abu Bakr's time, this silent form of dhikr has been handed down orally and is especially favored today within certain branches of the Naqshbandi tarikat, whose dervishes trace their *silsila* not only to Hazrat 'Ali, but also to Hazrati Abu Bakr, beloved representative and transmitter of the contemplative way, known as *mushahada.*

Hazrat 'Umar al-Khattab was the second caliph of Islam, and was also, like Abu Bakr, a father-in-law of the holy Prophet. He possessed a very forceful personality and vigor for righteousness that helped spread Islam throughout Arabia, Syria and Jerusalem during his ten years as caliph. The Messenger of Allah used to joke that even the devil would hide if he saw 'Umar coming down the road with his sword drawn. The dhikr which was taught by the Prophet to 'Umar was a more *jalal* (that is, a more externally powerful, strongly accentuated) form of *jahri dhikr*. This outwardly chanted form of remembrance has been preserved to this day in many of the turuq, such as the Rifa'i Order. It is a boldly chanted form of *tawhid*, accompanied by a powerful swaying of the head and bowing of the upper body toward the heart, alternating with a rising motion to each side.

Hazrati 'Umar was well known for his strict austerity and penitential disposition. During his tenure as "Commander of the Faithful," the reigning caliph of all Arabia, 'Umar shunned every vestige of luxury and owned only a few humble garments and a patched woolen frock. In this, he and other companions followed the way, or *sunna* of Muhammad. The Prophet had his wife 'A'isha patch his cloak and said: "Wear woolen raiment, that you may feel the sweetness of the faith," in this way establishing a custom emulated by dervish ascetics after his time.[7] With his emphasis on poverty, 'Umar became an exemplar of the purgative way, the *mujahada*. In our time, there remain only one or two of the old dervish orders which are thought to represent a direct link with the spiritual influence of Hazrat 'Umar (i.e., the 'Uqailiyya, a Syrian Rifa'i branch, and the Kubrawiyya).

Hazrat 'Uthman ibn 'Affan, the third khalif of Islam, who was twice honored to be a son-in-law of the Prophet, was known for his great love of Qur'an and *salat* (prayer). In fact, he was often known to pass the entire night in prayer, during which he would chant the entire Qur'an from memory, dividing it evenly between the first two *raka'at* of the evening prayer. The Messenger of Allah taught him a shortened, inwardly penetrating form of the dhikr—

---

7 Al-Hujwiri, *Kashf al-Mahjub*, 45.

illallah—in which the head fervently bows toward the heart with the potent words meaning: "(none exists) except Allah." This dhikr was passed down and is still used by a number of mystic orders today.

There exists no extant tarikat from the line of 'Uthman (unless we accept Evliya Chelebi's identification of the Zainiyya, a tarikat of the Suhrawardi line, with 'Uthman). This noble caliph attained to the station of friendship *(khullat)* with Allah, and has become the patron of those who chant Qur'an or sing a slow meditative *durak* during the course of a dhikr ceremony. Often sung is the noble ayat from *Sura Imran,*[8] which commends those who remember the Source of Being continuously in every circumstance:

> Those who celebrate the praises of Allah, standing, sitting, and lying down and contemplate the wonders of creation in the heavens and the earth.

HAZRAT 'ALI

HAZRAT 'ALI IBN ABI TALIB, the fourth caliph and noble son-in-law and cousin of the Prophet, is considered the full inheritor of the rich transmission of mystic teaching in Islam and the "*murshid*[9] of the knowledge of Divine Reality." Imam 'Ali, who is known in the tarikat as the "fountain of the mystics," was confirmed in this exalted station by the Prophet, who said, "I am the radiant city of knowledge and 'Ali is its gate. Whoever wishes to acquire this mystic knowledge, let them enter by means of this open gate."

The traditions record a number of occasions during which the Prophet Muhammad instructed Hazrat 'Ali in the Mystic Way. In one instance (related by Jabir), the Messenger of Allah called 'Ali to him on the Day of Ta'if and spoke privately with him at some length. When some of the people commented that

---

8 Qur'an 3:190.
9 A *murshid,* like a sheikh, is a spiritual guide and leader.

the Prophet's secret talk with his cousin had been prolonged, the noble Messenger replied, "It wasn't me who had a secret talk with 'Ali; rather, it was Allah who spoke secretly with him." On another occasion, the Prophet taught Imam 'Ali to repeat aloud the mystic words of unity, *La ilaha illallah.* 'Ali was instructed to repeat it three times, while moving his head first to the right (on *La ilaha*—nothing exists, no deity nor independent agent of power of any kind), and then downwards to the left, toward the heart (on . . . *illallah*—except the One Universal Source, known as Allah).

Imam Ali with sons, Hasan and Husayn

Hazrat 'Ali also transmitted a tradition—said to have come directly from the unseen mystic guide *Khidr*—in which the Arabic letters of the word Allah are removed one by one, revealing progressively deeper meanings. Thus *ALLAH*, which in Arabic is spelled: *alif, lam, lam, ha*, has the initial meaning of "*the One*" (Divine Source). When the first letter *(alif)* is removed the word becomes pronounced *LILLAH*, meaning "(everything is) *for Allah*". When the next letter *(lam)* is removed, the word becomes *LEYHU*, meaning "(everything in heaven and on earth) *belongs to Allah*." When the next *lam* is removed, leaving the single letter *ha*, only the word *Hu* remains, meaning "the formless *Divine Essence* (is the only Reality)."

Allah, in Arabic script;
reading right to left:
alif, lam, lam, ha.

'Ali's wife, Hazrat Fatima, the illuminated daughter of the Prophet, was the first to receive from the Messenger of Allah the *tasbih* which was to become recommended for all Muslims to recite after their daily prayers: 33 times, *Subhan Allah* (Glory to God); 33 times, *Alhamdulillah* (All praises are flowing to Allah); and 34 times, *Allahu Akbar* (Allah is greater... surpassing all human comprehension).

Hazrat 'Ali was a young boy of nine when his elder cousin, Muhammad, announced his prophethood in Mecca at a special feast among the members of his own clan. Though most of Muhammad's relatives and acquaintances reacted to his announcement with scorn, Hazrat 'Ali stood up and declared his acceptance of the prophethood of Muhammad. Later, in Medina, during the defensive battles against the enemies of Islam, 'Ali's reputation grew as a valiant warrior and chivalrous swordsman. His physical prowess and brave character formed a beautiful balance to his well-known mystic gifts.

'Ali was in his mid-thirties when the beloved Prophet, his cousin and father-in-law, made his transition to the Realm of Beauty (632 CE). By the time Hazrat 'Ali was accepted as the fourth caliph and leader of the Muslims, he was well into his fifties. What follows are a few of his mystical pronouncements, gleaned from his mature years.

A tradition *(ahl al-naql)* preserved from the time of his caliphate, relates that 'Ali led Kumayl ibn Ziyad from the mosque into the desert and asked him to preserve certain teachings concerning mystic knowledge. Among his words were these:

Kumayl, knowledge *('ilm)* is better than wealth. Wealth is diminished by expenditure while knowledge is increased even by giving it away. Those who amass wealth die even as they live while those who possess knowledge will continue to exist for as long as time lasts . . . The heart is a container of knowledge and the best heart is the one which preserves knowledge. In this respect, there are three kinds of men: those who intimately know their Lord, those who seek knowledge in order to be saved, and the throng who follow every crower and bend with every breeze—these have no sure authority, nor do they seek illumination through the light of learning." He pointed at his breast and said, "Here indeed is much knowledge—if I could come upon those who would carry it.

Two final short exchanges from this same period, are worth recounting. Caliph 'Ali came across a man pointing skyward with a stick and swearing: "By Him who is veiled with seven layers (of heaven)." 'Ali said to him, "Woe upon you; for Allah is too exalted to be veiled from anything or for anything to be veiled from Him. Praise be to Allah, Whom no place contains, yet from Whom nothing on earth or heaven is hidden." The man asked, "Should I then redeem my oath, Commander of the Faithful?" Hazrat 'Ali answered, "No, for you did not swear by God...but by something else."

On another occasion 'Ali was asked whether he saw God when he worshiped Him. The noble 'Ali *Murtaza* answered, "I am not one who worships someone whom I have never seen." When the man inquired as to exactly what 'Ali saw, when he saw God, 'Ali corrected him: "Woe, for the eyes do not see Him through human eyesight. Rather, it is the heart that sees Allah through the inner realities of faith *(iman)*."[10]

The Prophet taught various ways of dhikr to each of the first four caliphs and to various other companions; however, the main Sufi lineages come only from Abu Bakr (Mevlevi, Bektashi, Yasawi and Naqshbandi) and 'Ali (most other *Sunni* and all *Shi'ite turuq* trace back to Imam 'Ali). These two caliphs initiated one another as well; 'Ali learned from Abu Bakr the inward silent dhikr, which aids meditation, while Abu Bakr learned from 'Ali the secrets of the spoken dhikr, which awakens not only one's self, but all others who hear it.

Next, we will look at the larger community of mystics who surrounded the Prophet during his own lifetime, a loose-knit group of ascetic companions who could well be considered the first Sufis of the Muhammadan community.

---

10 Sheikh al-Mufid, *Kitab al-Irshad,* 166-69.

THE ASHABI SUFFA

DURING THE LATTER PERIOD of the Prophet's lifetime, Hazrat 'Ali, the Exalted Gate of Mystic Knowledge, was closely associated with an assembly of mystically inclined *fakirs* (those who renounce the world through the practice of voluntary poverty) who used to pass much of their time engaged in divine contemplation and *dhikrullah* seated around the veranda of the Prophet's mosque in Medina. These devout ascetic companions of the Prophet became known as the *Ashabi-Suffa (Ashab as-Suffa),* or *Ahl-i Suffa,* the People of the Veranda, those who dwelt in the Prophet's mosque and filled their day with devotions. Even today, in the *Masjid an-Nabi,* the Prophet's Mosque in Medina, there is a special area, demarcated by a raised platform near the Prophet's enclosed tomb, where these *"suffa"* companions used to gather.

Some have suggested that the word *sufi* (which is used to describe the mystics of Islam) may have derived from the word *suffa*—from this original circle of mystic ascetics who dwelt in the Prophet's mosque. The word *suffa* is also related to the English word *sofa*, but not in the sense of a cushioned divan but as a plain bench or simply the area where the mystic companions of the Prophet sat when they gathered. Other possible etymologies of the word *sufi*, are: *safa* (purity), *sophia* (wisdom), and *suf* (wool), the latter referring to the patched woolen cloaks and robes which the early ascetics wore. We may note in passing that another type of traditional woolen garment, dating from that period, remains popular with dervishes in many turuq today: a long sleeveless vest called the *haydariyya*, named after Hazrat 'Ali, whom the Prophet gave the epithet, *Haydar-i-karrar* (the Lion of Allah).

The *Ashabi-Suffa* were given to voluntary poverty and fasting, some occasionally, in their spiritual zeal, completely ignoring the duty of supporting themselves through a livelihood. Eventually, a question arose among some of the Muslims as to whether these contemplative companions were not becoming too idle and ascetic in their lifestyle. After all, the Qur'an discouraged Muslims from following the encratic orientation of the Christian monks and, in the early Meccan years, the Prophet had forbidden the ascetically inclined 'Uthman ibn Maz'un from taking a vow of chastity (probably including self-castration), before he emigrated to Christian- ruled Abyssinia.

On the other hand, the Messenger of Allah did himself engage in occasional periods of solitary retreat *(khalwa),* as had the prophets before him, when he would go to meditate and pray in the caves at Mt. Hira during the month of Ramadan. Also well-known was the Prophet's saying: "Poverty is my pride." The ideal was "to be in this world but not of it"—to marry, to have family, to live, work and pray together in society while always remembering Allah and the perspective of Divine Unity.

Ultimately, divine approval and blessing came for the *Ashabi-Suffa* in the form of a Qur'anic revelation (6:52) which said, "Do not drive away those who morning and evening call upon their Lord, desiring His face." The Prophet echoed this endorsement by saying to them, "Rejoice! for whoever of my community perseveres in the state you are in, and is satisfied with his condition, shall be one of my comrades in Paradise."

It is related that the Messenger of Allah was in his house when he received the noble Qur'anic verse, "Keep yourself bound to the company of those who invoke their Lord morning and night." Upon hearing the revelation, he went out in search of them and found a group of *Sahaba* (companions), including Salman Farsi, engaged in dhikr in the farthest part of the mosque. (Some of them were said to have had disheveled hair, parched skin and very little clothing to wear.) When they saw the Rasulullah approaching they became silent. He inquired as to what they were doing and they answered, "We are engaged in the remembrance of Allah, and are glorifying Him for His extreme generosity toward us, inasmuch as He has blessed us with the wealth of Islam." The Prophet prodded them, "By Allah, are you only here for this purpose and none other?" When they affirmed, by the holy name of Allah, that this was indeed the case, he replied, "I asked you to swear not out of any misunderstanding, but because Gabriel had just now come to me and informed me that Allah was speaking highly of you before the angels. When I saw that the mercy *(rahmat)* of Allah was descending upon you, I desired to join you. *Alhamdulillah*, all praise is for Allah who has raised such people in my community during my own lifetime, that I have been ordered to sit with them. You are my companions in life and death."[11]

Another important hadith has come down to us in the *'Awarif ul-Ma'arif* (reported by Anas ibn Malik) concerning an occasion in which the Prophet himself, may peace and blessings continually be upon him, was, in private quarters, leading some of these companions in chanting the dhikr while they stood, swayed and moved in a circle along with the words of remembrance. Just then, Mu'awiya, the son of Abu Sufyan (Muhammad's recently-converted former enemy), happened to pass by and, hearing them, entered the room. "O Rasulullah! What a lovely dance this is!" he exclaimed in amazement. "Shhh! O Mu'awiya!" was the Prophet's

---

11 Muhammad Kandhalvi, *Virtues of Zikr*, 44, 68.

reply. "This is no dance; it is the dhikr of the Beloved. When one hears the name of one's Beloved is it not good to turn in worship?"[12]

This way of making dhikr, in which the circle of lovers "turn" in a ring *(dawran* in Arabic; *devran* in Turkish) has been adopted by many of the Sufi turuq. Some simply sit together, kneeling in a circle (or in lines) chanting dhikr, while some also stand and sway in place, while still other turuq have permission for the circle to turn, while the lovers hold hands or join arms in a shoulder-hold or waist-hold. Thus, while physically uniting in a circle of remembrance, these lovers anticipate and experience in the present "the circling that takes place in paradise every Friday" (the day of congregation). This tradition, revealing that there are dhikr circles in paradise, is related on the authority of the Prophet himself, who was directly apprised of this knowledge by the Angel Gabriel, after a bedouin came to the Prophet inquiring about it.

Thus, making dhikr in a circle became a firm tradition, practiced in all of the turuq, rooted as it was in the *sunna* of the Prophet Muhammad. However the formal practice of individual dervish lovers whirling in place has historically become associated with only one tarikat, the Mevlevis, who follow the rules of whirling established by their 13th century master in Konya, Hazrati Mevlana Jalaluddin Rumi. In this case, the precedent for whirling is also traced back to the Prophet, who, when told by Gabriel that the poor of his community would enter paradise five hundred years before the rich communities, became ecstatic and began to whirl, spinning around so much that his cloak fell from his blessed shoulders. Seeing this, the companions around him were also caught up in his exultation and joined him in whirling with abandon. There were other separate instances in which Hazrat 'Ali, his brother Ja'far, and Hazrat Abu Bakr Siddiq were also inspired to whirl spontaneously in response to various reports from the Prophet of their acceptance from on high. (Please refer to Appendix I for a complete discussion of the Prophet Muhammad's intercessory role in Islam.)

---

12 Muzaffer Ozak, *The Unveiling of Love*, 75-76; it is also quoted in *Zad ul-Ma 'ad.*

Besides Imam 'Ali, there were a number of other notable companions among the *Ashabi-Suffa.* The list includes the venerable Salman al-Farsi, the famous Persian convert, Bilal ibn Raba, the noble black Ethiopian who became the first muezzin of Islam, Zayd ibn al-Khattab, the brother of Caliph 'Umar, the noble ascetic Abu Dharr, and Abu Hurayra, who transmitted thousands of ahadith. (Abu Hurayra was one of the companions known, during the Prophet's lifetime, to count divine names on a *tesbih* rope tied with 99 knots, a practice to which the Prophet never objected, though he himself preferred to count the *esmas,* or divine names, on his fingers.)

One further member of the *Ashabi-Suffa* bears special recognition: Abu 'Ubayda ibn al-Jarrah, who was one of the ten companions promised paradise by the Prophet, and an ancestor of the noble 18th century Turkish saint and Seal of Pirs, Hazrati Pir Nureddin al-Jerrahi.[13] Because of his connection with Pir Nureddin, we will pause here to chronicle a few episodes from Abu 'Ubayda's life, followed by a brief consideration of Salman Farsi. Our discussion of the foremost early Sufis in the community of Muhammad would be incomplete without including Salman the Persian, the great mystic companion and universal seeker of Truth whose destiny it was to be involved with three of the major world's religions during his long and illustrious life.

ABU 'UBAYDA IBN AL-JARRAH

AMONG THE FIRST PERSONS to accept Islam from the hand of the holy Prophet were his first wife, Hazrat Khadija (the first woman and first adult to accept Islam), his nine year-old cousin and future son-in-law Hazrat 'Ali, and the Prophet's servant and adopted son Zayd. The first adult non-family member to accept Islam from the Prophet was the future first caliph of Islam, Hazrat Abu Bakr as-Siddiq. The very next day after he took *shahada,* Abu Bakr brought

---

13 According to Safer Dal.

four of his close friends to Muhammad, and they too embraced Islam. In the early days in Mecca, open support of the Prophet was an extremely harsh experience because of the hostility with which the Prophet was initially received in his home town. One of these four men was Amir ibn 'Abdullah ibn al-Jarrah, known as Abu 'Ubayda and also called *Amin*, the Custodian of the community of Muhammad.

Abu 'Ubayda's appearance was striking; he was a pleasing person to meet. Abu 'Ubayda was a tall, slim man with a sparse beard and bright face. He was extremely courteous, humble, and modest to the point of shyness, yet in a tough situation would become strikingly serious and alert, like a sharp and flashing sword blade. For thirteen years his father never accepted Islam, and after the hijra of the Muslims to Medina, Abu 'Ubayda had the painful experience of facing his father across the Meccan enemy lines at the Battle of Badr. Though Abu 'Ubayda tried to avoid him during the ensuing battle, his father, 'Abdullah ibn al-Jarrah, actually sought him out and attacked him; Abu 'Ubayda was forced to kill his father in self-defense. Elsewhere on the battlefield, the Prophet defended himself against his own uncles—now his avowed enemies—such as Abu-Lahab, who was also slain at Badr.

Later, at the Battle of Uhud, the Prophet narrowly escaped death when he was struck by a weapon across the face, breaking several teeth and embedding two discs from his shield into his cheeks. When the enemy onslaught had subsided, Abu Bakr attempted to extract the discs using his fingers. Abu 'Ubayda stepped forward, insisting that the least painful method was for him to use his own teeth to extract the disks from the Prophet's cheek. Thus, Abu 'Ubayda accomplished the excision but broke off two of his own incisor teeth in the process, an action which he never subsequently regretted.

Toward the end of his life, the Prophet sent out letters to the neighboring communities of Arabia, inviting them to Islam. One of these was the Christian community of Najran, who sent a delegation of their Byzantine priests and rulers to Medina to negotiate with the Prophet. For several days they tried debating religion, disagreeing on theological concepts such as the doctrine of the trinity and whether Jesus was, or had ever claimed to be God or his son. When these negotiations came to an impasse, the Prophet, acting on a revelation, issued them a challenge. He invited the Christians to participate in a contest of prayer called the *Mubahala*, a test of Divine Truth in which the two parties would assemble to invoke the response of heaven in a manner reminiscent of Elijah of old. The Christians agreed to the contest, but worried among themselves, "What if we are mistaken and Muhammad is an authentic prophet from God?"

The next morning, the Prophet, his daughter Fatima, her husband Hazrat 'Ali and their two grandsons, Hasan and Husayn, (known as the *People of the Cloak)* stood together under Muhammad's large green mantle while the Christian priests and the mayor of Najran took their place in another group facing them. Each party was to pray fervently to God Most High that a rain of fire would descend upon those who were farthest from teaching the Truth. Moments before the Prophet commenced his prayer the Christians called off the contest, explaining that they preferred to make peace with Muhammad and defer the divine judgment to the Last Day. Thus, recognizing the sincerity and integrity of the Prophet's character, the party from Najran negotiated permission to continue with their Christian faith (as People of the Book), while paying tribute to the Muslims in a traditional clan protection agreement.

Then their leader made a request: "O Abu-l Qasim (Muhammad), send one of your companions with us, one in whom you are well pleased, to judge between us on some questions of property about which we disagree among ourselves. We have a high regard for you Muslim people." The Prophet replied, "Come back to me this evening and I will send with you one who is strong and trustworthy." Hazrat 'Umar ibn al-Khattab heard this and went to the noon prayer hoping to be the chosen one, even raising himself a little taller as the Prophet looked around to make his selection. 'Umar said later, "By Allah, I never wanted an appointment more in all my life." 'Umar eventually became the *Commander of the Faithful* and was known as *al-Furqan*, the one who sharply distinguished the right from the wrong. Though possessing many noble, upright qualities, 'Umar also had a severe side to his personality and judgments.

Most probably, it was such considerations which led the Prophet to pass over 'Umar as ambassador for this delicate interreligious mission involving the settling of land disputes.

When the Prophet finished the congregational *zuhr* prayer that day, he began looking to his right and his left, saw 'Umar, but kept looking until he spotted Abu 'Ubayda ibn al-Jarrah. He called to him and said, "Go with them and judge among them with truth about that which they are in disagreement."[14]

After the Prophet's death Hazrat 'Umar actually went to Abu 'Ubayda and offered to take allegiance with him as caliph, saying, "Stretch forth your hand and I will swear allegiance to you, for I heard the Prophet, peace be upon him, say, 'every *umma* (community) has an *amin* (true custodian) and you are the *amin* of this community.'" But Abu 'Ubayda refused to put himself forward, deferring instead to Abu Bakr, whom the Prophet had made prayer-leader in his place during his final illness.

After Abu Bakr's death, Abu 'Ubayda also deferred to 'Umar and was given an assignment leading the forces in Syria, which he did very successfully. However, when the plague hit Syria and many began to die, Caliph 'Umar sent an urgent letter saying he had dire need for Abu 'Ubayda to return at once. But the motive of saving him from the plague was transparent and Abu 'Ubayda sent back a letter requesting to stay with his troops. 'Umar wept when he read the letter, for he realized that his friend and senior companion in Islam would soon depart this world. During his lifetime, the Rasulullah had foreseen the future station of Abu 'Ubayda and nine other companions; it was revealed that they would enter directly into paradise upon leaving this world. Even today there are ten plaques hanging in the inner courtyard of the Prophet's mosque in Medina, one to commemorate each of these ten companions of Paradise, known as the *Asharah al-Mubasharah*.[15]

---

14 The story of the Mubahala is recounted in a number of Muslim sources, including Tabari and the Shi'ite *Kitab al-Irshad* (see Sheikh al-Mufid's translation, 116-18).
15 Biographical information on Abu 'Ubayda was drawn in part from *Alim* software.

SALMAN AL-FARSI

WE HAVE MENTIONED SALMAN AL-FARSI as one of the *Ahl-i Suffa* but have not as yet sufficiently indicated the importance of his station in early Islam and the tarikat. Salman was so dear to the Prophet, that Muhammad enfolded him in his own green cloak and accepted him as an intimate member of his family. According to tradition, Salman lived to an extremely advanced age—some say two hundred years or more—finally dying in 656 CE during the caliphate of 'Ali.

Salman came from a long line of Zoroastrian priests in Jiyye, Iraq, but he could not find spiritual fulfilment within this hardened cult of fire-worship. Though it nearly cost him his life, Salman escaped the strict custody of his father, relinquished his incumbent vocation as a fire-priest, and converted to Nestorian Christianity, eventually settling in Damascus many years before the time of Islam. Salman learned from his Christian masters and their Aramaic Gospel targums, about the succession of holy prophets from Adam to Jesus *(Isa),* upon them all be peace, and the expectation among Jews and Christians of that time that still another prophet might be raised among them, perhaps in their own generation.

After Salman's last Christian teacher died, he moved to the Roman city of Ammura, still burning in search of Truth, and there heard rumors of a new prophet of the One God who had announced himself in Mecca in Arabia. Upon hearing this news, Salman set out walking towards Mecca with the next available caravan. But treachery was afoot; he was sold by his traveling companions into slavery and purchased by a rich Jewish merchant who lived in Yathrib (soon to become Medina and the home of the Prophet Muhammad). For a long time Salman's servitude isolated him from hearing any news about this longed-for prophet. Then one day he chanced to overhear his master speaking to a friend about a man named Muhammad who had just moved

 to Medina and was hailed by his followers as a new prophet. Overjoyed at this news, Salman arranged to travel into the city on the pretext of running an errand for his master. There, at last, he came face to face with Muhammad. It was profound mutual love at first sight. When the Prophet heard about Salman's cruel and unjust enslavement he immediately gathered money to purchase Salman's freedom.

Thus Salman entered Islam and, with his wide knowledge and experience, not only gave invaluable practical advice to the Prophet but also became one of the foremost mystic saints among the companions. In a later battle, his counsel helped stop an overwhelming Meccan enemy force when he advised the Muslims to dig a deep covered trench in advance of their attack. He was also said to have chanted Qur'an with a beautiful voice and was the first to translate the holy Qur'an into another language—in this case, Persian.

Salman embodied a wealth of esoteric knowledge, which he used to discuss with Muhammad. In turn, the Prophet explained how the current revelations of Islam renewed and clarified the primordial tradition of Divine Unity, the original inspiration for all the great traditions of the past. Salman could see from the Prophet's words that the reason he was never satisfied with these traditions was that the underlying unitive vision had become clouded over the centuries through the influence of limited human concepts.

In the time of Hazrat Abu Bakr's two-year caliphate (after the death of the Prophet), Salman was designated Abu Bakr's spiritual *khalifa* (representative and successor) in the mystic way of Islam. Thus, he is included in the Naqshbandi *silsila* (chain of transmission) as the inheritor of the mystic mantle which passed from Rasulullah to Abu Bakr to Salman the Persian. After Abu Bakr's death, Salman took hand with Hazrat 'Ali, who represents another spiritual link with the Prophet. Having received *bayat* directly from the Prophet as well, Salman was thrice covenanted into the Islamic tradition of Divine Unity, a direct knowledge of Reality which he passed on to many others in time. He is counted as one of the first great murshids in the tradition of Sufism and Universal Islam.

THE NEXT GENERATION

BESIDES SALMAN, there were three other "spiritual khalifas" from the time of the first four caliphs. After the passing of Abu Bakr, Hazrati 'Umar became caliph for ten years and designated Kumayl ibn Ziyad as his spiritual khalifa. Hazrat 'Uthman had Abdullah al-Ansari as his khalifa in the tarikat, and Hazrat 'Ali is said to have passed his mystic mantle to Hasan al-Basri (who appears directly after 'Ali in the *silsilas* of most Sufi orders). All four of these khalifas in the tarikat outlived the caliphs to whom they pledged allegiance, and eventually united in taking hand with Hazrat 'Ali ibn Abi Talib, who was the last of the four righteous caliphs and the one who is considered the head of all Sufi turuq.

All of the first four caliphs who succeeded the Prophet retained their sense of humility and simple lifestyle even as they ruled over vast lands. One person who came to visit 'Umar during the time of his caliphate, came across 'Umar wearing patched clothing and carrying wood; the man mistook him for a common laborer. All of the original four caliphs except Abu Bakr were destined to be martyred by extremists within their own Islamic community.

During the reign of 'Uthman, serious political divisions began to emerge which had previously been latent. Some resented the fact that the Rasulullah's relative from the noble house of Hashim, Hazrat 'Ali, had so far been passed over three times as candidate for caliph, even though the Prophet himself had endorsed him with the words: " 'Ali is to me as Aaron was to Moses." Also, though he was undoubtedly a pious and well-respected in-law of the Prophet,

'Uthman belonged to the Quraysh of Mecca, the old aristocracy which had vehemently opposed and fought the Prophet until Mecca was finally conquered. Thus Caliph 'Uthman's appointments of family and friends began to return power into the hands of those who were already suspected of professing Islam primarily as a means of gaining political control. For years, Caliph 'Uthman refused to seriously address any of the petitions from the faithful urging him to reform the nepotism and corruption which marred his reign. Tensions over these festering problems finally came to a head when a band of Muslim protestors stormed the caliph's house and murdered him while he serenely read from the Qur'an until his dying breath.

'Uthman's cousin, Mu'awiya ibn Abu Sufyan, who had been appointed the commander of the powerful Muslim forces in Syria, vowed revenge and accused Hazrat 'Ali— in line to become the next caliph—of having done little to save 'Uthman, nor track down his murderers. Unfortunately, such infighting became the focus of much of 'Ali's time as caliph, finally culminating in a civil war among the Muslims which ended more or less in a draw, with each side claiming some legitimate right to rule. Even the Prophet's widow, 'A'isha, the Mother of the Believers, became involved in an ill-fated revolt against 'Ali, known as the *Battle of the Camel*. Though famous as a formidable swordsman and fearless warrior for righteousness, Caliph 'Ali now found himself on the horns of a dilemma, ruling over a sharply divided population, all at war with one another in the name of Islam. He was deeply distressed by the thousands of Muslim lives which were lost in this ongoing struggle for power.

In one key battle against Mu'awiya's Syrian forces, 'Ali's sense of mercy and adherence to the Qur'an prevented him from consummating the war with a ruthless massacre of fellow Muslims that could have consolidated his power as caliph. A man of high principles, Caliph 'Ali attempted to approach every situation with honor, dignity and restraint worthy of the noble Prophet; but there were many other forces at work, determined to prevent rapprochement and unity among the Muslims.

Someone complained to Caliph 'Ali that he didn't rule as Abu Bakr and 'Umar had in earlier days. He responded, "If you people would behave the way people behaved during their caliphate, I would be happy to rule as they did."

Hazrat 'Ali's life came to an end in the fourth year of his caliphate in 661 CE, when he was stabbed by a Kharijite extremist with a poisoned sword, while kneeling at prayer. 'Ali lived a few more hours and, true to form, made those present, who had captured and tightly bound the assassin, promise not to beat the man, to loosen his bonds a little, and to administer fair judgment in meting out his punishment.

After the assassination of Imam 'Ali (may his soul be ennobled), his eldest son, Imam Hasan, succeeded him as the fifth caliph. Six months into his term, Mu'awiya brought his powerful troops from Syria and usurped the caliphate. Imam Hasan brokered peace terms with Mu'awiya and abdicated his claim, living on in Medina for another eight years. This exchange of power marks the end of the thirty year period of the *Khilafat-i-Rashida,* or rightly-guided caliphs, and the beginning of the Umayyad dynasty, a series of wealthy king-like caliphs who moved the capital to Damascus and ruled from Syria for the next ninety years.

After Caliph Mu'awiya's death in 679 CE, his degenerate son, Yazid ibn Mu'awiya, claimed succession to the caliphate, though 'Ali's second son, Imam Husayn, the Mystic Moon of Islam, was the more legitimate spiritual claimant. When Imam Husayn refused to renounce his right to the caliphate, Yazid ordered his soldiers to bring him the head of the Prophet's grandson. At Karbala, Husayn and a small party of family and devout followers took their stand against Yazid's forces and were brutally massacred. Vastly outnumbered, yet refusing to flee the field, Husayn futilely attempted to defend the true Islam against this tyrannical and debauched false caliph. Holding his infant child, Imam Husayn faced Yazid's troops and called out to them, trying to persuade them of the justice of his cause.

As he listened to Husayn's noble words, Hurr ibn Yazid at-Tamini, the Kufan calvary leader of Yazid's huge army, came to realize what a heinous deed they were perpetrating against the beloved grandson of the Prophet and went over to Husayn's side. Hurr died fighting in defense of the small band of martyrs.[16] According to tradition, years earlier the Prophet Muhammad had foreseen and spoken of an inevitable tragic end for his beloved grandsons (Imam Hasan is believed to be have been poisoned), and much sorrow in this for their surviving sister, Zaynab. This infamous scene of martyrdom at Karbala has assumed a profound sacrificial, almost messianic place in the annals of Islam, observed each year with mourning and fasting by Shi'ites and Sufis alike during the month of Muharram.

Yazid ruled as caliph for four years, after which a series of hereditary caliphs succeeded him. Several were poisoned and one dethroned. Thus for a time, while the Muslim political domains increased, exoteric Islam veered from the purity of the religious course established by the holy Messenger of Allah. For nearly a century, Islam was dominated by a series of wealthy, often despotic rulers. They, too, were overthrown and replaced by another line of claimants to the caliphate—the descendants of Muhammad's uncle, Ibn al-'Abbas, who established the 'Abbasid dynasty (750-1258 CE). During this period, the capital was moved from Syria and relocated in the cosmopolitan Iraqi city of Baghdad.

The partisans of 'Ali's family, supporting only those descended through Imam 'Ali and the Prophet's daughter Hazrat Fatima, split off from the *Sunnis* (the main body of Muslims) into the *Shi'ite* sect (now prevalent mainly in Iran, Iraq, India and Pakistan). Disgusted with the political milieu, many of the mystically-inclined Muslims began to withdraw from worldly pursuits, concentrating instead on inner, spiritual transformation. Within a few generations, organized Sufi orders would begin to emerge, particularly in Baghdad, representing in still another way the flowering of the mystical tradition from the lineage of Imam 'Ali.

It is related, in a casual anecdote from the days of the four righteous caliphs, that one day the robust Salman al-Farsi climbed up a date tree to pitch dates down to Imam 'Ali to eat. When

---

16 Sheikh al-Mufid, *Kitab al-Irshad*, 353.

'Ali began playfully throwing the date stones back up the tree at Salman and hitting him with them, Salman called down to 'Ali in jest, "Because of this you will be the last caliph."

THE NOBLE WOMEN
OF THE PROPHET'S HOUSEHOLD

SO FAR WE HAVE CHIEFLY emphasized the role of the men who surrounded the Prophet Muhammad. It is also important to consider the wives and female progeny of Muhammad and their contribution to scholarship and piety. The Qur'an (33:7) tells us: "The Prophet is nearer to the faithful than they themselves, and his wives are their mothers." Thus, as Mothers of the Faithful, the Prophet's wives held an important and highly honored place in the early Muslim community as educators and preservers of the Islamic traditions, as well as care-givers for the sick and suffering.

Muhammad's first wife, Khadija bint Khawalid, was a wise, compassionate, and wealthy business woman of Mecca, a widow who employed the young Muhammad, perhaps fifteen years her junior, as leader of her caravans. They soon developed a deep bond of trust and affection and were married. She was his first declared disciple—and his initial prayer companion during the early years of Islam—Muhammad's greatest  support during the trying times that accompanied his initial call to prophethood in Mecca. Through twenty five years of monogamous marriage until her death, Khadija provided both financial and moral support to the Prophet, and was always remembered as his most beloved wife.

Hazrat Umm Salama, Hazrat 'A'isha, Hazrat Fatima and
(unveiled) maidservants with the Prophet Muhammad
in Medina (16th century Turkish miniature).

After Khadija's passing and the hijra to Medina, Muhammad married Sawda, another widow, then gradually began to take multiple wives. The first and most beloved of these was 'A'isha (*as-Siddiqa*—the truthful), the young daughter of Abu Bakr Siddiq. She was an enthusiastic preserver of the Islamic tradition, who learned the Qur'an by heart, witnessed thousands of important sayings of the Prophet and transmitted them to the faithful after his passing. Muhammad himself advised the people to "learn a portion of your religion from this red colored lady (an endearing epithet by which he referred to A'isha)."

In later years, a companion named Abu Musa al-Ashari would attest: "If we companions of the Messenger of God had any difficulty on a matter, we asked 'A'isha about it." As "Mother of the Believers," she became an important teacher in the early Muslim community, possessing knowledge not only of law *(fiqh),* but of medicine *(tibb)* and poetry. Of her oratorical skills another contemporary, al-Ahnaf, reported: "I have heard speeches of Abu Bakr and 'Umar, Uthman and 'Ali and the Caliphs up to this day, but I have not heard speech more persuasive and more beautiful from the mouth of any person than from the mouth of 'A'isha."

In the fifty years of her life after the Prophet's passing, Hazrat 'A'isha became an active educator and social reformer, attracting men and women from far and wide to partake of her knowledge. Her house became effectively a school and an academy, producing respected hadith scholars such as her cousin, Urwah, and her secretary, Umra bint Abdur Rahman. She was also known to take orphaned children into her care, providing them with guidance and training. To this day, 'A'isha remains a highly respected authority in issues of Islamic theology and law.[17]

Hafsa, the daughter of 'Umar, was another of the Prophet's wives who excelled as a scholar, teacher and *hafiz* (one who has memorized the Qur'an). After Muhammad's death, the community entrusted her as guardian of the original written Qur'an collection, the master reference copy from which all other Qur'ans were carefully duplicated and disseminated.

Another wife of the Prophet, a mature widow named Umm Salama, became a teacher in the community and brought into Muhammad's household several young step-daughters, one of whom, Zaynab, came to be ranked among the best scholars of her time. Umm Salama, also a *hafiz*, accompanied the Prophet on several expeditions, often discussing theological and political questions with him. It was she who queried Muhammad as to why only men were mentioned in the Qur'an to the exclusion of women. The answer came soon in the form of a revealed *ayat*, proclaimed by Muhammad from the *minbar* of the mosque: "Lo! men and women who surrender to Allah, and men and women who believe, and men and women who speak truth,... and men and women who remember Allah—for them Allah has prepared forgiveness and a vast reward." (Qur'an 33:35) Around this time, *Surat an-Nisa* ("The Women") was also revealed,

---

17 Based in part on the internet source: *The New Muslim Woman.*

addressing women's rights of inheritance and other issues that helped elevate the status of women in the Islamic community.

The Prophet's youngest daughter, Fatima, known as *az-Zahra* ("The Radiant"), married the Prophet's cousin, 'Ali ibn Abi Talib. While Hazrat 'Ali was the primary inheritor of the knowledge of mystical realities, Hazrat Fatima, renowned for her piety, wisdom and courage, was divinely revealed as the intercessor for all the women of the community. Her sanctity was such that the Prophet included Fatima, along with her mother, Khadija, as two of the four perfected women foremost in paradise (the other two were the Virgin Mary and Asiya, the Pharaoh's wife who saved Moses). Shi'i tradition extols Lady Fatima as the secret khalifa of the Prophet, of whom Muhammad said: "Fatima is my spirit, which I hold in me . . . She is the light of my eye and the fruit of my heart . . . She is the mistress of all women."

Her eldest son, Imam Hasan, reported that one Friday night he saw his mother, Hazrat Fatima, standing in her prayer niche. She knelt and prostrated continuously until dawn, and he heard her praying for all the faithful men and women, but never for herself. When her prayers were completed, he inquired of her, "Oh mother, why did you not pray for yourself like you prayed for others?" She replied, "Oh my son, first your neighbor and thereafter your own house."

After Muhammad's passing, Hazrat Fatima used to gather the Muslims and recite what she had heard from the Prophet; she even preached in the mosque, edifying the people on the principles of Islam and enjoining them in those troubled times to behave justly toward one another. She firmly believed that Muslim women should be knowledgeable in Islamic culture and able to guide fellow Muslim women. Her early demise, just six months after her father, represented a great loss for the community, but to Fatima it was a homecoming anticipated with great joy.

Besides their two sons, the noble martyrs, Hasan and Husayn, Hazrat 'Ali and Hazrat Fatima had a gifted third child, a daughter named Zaynab. While the sons were brought up as heirs to the khalifate of their grandfather Muhammad, Lady Zaynab also received a strong education, whose foundations were laid by the Prophet and extended by her mother. After Fatima's passing, Imam 'Ali took great care to continue Zaynab's education.

By the time of his khalifate nearly two decades later, she was a well-known and respected teacher in the community, a recognized authority in Qur'an exegesis, hadith and Islamic law. Her knowledge was such that she was called the "Proxy of the Imam," and *Alimah Ghayr Mu'allamah* ("she who has spiritual knowledge without being taught"). She was also known as *Balighah* (intensely eloquent) for her clarity and eloquence of speech. A gifted teacher, Zaynab held a special place in the community as an educator, for many years holding well-attended classes to educate the women of Medina. She married and raised five children, but preferred the bliss and comforts of the next world to adornments in this, saying, for her, the life of this world is a resting place to relieve fatigue along a journey.

Her life was marred by great sadness when, in her fifties—a few years after the assassination of her father and subsequent death of her eldest brother, Imam Hasan—she traveled to Karbala with her dearly beloved remaining brother, Imam Husayn. There, under most trying circumstances, she witnessed his brutal massacre and the slaughter of most of her extended family, including her two sons. She and a few other family members, including Husayn's son, 'Ali Zayn ul-Abidin, survived the ordeal only to be thrown into prison, her brother's noble head gruesomely displayed in public on a stake. Taken before Caliph Yazid for arraignment, Hazrat Zaynab fearlessly accused him of his wrongs, apprised the court of the Prophet's great love for the martyred Husayn, and ultimately secured her own release as well as freedom for her remaining kin.

All of the noble women we have mentioned, in one way or another, took an active part in sharing religious knowledge and contributing to the educational system of their day. They stand as beautiful and authentic models of Islamic womanhood, balancing refined inner realization and piety with active divine service on behalf of the greater community.

We are now leaving the time of Rasulullah, and moving into the next generation of those who never saw the blessed Prophet in person, but received the benefit of his exalted spiritual influence and the teaching of Islam through the Qur'an, and through the guidance of his noble successors. One figure stands at the threshold of this era, a hidden friend of Allah whose reputation has assumed near-mythic proportions. He is the direct mystic link with the spirit of prophecy and the fullest intensity of the ascetic life characteristic of the first Sufis of Islam. Representative of all desert ascetics, all hidden saints and intercessors, all channels of mystical communion and disciples of Khidr , his intense spiritual gaze is transfixed beyond this world; this sun-parched desert mystic of Yemen, dressed in robes of burning white, is Uways al-Qarani.

UWAYS AL-QARANI

AMONG THE MEMBERS of the Prophet's extended community the near legendary Uways al-Qarani certainly ranks as the most intriguing of Allah's hidden friends. Known for his austerity, his prayers, and his intercessions on behalf of others, Uways is one of those who is said to have received instruction from the spirit *(ruhaniat)* of Muhammad; he also occasionally received communications directly from the Archangel Gabriel.

Uways bin Amir al-Qarani was born in the village of Qaran in Yemen. He was one of those who heard of the Prophet Muhammad and accepted Islam while the Prophet still lived in Mecca. Though he burned with love for Rasulullah, Uways was destined never to meet him in the flesh, nor would he be known as a *sahaba* (companion of Muhammad). Through mystic channels of communion the Prophet also possessed intimate knowledge of Uways and expressed great appreciation for him, calling him a great *waliyullah* (saint or mystic friend of Allah) among his *tabi'un* (believers). Thinking of Uways, the Rasulullah would sometimes turn his face towards Yemen and say, "Just now, I feel a sweet breeze (or breath) of Divine Mercy *(nafas ar-Rahman)* blowing to me from Yemen."

In Yemen, Uways tended camels for a living, accepting whatever people gave him for services rendered and never charging the poor. He distributed half of what he received to the needy, and used the rest to care for himself and his aged mother who was infirm and blind. In her helpless condition, she had no one to look after her except her son, a duty of love which he observed with great faithfulness; in turn he received the benefit of her loving prayers. After he learned about Rasulullah, Uways longed to make the journey to meet him in person. As his mother was totally dependant on him, she was extremely reticent to give him permission to make the long journey. In the end, she decided to allow him to go, but only on the condition that Uways return immediately if the Prophet was not there when he called upon him.

Uways agreed and traveled to Mecca where he knocked at the door of the Prophet's house. Fatima answered the door and they exchanged greetings of peace. She informed him that her father had gone to the Ka'ba and would be back later if he wished to wait. Uways asked Hazrat Fatima to convey to her esteemed father his heartfelt salaams from Uways of Qaran in Yemen, and then he bid her farewell. After that, he returned straightway to his mother in Yemen.

Later, when the Prophet returned, he immediately sensed a special quality of light as he entered the house. He asked, "O Fatima, has some radiant soul visited us today?" She replied that indeed someone named Uways al-Qarani had come to see him while he was out, and wished to convey to the Prophet the light of peace from Yemen. (An alternate version of this story, places it in Medina, with the Prophet's wife, 'A'isha answering the door. In either case, the Rasulullah afterwards spoke highly of Uways.)

One day, the Prophet remarked to his companions, "There is a man in my *umma* (community) who, at the resurrection, will intercede for a vast multitude of my people; his intercession will extend to as many souls as there are hairs on the sheep of the Rabi'a and Mudar tribes." When the companions asked this person's identity, the Prophet replied simply that he was one of Allah's servants. "But we are all servants of Allah," they countered. "Can you tell us his name?"

"His name is Uways," the Rasulullah told them, "and he lives in Qaran in Yemen."

"Has he seen you, then?" they inquired.

"He hasn't seen me with his physical eyes."

At this, the companions expressed their surprise that such a person, who obviously had great love for the Prophet, had not come to serve him and be in his presence. "There are two reasons for that," he replied. "One is that Uways is absorbed by his spiritual states *(ahwal);* and the other is his immense respectfulness towards the precepts of my religion. He has an old mother who has also declared her *shahada* (accepting Islam). She is blind and cannot move her hands and feet, so Uways stays with her and supports her by tending camels."

Hearing this, one of them asked if the Prophet thought any of them might ever meet Uways. He looked at Abu Bakr and said, "You will not see him in your lifetime." Then turning towards 'Umar and 'Ali he added, "But you will. He is a lowly, hairy man, of medium height; he can be identified by a patch of whiteness the size of a *dirhem* (coin) on his left side and another one on the palm of his right hand. When you see him, relay my salaams to him and ask him to pray for my *umma*." Toward the very end of his life, the Prophet also expressed the wish that Uways be brought one of his own cloaks.

During the caliphate of 'Umar (after Rasulullah and Abu Bakr had passed away), Hazrat 'Umar came to Mecca bringing with him Hazrat 'Ali and the cloak of Rasulullah. There, he gave the Friday *khutba* and, in the course of that sermon, cried out to the congregation, "O men of Najd, are there any natives of Qaran amongst you?" When some of them answered, "Yes," 'Umar sent for them and asked them about Uways. Indeed, they knew of him, but they assured the caliph that this person was an extremely odd and unkempt man who was given to hiding out in the desert, far from other people. They said, "He doesn't eat what we eat nor does he feel joy or sorrow as we do. When others smile, he weeps; and when others weep, he smiles. Sometimes, if they see him, the children throw stones at him, but he only speaks gently to them, entreating them only to throw tiny stones so that he won't be distracted by wounds bleeding during his prayers." When 'Umar insisted upon finding him, some of the people agreed to take them to the Valley of Arnah where Uways was tending their camels.

When 'Umar and 'Ali arrived there, they found Uways engaged in prayer, and waited for him to finish. (Tradition adds that an angel, appointed by Allah, was tending the camels for him while he prayed.) When Uways arose from prayer, 'Umar and 'Ali approached him, exchanged salaams with him, and asked him his name. "*Abdullah* (God's servant)," was the reply.

"We're all God's servants," 'Umar told him. "What is your real name?"

"Uways," he responded. Then they had him show his right hand.

"Our master, *Sayyidina* Muhammad, sends his salutations to you as well as his blessed cloak. He said, 'Wear this and then pray for my *umma*.'" But Uways protested, telling 'Umar that this request must have been meant for someone else, since he, Uways, was but a weak, sinful and incapable servant. 'Umar assured him there was no mistake. Then Uways reverently accepted the cloak, kissed it and held it to his face, breathing the rose fragrance which still slightly lingered on it.

"Please wait here for a while," he said to them, and went off a short distance. Laying the cloak reverentially upon the earth, Uways prostrated on it and prayed for the community *(umma)* of Muhammad. "O Lord," he said, "this cloak is the cloak of Your beloved Messenger. He has presented it to me, but I refuse to wear it unless you pardon his *umma*." After some time, he received inward Divine confirmation that one third of the community of Muhammad had been accepted. More long prayers followed, along with confirmation of another third of the community. Finally, after a very long wait, 'Umar and 'Ali approached him. "O, you've interrupted me!" Uways sighed. "I had received Allah's intercession for two-thirds of the Muslims and was very near receiving pardon for them all when you came up." However, since so many had received divine acceptance as a result of his prayers, Uways was willing to put on the cloak.

They spoke further, and Uways asked 'Ali what he was able to *see* (spiritually) when he looked at Muhammad. 'Ali mentioned one occasion when they were destroying the idols in the Ka 'ba at Mecca.

Hazrat 'Ali and the Prophet Muhammad destroy the idols in the Ka'ba.

The Prophet instructed 'Ali to stand on his shoulders in order to destroy some of the idols which were out of reach. When 'Ali protested that, rather, the Prophet should stand on his shoulders, the Messenger of Allah declined, saying, "Believe me, If I did, you would be crushed by the weight; so please do as I have asked." Only then did 'Ali reluctantly consent to stand upon the blessed shoulders of the Prophet. But when he climbed into place and looked up through the open roof of the Ka 'ba, he was amazed by what he saw. Above him, he witnessed an unveiling of the entire cosmos, shining through the form of Rasulullah's face. "Ah," Uways remarked, "What you saw was just a small glimpse of him."

Sufis find a profound symbolism in this act. The Prophet Muhammad, profound embodiment of the sacred law or *shariat* of Islam, revealed himself as the living foundation of the religion which raises up and supports the mystic *tarikat*. The *tarikat* (Sufism), represented by Hazrat 'Ali, leads to a direct spiritual revelation of the Divine Truth *(hakikat)*.

After 'Umar and 'Ali had visited with him for some time, Uways told them: "You have taken trouble (to come see me); now return, for the resurrection is near, when we will see each other without having to say farewell. At present, I am myself preparing for the resurrection."

After 'Umar and 'Ali's visit, the men of Qaran began to show great respect for Uways. Meanwhile, his mother having died, Uways moved to Kufa and became even more reclusive so that very few people ever saw him. Later, he was reported to have told someone that the people with whom he had spoken the most were Hazrat 'Umar and Hazrat 'Ali. He was also quoted as saying, "In this passing life, do not ever banish the fear of Allah from your heart. The only way to salvation is to obey him."

One man who did manage to find Uways and converse with him was Harim bin Hayyan. He reports:

When I heard the hadith of Rasulullah, peace and blessings be upon him, about the intercessory power *(shafa'a)* of Uways' prayers, I longed to meet him and traveled to Kufa in search of him. I found Uways taking his ablution by the side of the Euphrates River. Recognizing him by his description, I approached him with the greeting of peace, *"As-salaam 'aleikum."* He returned my salaams, but wouldn't allow me to kiss his hand [the traditional way in which they used to show respect for the Prophet, and later for sheikhs in many of the Sufi orders]. I said, "O Uways, may Allah's mercy be upon you. How are you?" He was extremely emaciated and as I gazed upon him, pity began to well up in me until I burst into tears. Uways began to weep as well, and then surprised me by calling my name: "O Harim bin Hayyan! How are you, my brother? May Allah grant you a fruitful life. Who pointed me out to you?" Ignoring his questions, I blurted out, "How did you know my name and my father's name without having ever met me?"

"The All-Knowing, All-Aware One told me. My soul recognized your soul, because the souls of the believers recognize one another even if they have never met." I asked him to share with me any saying of the Prophet known to him, but he deferred, saying, "I never saw him and only heard his words from others. It has never been an occupation of mine to collect ahadith." So I asked him to at least chant with his own voice an ayat from the Qur'an. He grabbed my hands and intoned the traditional introductory formula, *"A 'udhu billahi min ash-Shaitan ir-rajim."* ("I take refuge in Allah from the evil influence of Satan, the accursed.") At this he began to weep, but then continued with *Sura Zariyat* (51:56): *"Wa ma khalaqtal-Jinna wal-'insa 'illa liya 'budun."* ("I have created the *jinn* and human beings only for the purpose of knowing and worshiping Me.") Then he added an ayat from *Sura Enbiya* (21:16): "Not for idle sport did We create the heavens and earth and all that lies in between!" At this he gave out a loud cry, causing me to wonder whether he had taken leave of his senses.

"O son of Hayyan!" he said suddenly. "Why did you come here?" I replied that my purpose was to make *sohbet* (conversation) with him and to get to know him. Then he mused, "I could never understand why, after someone meets with Allah Most High, they would crave the company of other created beings."

I decided to ask him for advice and received this animated reply: "When you go to sleep, know that death is under your pillow. When you awake, also keep its awareness right in front of you. Don't ever dismiss your sins as being insignificant; rather, consider that no matter how small they might be, they are acts of disobedience which separate you from Allah, so keep your attention on that. If you think your sins are small, you make your Lord who prohibited these acts small as well."

"Could you advise me on where I should settle?" I

ventured. "You should go to Damascus," he replied. "And what would I do there?" I queried. "I pity your heart," he told me, "which is filled with so many doubts." I asked for a little more advice.

"Look, O son of Hayyan! Your father died, Adam died, Noah died, Muhammad died. They all died, as did Abu Bakr and my brother 'Umar." He stopped and drew in his breath. "Ah! 'Umar! Ah, 'Umar—may you be in the Mercy of Allah!"

"But Hazrat 'Umar has not yet passed away," I informed him. "Allah Most High informed me that he has passed away," he said quietly, and then offered a *salawat* (blessing upon the Prophet) and a short prayer for the soul of Caliph 'Umar [who had indeed been assassinated in Medina just days before].

Then Uways looked straight at me and offered these parting words of advice: "We are amongst the dead, you and I. Never let the Book of Allah slip from your hands, nor the *sirat al-mustaqim* (straight path) which is mentioned in it; and never forget about death. When you go back to your people, advise them well, and cling to the teachings of the *Ahl-i Sunna* (the People who know the way of Muhammad), so that you won't lose your religion and, without realizing it, end up in hell." He offered a short prayer and then said sternly, "Go, Harim bin Hayyan! From this point on, neither of us should see the other again. Remember me in your prayers and I will remember you in mine. You go this way and I will go the other."

I still longed to walk with him a little more but he wouldn't allow it. He ran away and began weeping as he ran. I also wept as I gazed after him, a tiny figure disappearing on the horizon and finally entering into the city. I never heard from him again.

After this, Uways continued to dwell alone in the wilderness, avoiding all contact with society. He did make a pilgrimage to

Mecca and Medina in subsequent years, but fainted at Rasulullah's tomb, saying when he awoke, "Take me away from here! I don't have the taste for living in a place where our holy Prophet is buried."

One man, named Rebbi bin Haysan, tried to visit Uways, but found him doing morning prayers that lasted till the commencement of noon prayers, which continued until the beginning of the afternoon prayers, and so on, so that there never seemed to be an end to them. For three days, Rebbi did not disturb Uways but observed that he neither ate nor slept, but only engaged in continuous prayer.

He had heard that Uways entered great states of ecstasy in prayer and desired to emulate the worship of the angels. Tradition has it that, after the Prophet's heavenly ascent *(miraj),* he introduced the form of Islamic prayers to his followers, basing the motions upon the postures assumed by the angels on various levels of the seven heavens. Taking the angels as his model, Uways would one night declare to himself, "This is the night of *sajda* (prostration)," thus aspiring to enter into the consciousness of the ones who are in eternal prostration. The following night would be the night of *qiyyam* (standing prayer), then the night of *ruku* (bowing with hands on the knees), and so on.

Rebbi watched him for three days, and noticed on the fourth day that Uways showed signs of fatigue. Finally, Uways began to doze off at prayer; but he quickly awoke and beseeched his Lord, *"Ya Rabb!* Please protect these eyes from wanting too much sleep and this stomach from wanting too much to eat!" Rebbi, who had waited for days to hear some utterance from Uways, heard these words and said to himself, "This is good enough for me." He left without ever having spoken with Uways.

Some others did manage to converse with Uways and inquire as to how he was able to endure such long devotions without food or sleep. He said, "Actually, I don't have the strength necessary to do it. I spend all night in prostration and by morning, I still haven't even said the first *'Subhana Rabbil 'ala'*. [During prostration in prayer, the worshiper is supposed to utter this phrase of divine glorification at least three times.] I often can't say even one of them. I keep attempting because I want to enter into the angelic way of worship."

"But how about the ecstasy and joy in *salat*?" they asked. "If someone put a needle through your throat, you wouldn't feel it if you have that ecstasy in *salat*," he answered. "And what do *you* feel?" they continued. "Do you know the state of a person who wakes up in the morning and doesn't know whether he will be alive by nightfall?" he replied. "What is this way like?" they asked. He looked at them and said, "O, there is much pain on the long road of meager sustenance." Then he gave them a parting piece of advice: "If you are able to know Allah Most High, then that is all that matters; may you forget about everything else. And if Allah Most High knows you, then may He alone know you. That in itself will suffice."

Uways died a martyr in 657 CE, while fighting on the side of Hazrat 'Ali at the battle of Siffin during the Muslim civil war. No direct disciple is known to have succeeded Uways, and yet over the centuries, a loose tradition of Uwaysian independent mystics has flourished, all of them led  by the spirit without the aid of living guides or sheikhs. Each of them in turn look to the great mystic intercessor of Qaran as their spiritual Pir.

REPENTANCE, LOVE AND MASTERY

WE HAVE GIVEN a rather detailed portrait of the mystic life of prayer and intercession lived by this enigmatic and reclusive saint from the time of Rasulullah, Uways al-Qarani, in some cases drawing upon Turkish source material[18] previously untranslated into the English language. The cloak of the Prophet which was given to Uways eventually made its way to Istanbul (as have many other relics from the Prophet's time) and was enshrined by Sultan 'Abdul Majid in a special mosque in the Fatih area called "The Mosque of the Blessed Cloak." There the cloak, which is not the green one but the camel-colored cloak of the Prophet, can be seen on display during the holy month of Ramadan.

We may take Uways himself as a classic representative of the severe style of desert spirituality that flourished from the time of the Christian Desert Fathers and anchorite hermits, such as St. Anthony of Thebes, throughout the period of the early Sufi masters. This Uwaysian way, the austere path of the world-renouncing *fakir*, emaciated and disheveled—seemingly half-mad through absorption in divine contemplation, appears extreme to modern eyes, even as it did to the conventional minds of his own time who could not appreciate the nature of his *fana*, or inward absorption, in the Divine Reality.

His state is characterized by an intense love of Allah manifesting as divine awe and the fear of lapsing into divine disfavor through heedlessness and sin. The brevity of this life is ever before his eyes as is the glory of the resurrection. For such souls, the path abounds with intense weeping and repentance, long solitary periods of prayer, fasting, and great ecstasy.

When Uways advises Harim bin Hayyan to always remember that death is under his pillow, he is not advocating some morbidly fatalistic world-view. Rather, he is prescribing an age old medicine for spiritual complacency. While the soul lives in this world, it often tends to procrastinate in the pursuit of its ideals, secure in the illusion that physical death is always far away. The antidote to this instinctual blind spot in the psyche is called by the Sufis *dhikr al-mawt*, the constant remembrance of death, which puts the priorities of one's life into clear perspective as nothing else can. A Turkish proverb sums up the relative brevity of human life in the spirit of Uways al-Qarani:

18 *Evliyalar Ansiklopedisi*, vol.12, 141-53.

Mystic Love: The Heart of Islam

*I come from my mother's womb, I go to the bazaar and buy
my shroud; then I enter my grave.*

There are seven levels on the mystical path. The first step is
repentance: awakening from life's intoxication and overcoming
the negative patterns of behavior arising from the limited self.
This is accomplished primarily through remembrance of one's
own Essential Source. Through prayer, dhikr, alms-giving, the
wise guidance of Qur'an and one's sheikh, and by identifying with
one's divine inheritance, one gradually becomes free from the
control of one's aggressive animal qualities, becoming more fully
human and humane. This is the initial station or *makam* which
played so important a part in the lives of the earliest followers of
the Prophet *(ummati Muhammad)*.

The second step, abstinence, is an equally important part of the
path, a stage whose prescriptions involve retreat and fasting—
from food as well as from impure habits and thoughts. It is the
makam of spiritual discipline, of standing back and saying "no"
to one's habitual self-indulgent tendencies, of awakening from
the sleep of unconscious behavior. For the early Sufis, this was
frequently linked with a sense of divine awe and the fear of falling
out of grace, through transgressions born of heedlessness *(gaflet)*.
In more modern terms, we might speak about healing spiritual
alienation and turning away from negativity toward the Source of
Love. Divine awe, in contemporary terms, balances our natural
narcissism with a greater perspective, allowing us to sense how
small one individual is in the larger scheme of things in a vast,
infinite universe. The perspective of unity, in turns, avoids the
isolated feeling of the existentialist, in favor of a realization of
connectedness with all life. By serving others and the collective
good, and not just our own personal needs, we help ourselves and
render divine service.

Neither Qur'an nor hadith ever present Allah merely as a purveyor
of severe judgment upon the soul. Rather, absolute justice and
fairness, tempered with loving-compassion, is promised to every
soul by Allah, the Primal Source of Being, who is also known by
the name, *As-Sattar*, the One who covers for our faults.

Throughout the Qur'an, Allah continually reveals Himself as the Merciful *(Rahman)* and Compassionate *(Rahim)* Source, and this same Supreme Reality conveys to humanity, through His beloved Prophet (in a *hadith qudsi*) the good news that "My mercy prevails over my wrath." In another hadith the Prophet revealed to a companion named Mu'adh that he had received word from Allah that whoever sincerely says *"La ilaha illallah"* and has even a drop of goodness in them, Allah will save them from perdition and accept them in Paradise. Elated with this revelation, Mu'adh asked whether he should immediately go and spread the good news to everyone. "You'd better not," replied the Messenger of Allah, "lest they become complacent through too much reliance on it." (Several other companions, including 'Uthman and Ibn 'Abbas, also reported hearing such tidings independently from Rasulullah.)

In moderation, all the ascetic qualities of Uways al-Qarani and various other companions can also be found in the noble Prophet Muhammad; but in the Prophet we see a greater perfection and balance, a personality permeated by the sweetness of divine love, mercy and the joy of human companionship. It is this sweetness of divine love and attraction—manifested in the Qur'an as *Bismillah ir-Rahman ir-Rahim*—that has drawn countless souls to follow the exalted way of Islam and the *sunna* of the Prophet Muhammad, and has blossomed over the centuries as the Sufi path of love, a rich spirituality capable of attracting the modern spiritual aspirant as well as the more traditional mystic.

In the centuries following the passing of the Seal of Prophets *(Khatem-un-Nabiyin)*, a number of saints *(awliya)* of mystic love began to appear among the community of Muhammad. The first generation emphasized the station of repentance and awe of the divine. As the perception of the mystics penetrated deeper, the gates of divine mercy began to open wider, revealing a vast ocean of mystic love in which the lover is intoxicated by the wine of love—the revelation of the Divine Presence itself. For the lover, Allah becomes idealized as the Beloved, the true possessor of the heart, the One who is nearer than near and is actually the innermost secret of one's true Self. We shall see the unfurling of this station of passionate divine love evidenced in the lives of a number of saints of mystic love: the enlightened lady, Rabi'a al-'Adawiyya, of ninth-century Basra, the tenth-century martyr of love, Mansur al-Hallaj, the thirteenth century poet of Anatolia, Mevlana Jelaluddin Rumi, and the seventeenth century Seal of Pirs, Nureddin al-Jerrahi.

This great love has become the central motif of Sufism which balances and beautifies the rugged asceticism of times past, when only the door of repentance and fear of judgment seemed to beckon the believer, when few would have thought of speaking of God as "the Beloved." In fact, Muhammad's enemies in Mecca originally challenged his very linkage of Allah with the quality of mercy, saying, "Who is this *Rahman* of whom he speaks?"[19]

While the vessels of spirituality in Sufism have undoubtedly broadened over the course of time, the essential foundations of *tasawwuf* (mysticism) remain the same today as in the past. The initial step on the path is still repentance—the desire to extricate oneself from negative, alienating patterns of behavior—while the false self (or limited ego-identity) continues to be the veil that clouds our realization of who we really are and diverts us from the direct experience of paradise consciousness.

Thus the Sufi draws upon the energy of the spiritual warrior in order to overcome the intoxicating pull of the world and the conventional paradigms of society which lull us away from remembrance *(dhikr)* of our divine inheritance. But this interior spiritual warfare does not involve a battle in which one attempts to slay the ego. Rather, Sufism aims to transform the tyrannical attributes of the ego and the animal characteristics of one's nature through the energies of the divine qualities, causing them to blossom forth in useful service to the whole Self. The ego, or personal self, with all its desires and aversions, constitutes a relatively narrow setting of consciousness which longs to be transcended and transformed for use by the higher levels of soul rather than starved, despised or repressed. When the nineteenth century Sufi murshid, Abu Hashim Mandani, was asked about austerities such as all-night vigils by his young disciple, Hazrat

19 Qur'an 25:60.

Inayat Khan, the master simply replied: "Whom do you torture?"

Where the rishi or monk may dedicate their whole life to retirement and denial of the flesh, the contemporary Muslim or dervish, still following the example of the blessed Prophet, is only expected to set aside one month out of the year (the month of Ramadan) for intense inner purification and outward fasting (from sunrise to sundown). Furthermore, this is done in community and is never to be engaged in with a long face. Ramadan is considered the month of Allah's great mercy and boundless generosity.

The path begins as a spiritual struggle in the soul *(jihad)* in which the individual attempts to use the personal will to better oneself and to come closer to Allah; at a further stage, the path becomes an alchemical transformation of one's whole being in which the perceived dualism of "self" and "Lord" is unmasked to reveal that no will nor separate self exists apart from the one Divine Will. It is Allah who mysteriously puts it in one's heart to change and then effects the change, though the individual may have the feeling of putting personal effort into it and deserving some credit. One way in which the Qur'an expresses this mystery is to say: "Let whoever will, take the right path to their Lord. Yet, in reality, you cannot will, except by the will of Allah." (81:29) At the highest level on the mystic path of God-realization, the language of servanthood *('ubudiyyat)* is still retained, even though there is no thought of separation. In fact, according to the science of *tasawwuf*, to consider oneself as a discreet entity, separate from the One Reality, is actually the highest and most subtle form of idolatry *(shirk)*.

As Hazrat 'Ali nobly stated: "Man is a wave in the boundless Sea of God. As long as man's vision is clouded by ignorance and sensuality he will consider himself a separate entity, different from God. But when the veil between him and God is lifted he will know who he really is. The wave will merge with the ocean."[20]

---

20 Masud-ul-Hasan, *Hadrat 'Ali*, R.A., 355.

We would ask the reader to take time at this point to read Appendix II which examines in some detail the structure of the mystical path, with its four worlds and seven levels. Many of the basic concepts of Sufism which are referred to in the remainder of this book are thoroughly explained there.

SECTION TWO
The Rise of Sufism

THE HALVETI-JERRAHI SILSILA

EVERY TARIKAT *(TARIQA)* traces its lineage of transmission though various grand-sheikhs and pirs on a time-line beginning with the Prophet Muhammad, peace and blessing be upon him, and continuing down through the founding pir of their specific Sufi order to the present day head of the order. While a tarikat may have many sheikhs and sheikhas, the grand-sheikh is the living spiritual head of the order who sits on the *asitane* post, which is the headquarters of the tarikat, usually situated in the city where the tomb of the founding pir of that order is located.

Traditionally, when a dervish has gone through a training and is made a sheikh or sheikha in an order, that dervish is given an *ijazet* or diploma, which is often a long scroll listing, usually in Arabic, the chain of spiritual transmission (or *baraka)* from the Prophet Muhammad, through each grand-sheikh, down to their own spiritual guide. Their name is listed at the bottom as a *khalifa* of their sheikh and is stamped with the special seal of the order. The term *khalifa* is used in the tarikat to denote a certain spiritual level in which a dervish is designated a deputy or representative of their sheikh and is given special practices, but does not necessarily have permission to initiate others. The term *sheikh* normally denotes a further level of autonomy: one who has full permission to open their own tekke, teach, and give *bayat* (initiation) to others.

Though most dervish orders have, in the past, emphasized male participation, some turuq have, over the centuries, been open to women's participation. In modern times especially, one can observe more sheikhas and murshidas becoming active participants and teachers in the orders. (It is worth noting that women have always been empowered to lead other women in Islamic ritual prayer— for over a thousand years—during which time, by comparison, Christian women were only permitted to receive the sacraments from a male priest.) Though this recognition of the feminine contribution is becoming more pronounced in recent decades, history shows that there has never been an absence of enlightened women teachers and saints during any period of Islamic history. Though not well-known, Sufi tradition speaks of a highly advanced black woman in the time of 'Abdul Qadir Gaylani, whom the saint recognized as a *qutb*. Rabi'a al-'Adawiyya is undoubtedly the most celebrated of women mystic saints and one very close in time to the Rasulullah.

In this chapter, we will historically survey the lives and historical times of some of the most notable sheikhs and founding pirs of the Halveti-Jerrahi order, as well as other saints and important pirs whose contributions to the development of Sufism are relevant to the broader context of this spiritual family tree. The emphasis will be on the evolution of major trends and ideas in Sufism as well as stories from the lives of these masters of the mystic way.

Occasionally, when presented with elements of the miraculous in these stories, it is best to observe the point the story makes and any allegorical teaching that it conveys, rather than focusing on how literally the account should be taken. Although anything is possible for Allah, not every teaching story is meant to be taken literally. It has been said that if one is impressed with someone who walks on water, a piece of wood floats in water with more ease; if to fly in the air is considered great, a bird can do it better. Rather, what is truly miraculous and marvelous is the person who becomes fully human and establishes their heart as the throne of Divine Love.

The Halveti-Jerrahi *silsila* (chain of transmission) divides naturally into three sections. The first covers from the time of the Prophet and Hazrat 'Ali through the pir who founded the *Khalwati (Halveti* in Turkish) line, Hazrati Pir 'Umar al-Halveti (and his immediate khalifas in fourteenth century Anatolia). The second period reaches from Pir 'Umar's successor, Pir Yahya Shirvani through Sheikh 'Ali Alauddin Kostendili and his successor, Hazrati Pir Nureddin Jerrahi, in Istanbul around the beginning of the eighteenth century CE. The third section is the line of the Jerrahiyya, starting with Pir Nureddin and his seven main khalifas, coming down to Fahreddin Efendi, who presided as the Jerrahi grand-sheikh at the beginning of the twentieth century, when the all the tekkes in Turkey were officially closed.

For those who are interested in Sufism, as well as those in the West who are connected with the Halveti-Jerrahi path, or one of the other noble *turuq* of Islam, it is our intention to provide a broad overview of the order's history and teachings up to the modern era.

What has been presented so far is but a small drop from the vast ocean of knowledge which flows from the Rasulullah's time, when the divine power and wisdom descended to earth in the form of the holy Qur'an. The divine message has been given to humanity in the form of the written Qur'an *(kitab)* and the interior wisdom *(hikma),* mentioned in *Surat al-Jumu'ah* (62:2), a two-fold revelation which manifests both as the *shariat (shari'a),* the sacred law of the Islamic religion, and the *tarikat (tariqa),* the spiritual path of the mystics. According to tradition, during the *mir'aj* (ascension of the Prophet Muhammad), 90,000 words or teachings were communicated to the Prophet. However, only 30,000 would he publicly mention; these dealt with the general understanding, suitable for everyone *(umum)*, while another 30,000 involved a deeper, more mystical level, suitable for the intimate friends of Allah who have a deeper understanding of Reality *(has)*. The last 30,000 were for the mystic heart of the Rasulullah alone, and could not be told nor put into words. The mystic tradition then, verbally and non-verbally, was transmitted by the holy Prophet to men like Salman al-Farsi, Uways al-Qarani, the Prophet's daughter, Fatima, and to his four khalifas, especially Hazrat 'Ali ibn Abi Talib, the gate of the city of esoteric knowledge.

Hazrat 'Ali had seventy disciples, and after his death these disciples appointed four persons from among themselves to be pirs or elders. These four consisted of: Kumayl, Hasan and Husayn (Ali's two son by Hazrat Fatima), as well as Hasan Basri, who is today recognized as the spiritual head of three great turuq: the *Qadiriyya*, the *Chistiyya* and the *Suhrawardiyya*. Hasan of Basra grew up in Medina where his mother was a maidservant of one of the Prophet's wives, Umm Salama. During his lifetime, Hasan was able to visit some 130 of the companions of the Prophet and, though rather young at the time of Imam 'Ali's passing, received the spiritual transmission from 'Ali and was appointed as one of his chief successors to carry on the esoteric teaching of Islam. Later, when Hasan moved to Basra, he became a close acquaintance of Rabi 'a al- 'Adawiyya, who also lived there.

The two most prominent disciples of Hasan Basri (d.728 CE) were 'Abdul Wahid ibn Zayd and Habib al-Ajami. These men in turn stand at the head of two main lines of the tarikat of 'Ali. From 'Abdul Wahid comes four branches, including the *Adhamiyya*, connected with Ibrahim Adham, the famous king of Balkh who gave up crown and throne to become a humble dervish ascetic *(zahid)*, and the *Chistiyya* (through Abu Ishaq Shami Chisti). From Habib al-Ajami (d.773) came eight further branches. These include the ecstatic line of the *Tayfuriyya* (or *Bistamiyya)* from Abu Yazid *(Bayazid)* Bistami of Khurasan (d.874) and the famous Baghdad school of sobriety known as the *Junaydiyya*, from Abu'l Qasim Junayd (d.910), from which sprung the *Qadiriyya* and *Rifa'iyya* lines as well as the *Suhrawardiyya* line, all in Mesopotamia.

Habib al-Ajami taught Da'ud at-Ta'i (d.777), who taught Ma'ruf al-Karkhi (d.815). All of them were ascetics and teachers of great renown in their time. Ma'ruf al-Karkhi taught Sari as-Saqati (d.867), who was the first man to preach in Baghdad on the mystic truths and the Sufi unity, and may be considered along with Muhasibi as the founder of the Baghdad school. Sari as-Saqati taught his spiritually-gifted nephew (his sister's son), Junayd, who built on the foundations of his teachers to became one of the most formative and influential figures in the history of early Sufism. Through Junayd, the chain of transmission passes to many, many orders, including the *Khalwatiyya* and the *Jerrahiyya*, whose lines we are tracing down to the modern times.

Again, the earliest phase of Sufism took the form of asceticism, a renunciant lifestyle characterized by a strong consciousness of the sin of divine disobedience and the need to repent. (Later on, a stage would be recognized in which one repents of repentance.) One of the reasons for the ascetic approach is to be found in the political conditions of the Ummayad period, after the time of Hazrat 'Ali, when disgust with the impious tyranny of wealthy so-called Islamic rulers led the pious to renounce the world in favor of a life of seclusion far from the decadence and intrigues of the royal palaces and harems.

At first, voluntary poverty was considered practically a prerequisite for paradise, but later the idea of salvation through literal poverty was replaced by an ideal of simply being unattached to worldly possessions. The lovers of God might legitimately have money in their pockets as long as God, not money, was in their hearts. A wealthy man tried to give Hazrat Junayd some money, but Junayd refused saying that the rich man had a better right to it than he. When the rich man looked puzzled, Junayd asked him, "Do you have more than this?" The man replied, "O yes, a lot more!" Junayd led him on: "And would you like to have more money?" When the man affirmed that he would, Junayd told him, "Then please keep your money. As for me, I possess nothing and need nothing."

A HISTORICAL OVERVIEW
OF THE EARLY PERIOD OF ISLAM

AT THIS POINT, before looking in more detail at the lives of the early masters of Sufism, a brief review of the geographical and political growth of exoteric Islam after the Prophet's death will serve us well, furnishing a cogent context for understanding the ascetic period and the subsequent rise of organized Sufi turuq as they emerged in Baghdad and elsewhere around the close of the second century (Islamic calendar).

In June 632 CE, upon receiving news of the death of the Prophet Muhammad, upon him be peace, many of the Arabian confederates declared their prior agreements with the Rasulullah nullified and thus refused to pay further taxes. As the newly-appointed caliph representing the Prophet, Abu Bakr was immediately thrust into war against them in order to re-establish Islamic sovereignty. One of the Islamic army commanders, Khalid ibn al-Walid, was particularly successful in winning victories in Syria. Damascus was taken in 636 CE, followed by the conquest of Jerusalem in the Holy Land in 638, during the reign of Caliph 'Umar, and soon thereafter the rest of Byzantine Syria fell to the Muslims.

Syria became the eventual base of power for the Ummayad dynasty after Caliph 'Uthman installed his cousin Mu'awiya as governor of that region. With thousands of troops at his command, Mu'awiya became too powerful for Caliph 'Ali to dislodge during his term. This left Mu'awiya free to simply take over the Caliphate after 'Ali's passing. Over the next half century, Egypt was taken from the Byzantines and gradually much of the rest of North Africa. Another contender who revolted against the Ummayads and declared himself caliph, 'Abdullah ibn az-Zubayr, held Mecca for better than a year before being defeated by the infamously cruel and forceful leading general of the Ummayad caliphs, Yusuf ibn al-Hajjaj. Under the command of Hajjaj, the Arab armies expanded into India and Central Asia, up to the borders of China.

The Byzantine Christian capital, Constantinople was attacked several times between 660 and 717 CE, but was not taken. There the aged standard-bearer, Abu Ayyub Ansari *(Eyüp Sultan)*, a prominent companion of the Prophet, was martyred. His tomb and mosque in Istanbul have attracted the pious for centuries. In Ottoman times, the Mosque of Eyüp Sultan became the site where the sultans would ceremoniously gird their swords. The Byzantines were also able to hold Anatolia and the Balkans during the early Islamic period, keeping them in Christian hands.

By the seventh century CE, the two superpowers of the time, the Byzantine heirs of the "Holy Roman Empire" and the Sasanian empire of the Zoroastrians in Persia had become militarily exhausted by many decades of warfare (frequently against one another). Both parties had become highly unpopular with the subjects they ruled. Thus, when the Muslims invaded, it was often without much bloodshed or resistance from the populace; in fact, many of the people welcomed them with open arms and joined them against their former overlords.

The Rise of Sufism

The Zoroastrian state-sponsored religion of Persia had hardened into a very degenerate and dualistic teaching. Upheld by corrupt ministers and ritual-bound fire-worshiping priests, it could not compete with the fiery missionary zeal of the Islamic renewal of the Abrahamic faith. Having become a largely Europeanized, state-sponsored religion, seventh century Christianity had also lost much of its purity and spiritual power. However, it managed to hold on to many of its lands, while the older Zoroastrian cultures seemed completely spent and soon crumbled before the Muslim invaders.

The Islamic capital was moved to Damascus during the period of the Ummayad Dynasty (661-750 CE). Early on, the Muslims had taken the relatively new Iraqi cities of Kufa and Basra as bases of attack northward. Soon Spain was taken (711-759 CE) as well as Transoxania and Sicily—indeed the whole of the Middle East fell into Muslim hands in a surprisingly short period of time.

Caliph 'Umar had set the precedent of shielding the native populations from too much disturbance after their conquests, and maintained the Qur'anic policy of not forcing conversions to Islam. Instead, a great deal of autonomy was left to the native social and religious leaders and their people, who simply paid taxes to an unobtrusive Arab elite class of governors. The Muslims even helped to reorganize the Nestorian Church and made use of Nestorian Christians as educators in their system. Assimilation occurred naturally as large numbers of non-Muslims converted to Islam. There were a number of practical incentives for accepting Islam: doing so allowed converts not only to avoid the *dhimmi* tax[21] but to share power and equal-standing with the Muslim Arabs.

During the reign of 'Abdul Malik (685-705 CE) many great mosques were built, such as the Dome of the Rock in Jerusalem and the Grand Mosque at Damascus. Muslim conquests reached as far as France and the English Channel before being halted. As the period of expansion reached its farthest limits in the West, the

---

21 The *Jizya* tax was required by the Qur'an (9:29), a poll-tax to be paid to the Muslim authorities by the *dhimmi* (Jews and Christians) in "compensation" for their protection by the ruling Islamic government. Muslims were protected for free.

Ummayad power began to wane and especially suffered in Syria where it had become spread too thin.

When the Ummayads first came to power after the death of Caliph 'Ali, Mu'awiya was accepted as the next caliph by the majority of Muslims because he wielded the strong military might needed to re-unite the warring factions of Muslims. Rival factions who resented the Ummayads as tyrannical usurpers bided their time, waiting for an opportunity to revolt and expel them. This moment finally arrived in August, 750 CE, when the descendants of the Prophet's uncle al-'Abbas disposed of the last Ummayad caliph, Marwan II and his family, and assumed power, coming in on a wave of messianic popularity.

The Dome of the Rock in Jerusalem.

With the 'Abbasid revolution, the Islamic capital was moved to Baghdad in Northern Iraq, an international city which swelled to the size of half a million people, the largest in the world outside of China. This cosmopolitan city contained Persians, Iraqis, Nestorians, Jews, people of every persuasion, and is known to the Western world as the backdrop of the Arabian Nights lore, with its famous 'Abbasid caliph, Harun ar-Rashid (786-809 CE). The 'Abbasids encouraged art, poetry and religious debate, and glorified the role of the caliph to near divine proportions. Arabic poetry was collected and traditions of the Prophet codified; Hellenistic philosophy and learning was studied along with Persian culture. While the West languished in the "dark ages," science, algebra, history, and astronomy were all flourishing under the 'Abbasids. They supported Islamic customs such as the pilgrimage to Mecca, while subjecting heretical doctrines to increased government suppression and persecution. Incidentally, the word *algebra (al-jabr)* comes from the name of an Arabic book, *Hisab al-jabr wa al-muqabala*, written by a Persian Muslim scientist, Al-Khwarizmi (ca. 780-845 CE). He developed the mathematical concept of algorithms (the word is a corruption of his name), popularized Arabic numerals, and introduced the number zero to the West at a time when the Latins and Greeks were using neither zero nor the decimal system (the concept of zero or nothingness, *shunya*, being previously known in India).

THE FOUR SCHOOLS OF ISLAMIC JURISPRUDENCE

IT WAS DURING THIS PERIOD, approximately two centuries after the Prophet's death, that the Sufi turuq began to emerge as discreet entities, especially in the capital, Baghdad. At approximately the same time and place the Islamic *shari 'a* was being codified into a clear legislation through the science of *fiqh*. In certain ways, this development parallels the work of the fourth and fifth century ecumenical councils in the early Christian Church; but where the Christian Church insisted on legislating one orthodox set of dogmas, to be professed by all its members, Islam, as an orthopraxy, allowed for somewhat more leeway in the interpretation and expression of its religious practice.

Thus, the four major schools of Islamic jurisprudence came into being during the eighth and ninth centuries CE, based on the sayings and revelations of Muhammad, as well as extrapolated principles drawn from Qur'an, hadith, and the actions of the Prophet and his companions. (In cases where no clear precedent from the Qur'an or the *sunna* of the Prophet exists to guide one's action, Muslims are encouraged to pray for guidance and use *ijtihad*—personal reason and judgment—reflecting as much as possible in their decisions the spirit of the Qur'an.)

The four Sunni schools, or *madhahib*, were headed by Imam Abu Hanifa (d.767 CE) of Kufa, Imam Malik ibn Anas (d.795 CE), a Palestinian who grew up in Medina, and his Syrian student who spent much of his life in Egypt, Imam Muhammad ibn Idris ash-Shafi'i (d.820 CE), as well as Shafi'i's disciple, Imam Ahmad ibn Hanbal (d.855 CE). All four of these imams settled in or spent time in Baghdad studying and teaching. Their schools of law are known respectively as the *Hanafi*, the *Maliki*, the *Shafi'i,* and the *Hanbali*. (There are also Shi'ite schools such as the *Ja'fari* Twelve Imam school and the *Zaydis*, as well as the old *Kharijite* school, which was neither Sunni nor Shi'ite.) The authoritative hadith collections of Bukhari and Muslim were also compiled during this important and formative era of Islamic history.

At the time when the four schools of jurisprudence were coming into being the 'Abbasid caliph still had popular consent to govern the empire and to interpret law from the Qur'an as he saw fit. A new development, which could scarcely have foreseen, was set into motion when Caliph al-Mu'tasim ordered Imam Ibn Hanbal scourged and imprisoned for disagreeing with the *Mu'tazilite* doctrine which the caliph favored. This doctrine held that the Qur'an was not eternal but created, and thus under the caliph's control.

After al-Mu'tasim died, his son, al-Mutawakkil, proved to be a more tolerant successor,[22] freeing the persecuted doctor of law and honoring him and his anti-Mu'tazilite views in the royal court.

---

22 Though tolerant in this respect, al-Mutawakkil was known to persecute Jews and Christians, in violation of the spirit of the Qur'an, which advocates tolerance and respect for them as the People of the Book.

This signaled a swing of the pendulum toward viewing the Qur'an as eternal (at least in its heavenly prototype) and seeing the doctors of theology, rather than the temporal king, as the most appropriate interpreters of the uncreated divine word. Thereafter, the people held Ibn Hanbal in high esteem. Though he shunned the wealth of the court in favor of a reclusive lifestyle, the political events which had already involved him became pivotal in transferring the power of religious interpretative authority to the *'ulama'* (the Islamic theological scholars), causing the sphere of the caliph's influence to be relegated thereafter to the political arena.

It cannot be too deeply emphasized that the historical trend which gave rise to the codified legislation of the exoteric law in Islam under the control of the *'ulama'* also gave rise to its complimentary esoteric aspect in the form of organized *turuq* with their own sheikhs and mystical institutions. The emphasis of the Sufis lay with matters of the heart. Where the shariat prescribes how to technically perform obligatory acts of worship and moral codes of behavior, the tarikat provides the key to the intention and deeper significance which underlies them. Sufism thus provides a much needed alternative to the legalistic approach.

With this background in mind we can now return to our primary theme, the consideration of the tarikat and its mystic guides after the time of Hazrat 'Ali, beginning with Al-Hasan ibn Abu'l Hasan al-Basri.

HASAN AL-BASRI

THE PARENTS OF HASAN (642-728 CE) lived as freed slaves in Medina shortly after the time of the Prophet, peace be upon him. Hasan's father, who had been captured in Maisan, worked as a servant of the Prophet's secretary, Zayd ibn Thabet al-Ansari, while Hasan's mother was in the service of the Prophet's wife, Umm Salama. Though neither of the parents had accepted Islam at the time of Hasan's birth, they took the new-born child to Caliph

'Umar, who was impressed with the baby's beauty and gave him the name which means "beautiful;" Hasan. Though elderly, Umm Salama was able to occasionally nurse Hasan and was known to have prayed special *duas* on his behalf. She prayed: "*Ya Rabb* (O Lord)! make this child an imam to the world and a person who will be followed by humanity." Hasan's spiritual rank has been attributed to this supplication from one of the most holy mothers of the community.

As Hasan grew up, he attended the *sohbets* (spiritual conversations) and *khutbas* (sermons) of Caliph 'Uthman, and became a *hafiz*, one who has memorized the entire Qur'an. He sought out as many of the living companions of the Prophet as he could find in order to learn from them and collect ahadith. Foremost in knowledge among these was Hazrat 'Ali, who helped train Hasan in the mystic way of Islam and issued him an *ijazet* authorizing him to teach in the masjid as well as to give more intimate teachings to the *ikhwan* (brotherhood) in his own home. Hasan is thought to have been between 15 and 19 years old at the time of Caliph 'Ali's assassination (661 CE).

Following his years in Medina, Hasan moved to Khurasan in Iran for about 10 years and there met many more of the *sahabi* (companions of the Prophet). After that he moved to Basra where for some time he held public office, had dealings with high Byzantine officials and even worked as a jewel merchant. Though an ascetic by temperament, Hasan also took part in several battles and was once forced to flee for his life from the notorious Umayyad general, Al-Hajjaj.

Hasan was famous for this saying, which well exemplifies his attitude toward life: "The world is a bridge over which you must cross, but do not linger to build your dwelling." The saying has also been ascribed to Jesus in various late inscriptions in the Middle East. Like the Master Jesus, Hasan left no writings but was widely quoted by others. Hasan attracted a wide circle of students, including several who would become well-known masters of the mystic path, as well as a contingent who broke away from him to found the *Mu'tazilite* school, a rationalist movement influenced by Hellenistic and Persian philosophy. While the *Kharijite* school of thought maintained that a Muslim who committed a grave sin was no longer a Muslim but an infidel or unbeliever, Hasan maintained that such an act simply made them a hypocrite, yet still basically a Muslim believer. The *Mu'tazilites* ("those who stand apart") adopted a position somewhere in between calling such a person neither a believer nor an unbeliever and "took their distance" from Hasan, as the meaning of their name implies. Their philosophy of human free will was greatly favored by the early 'Abbasid dynasty, whereas the Umayyads favored the doctrine of divine predestination.

During this popular upsurge of Rationalist thought, Hasan of Basra wrote to Hasan ibn 'Ali, the grandson of the Prophet, asking for his guidance in regard to the polarized debate between the advocates of total divine predestination and total human freewill. Hasan ibn 'Ali wrote back that, in his opinion, those who did not accept *qadar* (the idea that our destinies and actions all originate with Allah) were unbelievers, while those who impute their own personal sins to Allah were miscreants. Rather, he concluded, the true teaching of the religion and the Qur'an grants that humans are free to acquire their actions according to the power given to them by Allah, and thus takes a middle course between either of the extremes advocated by these opposing groups.

In Basra, Hasan preached publicly to the people, calling them to repentance and to abstinence from worldly desires, admonishing them stand in awe of Allah and transfer their love of the transitory things in this world to the eternal bliss of the world to come. "It is a wise person who regards this world as nothing, and thus seeks the other world, rather than thinking nothing of the eternal realm in favor of gaining this one. Whoever is drawn to Allah knows Him as a Friend, but whoever is drawn to this world regards Him as an enemy." He also emphasized meditation (*fikra*) as a means to self-knowledge, saying: "Meditation is a mirror which reveals to you your virtues and your vices."

In a more mystical vein, the sheikh speaks of the relationship between Allah and humanity from the divine standpoint:

When my servant becomes completely absorbed with Me, I allow his happiness and his delight to consist in My remembrance; and when he has delighted in My *dhikr* (remembrance), he is filled with desire for Me and I for him; and when that takes place, I raise the veils of separation between Myself and him, and I become manifest before his eyes. Such people do not forget Me when others forget. Their word is the word of the Prophet; they are the true heroes, those whom I will remember and spare, whenever I must bring punishment and affliction upon the people of the earth.[23]

In the case of Hasan, it is not always easy to separate the kernel of historical fact from the abundance of legendary material. However, we will relate two stories about Hasan Basri which quite possibly reflect authentic episodes in the life of the saint. The first story, concerning Hasan and his Zoroastrian neighbor, Simeon, is recounted by Fariduddin 'Attar in his *Tadhkirat al-Awliya* (Memorial of the Saints).[24]

Simeon was of the Zoroastrian faith, a religion which emphasized the struggle between the Spirit of Truth and the Spirit of Falsehood which is played out in the arena of this world. The religion's founder, Zarathustra (Zoroaster), taught that the light of the Ultimate Source of Truth shines spiritually upon creation, just as the fire of the material sun illuminates and nourishes the earth. From such core teachings, Zoroastrian worship developed along the lines of sun worship and ritual fire worship, offered by a caste of priests, after the manner of the ancient Aryans. What had perhaps originated as non-dualistic teachings revealed through an authentic Persian prophet (one of the 124,000 mentioned by the Prophet Muhammad), in time, hardened into an extremely dualistic conception of two separate gods, one good and one evil, encapsulated in a degenerated system of elemental ritual worship.

Although Simeon found little to spiritually sustain him in this faith, he was nevertheless hesitant to abandon it in his old age. Hasan used to supplicate Allah in tears that his neighbor Simeon

---

23 Abu Nu'aym, *Hilya*, quoted in M. Smith, *The Way of the Mystics*, 177-78.
24 'Attar, *Muslim Saints and Mystics*, 24-25.

would turn from worshiping fire to the realization of Truth. Though Simeon respected Hasan and knew of his saintly reputation, he nevertheless held out and seemed firmly tied to his tradition.

Finally, when Simeon became bedridden and ill, approaching the point of death, Hasan was urged by friends to go visit Simeon. Hasan went and found Simeon blackened with fire and smoke. "Come, be in awe of Allah!" Hasan told him. "You have been surrounded by fire and smoke all of your life. Accept Islam, that Allah might have mercy on you." Simeon explained to Hasan that from what he observed, most Muslims were hypocritical in that they didn't practice what they preached; so why join them?

Hasan responded that this was not the token of those who truly know. However, he added, those believers who act as he describes at least make some attempt to realize and acknowledge the unity of the One Being whereas Simeon had spent his whole life worshiping fire. "*Alhamdullillah*, I have never worshiped fire as you have," Hasan continued, "but let us suppose we would both die and enter the fires of hell, to be consumed by them. Allah is not likely to pay any regard to you, a life-long fire-worshiper, yet if Allah so wills, the fire will not dare so much as burn one hair of my body. For fire is a thing created by Allah, and all of Allah's creation is subject to His command. So come—you've worshiped fire for seventy years—let us both thrust our hands into the fire so that you can clearly see the impotence of fire and the omnipotence of Allah." Thus saying, Hasan placed his hand into the fire and, though he held it there, his hand was not burned in the slightest. Simeon was amazed and understood deeply that his years of fire-worship had been to no avail.

"But what can I do?" he asked. "Accept Islam," Hasan urged him. Simeon was tempted but told Hasan that he just couldn't see how Allah would accept a deathbed conversion to Islam. Hasan assured him it would be accepted, that it was the heart's intention that counts, not whether Simeon lived to put his realization into practice. "Would you be willing to put in writing a guarantee that Allah would not punish me?" Simeon asked. "If so, I would feel confident about this and would take *shahada* as a Muslim." Without hesitation, Hasan wrote a letter of guarantee and at

Simeon's request had witnesses come in and officially sign it. Then Simeon wept many tears and as his last earthly act affirmed the unity of Allah and accepted Islam from the hand of Hasan Basri. He also made Hasan promise to wash and bury his body with his own blessed hands and bury him with that contract in his hand as his proof before Allah.

That night, after Hasan had buried Simeon along with the guarantee as requested, Hasan began to wonder whether he had really been right to issue Simeon an ironclad guarantee in the name of Allah, since he well knew that he couldn't even guarantee his own salvation, as each soul's destiny is in the hands of Allah alone. Often enough had Hasan wept tears of repentance and had himself been seized by the fear of hell. "O Sheikh Hasan!" he berated himself, "By commanding the unseen you have shown arrogance and uttered strange words."

With such thoughts on his mind, he fell asleep and had a dream in which Simeon appeared before him walking in the garden of Paradise, radiant with light and wearing a crown studded with luminous heavenly jewels and a golden rope around his waist. "How are you, Simeon?" Hasan inquired. "You can see for yourself," he answered. "Allah's generosity is so great that even to drink one drop from His mercy forgives a thousand unbelievers like me at once. His favors showered upon me surpass all description; all my sins have been turned into good deeds and all the clouds that shrouded my heart have been cleared away by the acceptance of heaven. You certainly honored your guarantee, Hasan, but as it turned out, I didn't even need this paper, so here it is. You keep it." Then Hasan awoke and found that he was clutching that very paper in his hand.

"*Rabbi'l Alamin* (Lord of the worlds)!" Hasan cried, "Well do I know that You do what You will without any cause other than Your great bounty. Who then could be turned away from Your door unsatisfied? If You accept into Your presence a fire-worshiper of seventy years because of a single utterance from him, how could You reject a sincere believer of seventy years?"

Our second story involves a man who reported that another

person was speaking badly about Hasan. Hasan asked the informant why he had visited this person. The man answered that he was invited as a guest. Hasan probed him further as to what kinds of food and drink he had received from his host, and these were enumerated to him. "So," Hasan told him, "you were able to keep all of these refreshments inside you, but weren't able to do the same with a few words—is that it? You had to run up and report them to me?" Having said that, Hasan sent a plateful of fresh dates to the man who had slandered him, accompanied with a note of apology which read: "It has come to our attention that you recently transferred the merit of some of your good deeds to us. We are only too happy to reciprocate, though we must beg your forgiveness inasmuch as our gift is not nearly so large as yours!"

Though we may sense a tongue-in-check quality in the sheikh's note of reply, he is actually putting into practice the highest form of forgiveness among the four types of clemency. The lowest level which is allowed in Islam (but not encouraged in the tarikat) is to retaliate in kind (an eye for an eye), without exceeding to the slightest degree the injury that one received from the other party. For instance, the Prophet Muhammad, during his final illness, came one day to the masjid in a weakened condition and insisted that if there was anyone present to whom he owed anything he would now like to repay it. He also requested that if there was anyone present whom he had ever hurt in any way over the years, no matter how slight or even unintentional the injury, they should now come forward and retaliate in kind, in order that he, the Prophet, should not die without having redressed even the slightest acts of tyranny that he might have committed against another.

The second level of forgiveness involves the higher principle of turning the other cheek to one's enemy when one is insulted or injured and foregoing any act of retaliation, even though one might still secretly resent the other's actions. Such anger or resentment at another is often associated with the feeling that one's ego has been affronted.

At the third level, one is content regardless of whatever praise, blame or injury one receives (realizing that everything is ultimately from Allah, Who knows best what we should receive). A person who adopts this attitude is able to sincerely forgive without the slightest hidden resentment toward the other.

Finally, at the fourth level, one goes a step further and actually rewards the other—either with thanks, with prayers on their behalf or with a gift of reparation—because one is genuinely concerned for any trouble, inconvenience or spiritual loss that the other might incur as a result of attacking one, while one's own welfare is considered secondary.

Once an unbalanced individual verbally abused and attacked Sheikh Abu Yazid Bistami (d.874 CE), hitting him over the head with a staff with such force that it broke the staff in two. After recovering, the sheikh procured a better, stronger staff and sent it to the man, with a note of apology about the broken staff. He also sent the man a jar of honey with the intention that it might help sweeten his tongue and mitigate against such harsh words as he had uttered toward the sheikh.

We can draw another example from the family of Hazrat 'Ali (may Allah exalt his noble soul). When a maidservant accidently spilled a container of scalding soup all over Imam Hasan ibn 'Ali, while serving him and his family dinner, he jumped up quickly while the fearful maid recited a Qur'anic *sura* about Allah's love for those who show mercy even when they are severely tested. Upon hearing this, Imam Hasan calmed himself and refrained from any verbal or physical reprimand against the servant; instead, he surprised her by issuing her a declaration of freedom on the spot. Later, we shall see another example of such *adab* (spiritual etiquette) in the life of Ibrahim Adham.

OTHER NOTABLE EARLY SUFIS
Fuzayl ibn Iyad

AS WE HAVE PREVIOUSLY MENTIONED, Hasan Basri gave spiritual guidance to a number of pupils who subsequently became important teachers of *tasawwuf*. One of these was 'Abdul Wahid ibn Zayd (d.793 CE), founder of the *Zaydiyya* order, a preacher and ascetic who observed a forty year vow of chastity and founded a monastic community at Abbadan near Basra.

'Abdul-Wahid was the sheikh of the famous Abu 'Ali al-Fuzayl ibn Iyad (d.801 CE), who started his career as a banditti captain robbing caravans on the roads between Merv and Baward. A man of noble, even pious disposition, Fuzayl ibn Iyad had a Robin Hood-like reputation for dealing honorably with his victims. Indeed, he always avoided caravans which contained women and refused to rob anyone who was poor; he and his brigands would only take a portion of their victim's money or goods and Fuzayl even kept careful records of his victim's names and how much he had taken from them in his chosen profession as chieftain of the highwaymen. However, it was beyond most people to fathom how Fuzayl reconciled in his own mind a life of lawlessness with a nominal observance of Islam.

One day a merchant, who was aware of Fuzayl's reputation as a God-fearing man, set out from Merv with a caravan laden with goods. Instead of hiring a protective escort, he hired a Qur'an-reader to ride a camel alongside the caravan and read from the Qur'an throughout the journey. When they reached the spot where the bandits were waiting in ambush, Fuzayl chanced to hear the hafiz chanting an *ayat* of the *Qur'an al-Karim* (57:15) which asks: "Isn't it time that the believers open their hearts to compassion and submit to Allah's way?" The ayat had a profound effect upon Fuzayl, as though an arrow had pierced his soul. Filled with contrition, he fell from his perch on the wall crying, "Yes Lord! Surely it is high time, and even past that!" Dazed and bewildered, he began to run toward the road, causing the caravan to recoil in fright. Fuzayl stopped and announced to a relieved caravan his intention to repent from a life of crime.

He passed that night in great remorse and solemn meditation. The next morning he took his records and began repaying to the last dinar everything he had ever stolen. This included a Jewish merchant whom Fuzayl agreed to serve after running out of reimbursement money. This proved a great trial for Fuzayl, but with Allah's help, the Jew not only was amply satisfied with the debt payment but actually converted to Islam.

Having discharged his last worldly debt, Fuzayl made a pilgrimage to Mecca and began a new life as an ascetic, associating with the famous imam, Abu Hanifa in Kufa and submitting himself to the spiritual direction of Sheikh 'Abdul Wahid ibn Zayd at Abbadan. In time, his sanctity increased to the point that 'Abdul-Wahid appointed him as his own successor. At his sheikh's direction, Sheikh Fuzayl founded a new order called the *Iyadiyya*, which further emphasized the monastic aspect of dervishhood. Sheikh Fuzayl lovingly balanced his ascetic tendencies by supporting a wife and several children.

As his reputation grew, even the famous 'Abbasid caliph, Harun ar-Rashid came to seek out Fuzayl's advice. Once, when visiting Mecca, the caliph tried to call upon the sheikh in his lodging but was refused admittance. The caliph's courtier, Fazl the Barmecide, spoke through the door and finally persuaded the sheikh to admit the Commander of the Faithful. When he entered and laid eyes on Sheikh Fuzayl in the darkened room, Harun began to weep and pleaded with him for a word of spiritual counsel. Fuzayl answered, "O Commander of the Faithful, your ancestor 'Abbas was the uncle of Muhammad Mustafa. 'Abbas asked the Prophet to give him command over some of the men in Medina. The blessed Prophet answered him: 'O my uncle, I will give you command for one moment over yourself.' By this he meant that a moment's self-control—which is the obedience of the self to Allah's command—is better than a thousand years of being obeyed by others, as it leads to one's own repentance and redemption before one passes from this world and faces the great evaluation of one's earthly life.

After receiving other counsels and warnings that on the Day of Judgment all of the caliph's subjects will have the right to accuse him concerning the injustices he has perpetrated, the caliph fell into a fit of bitter weeping until he nearly collapsed.

"Enough!" said his courtier. "You have slain the Commander of the Faithful!" Fuzayl answered, "Be silent, Haman (the advisor of Pharaoh)![25] It is you and your creatures who are destroying him; then you tell me that I've killed him. Is that murder?" Recovering his composure somewhat, Harun gratefully attempted to donate money to Fuzayl to use either for himself or for others, just as he had done with the other Islamic scholars he had visited for advice. But where others had fawned before the caliph and gladly accepted his gold, Fuzayl was incensed at the offer and told the caliph that this unjust action showed conclusively that his counsels had been a complete waste of time. Harun exclaimed, "How so?" Fuzayl replied, "I wish salvation for you, yet you cast me into temptation. Is this not unjust? I'm trying to tell you to give back what you possess to its proper owner, but you distribute it to others to whom it doesn't belong. Its useless for me to speak with you!" And with that, he rose and flung the gold out of his house. With tears in his eyes, Harun departed, confiding to his courtier, "O Fazl, Fuzayl is a king of men indeed. His arrogance is extreme, and the world is very contemptible in his eyes."[26]

On still another occasion, Harun visited Fuzayl and ventured to asked him: "Have you ever met with anyone of greater detachment than yourself?" Sheikh Fuzayl replied, "Yes, O Caliph! Your own detachment far exceeds mine." Surprised by this answer, Harun ar-Rashid asked, "How can that be?" Fuzayl replied: "I have detached myself from this world which is doomed to perdition, but you seem to have detached yourself from the other world which is infinite and everlasting."

25 According to the Qur'an (28:6; 29:39 & 40:23-24: "And certainly We sent Moses with Our messages and clear authority to Pharaoh and Haman and Korah, but they said, "A lying enchanter!"). Although there is also a well-known biblical advisor named Haman (the son of Hammedatha the Agagite) who is minister to King Ahasueros and the villain of Purim stories (Esther 3:1, etc), he would seem to be a different person than the contemporary of Moses and Pharaoh who is mentioned in the Qur'an.
26 *Attar,* 53-60.

Ibrahim Adham

A very different situation unfolded with Fuzayl's famous dervish, Abu Ishaq Ibrahim ibn Adham (d.783), who renounced his kingship in Balkh in order to find himself within the Source of Being. The amazing love story of Ibrahim's parents is recounted in detail in Sheikh Muzaffer Ozak's *Irshad*.

The princess of Balkh, Ibrahim Adham's mother, fell into a long, death-like coma, was buried and fortuitously resuscitated in her tomb by a love-sick pauper named Adham. The couple married and the fruit of their union, Ibrahim, was born in Mecca. He eventually inherited the throne of Afghanistan, one of the most important and wealthy countries in the world during that era. His parents uttered many prayers for the newborn child as they circumambulated the Ka'ba, the holy shrine which had been constructed by his namesake, the Patriarch Abraham. In retrospect, it was clear that these prayers were divinely accepted, as Ibrahim became a great lover of Truth; but at first his spirit was like a nightingale trapped in a gilded cage of luxury and pomp.

The well-known story of Ibrahim's conversion and abdication of the royal throne took place in the following manner. One night as he slept on his magnificent royal couch, he was awakened around midnight by the sound of footsteps on the palace roof. "Who goes there?" Ibrahim called. "Friend, I am looking for my lost camel on this roof," a voice replied. "Only a fool would search for a camel on the roof," Ibrahim retorted. "O heedless one," came the answer, "are you any less foolish, searching for God in silken clothes, asleep upon a golden couch?" The words filled him with terror, and he could not go back to sleep.

Ibrahim Adham as an ascetic (17th century India).

The next morning, as the king sat on his throne, an awesome figure entered the palace with his camels and advanced to stand before him. "What do you want?" Ibrahim demanded. "I have just arrived with my people to set up camp at this inn *(caravanserai)*." An angry Ibrahim responded, "You must be mad! This is no inn! It's a royal palace!" The stranger replied, "No, it definitely seems to be an inn. After all, who was the last owner of this palace before you?" "My father!" the king snapped back. "And before that?" the stranger queried. "My grandfather; and before that, his father!" Ibrahim replied. "And where are they now?" the man asked. "They're dead! They're not here anymore!" Ibrahim answered. "Didn't I tell you it was a inn," the stranger said, "a lodge where one person settles after another one vacates? One day you will also go your way. I wonder what provisions you have made?"

With those words, the man turned and vanished from their sight, leaving the king shaken and confused. That being was Khidr, upon him be peace, an unseen guide who was to appear to Ibrahim and spiritually guide him at several crucial times in his life. It is he who appeared to teach the hidden mysteries to Moses in the Qur'an (18:65-84), and who has appeared to many of the Sufi masters and lovers throughout the centuries in times of need.

As a diversion, Ibrahim went fox-hunting, only to be startled from his horse by a heavenly voice, saying: "O Ibrahim, did I create you for this? Surely not in such idleness will you die." That very day, Ibrahim discarded his crown and royal garb and put on haircloth, leaving his palace to wander in poverty like a beggar. He set his face toward Mecca and traveled through the desert where Khidr, under the guise of still another person, appeared with food and provisions and accompanied him. He settled for a time in the solitude of a cave in Nishapur.

The period of his desert wandering was lengthy, perhaps several years or even fourteen according to one account. As Ibrahim finally neared Mecca, he traveled incognito, accepting a job watering the camels with a caravan bound for the holy city. The former king was still extremely famous and close to the heart of his people. Some of the elders of the Haram in Mecca, upon hearing that Ibrahim Adham was en route to their city, decided to give him a royal entry befitting a king. They began to check every caravan, trying to locate the king. Finally, they approached Ibrahim's caravan and even spoke to him; however, they didn't know him by sight. Ibrahim insisted that he was not a king but a poor dervish. When pressed, he admitted that he knew Ibrahim Adham, but added, "What do you want with that heretic? Believe me, you wouldn't think so highly of him if you really knew what a terrible scoundrel and tyrant he was!" This insult against the king so enraged them that they beat him savagely and left him in a pool of his own blood. Even the caravan deserted him after hearing what he had said.

When Ibrahim awoke, he spoke to his own *nafs* (ego): "You see, if I had told them that you were the Sultan of Balkh, they would have kissed your hands, acclaimed you and given you anything you wanted. But instead, I revealed to them that you are but a poor dervish and they gave you a good thrashing for it. Ha! You secretly wanted the elders to come out to meet you. *Alhamdulillah*, I've seen to it that you've gotten your wish." Then he arose and entered Mecca to perform the *hajj*.

Later in life, Ibrahim would regard this and several other such humbling episodes as his most satisfying moments on the spiritual path. In this way, Ibrahim prefigures the later masters of *malamat*, the Sufi Way of Blame, those who struggle against their egos by purposely showing themselves before others in the worst possible light. This safeguards against spiritual inflation in one's personal ego as a result of other's praise or adulation. Through such actions, the truly realized dervish is able to remain ever vigilant against the vice of *ujub*, a form of arrogance in which one partakes of the delusion that one is better or more pious than others due to one's spiritual efforts and experiences.

In Mecca, Ibrahim sought out Sheikh Fuzayl ibn Iyad and Sufyan al-Thawri. Later he was also to associate with Imam Abu Hanifa, from whom he learned some of the divine knowledge *('ilm)*. Abu Hanifa was one of the most celebrated imams in the annals of Islam and, although he was not a Sufi sheikh, many prominent Sufis studied with him. He was a great scholar who began to codify many of the traditions of the Prophet after he dreamed that he was collecting the bones of the Apostles, choosing some and discarding others. He also received permission from the Prophet in a dream in which he was told: "You have been created in order to revive my ordinances." When the famous sheikh, Da'ud at-Ta'i, came seeking Abu Hanifa's advice, he was told: "Practice what you have learned, for theory without practice is like a body without a spirit." To this day, the Halveti-Jerrahis, like nearly all Turkish Muslims, follow the *Hanafi* school which he founded.

There is another story concerning Ibrahim Adham which gives an important insight into the way a sheikh must sometimes deal with a prospective student. Ibrahim's first murshid accepted him as a dervish on probation. The teacher, recognizing the stench of the palace and the arrogance of being an "important person" which still clung to the former king, assigned him to collect garbage as a way of training his ego. After a time, he ordered some of the other dervishes to "accidently" run into Ibrahim and knock the trash from his hands in order to see what he would do. The first time,

Ibrahim muttered something about what he would have done with them if he was still the king. Then, catching himself, he silently picked up the trash.

"He's not ready yet," the Murshid said when this was reported to him. Later, the test was repeated. Ibrahim just glared at the offender for a moment, said nothing and picked up the refuse. "Still not ready," said the Murshid. When it was done a third time, Ibrahim did not even look to see who did it but humbly collected the garbage in silence. When the Murshid heard this, he called for Ibrahim to receive *bayat* (initiation) as a dervish. In such ways, Ibrahim grew in humility and divine realization to such an extent that the venerable Junayd of Baghdad would later proclaim: "Ibrahim is the key to the mystical sciences."[27]

Hazrat Ibrahim once asked a certain man whether he desired to become a *waliyullah*, a saint. When the man answered, "Yes," Ibrahim advised him: "Covet nothing in this world or the next, and devote yourself entirely to Allah and turn to Him with all your heart, untainted by any attachment to the things of this world or the life to come."[28]

Later in life, with his sheikh's permission, Ibrahim Adham returned to Balkh, where his son now ruled in his place. Ibrahim entered the royal city and found himself amongst a crowd of people at the gate of a newly-constructed palace, upon which no expense had been spared. Ibrahim listened as the people raved about the beauty of this new palace and marveled at its magnificent construction. Suddenly, he called out: "O people, this is not the real palace! Sooner or later it is bound to be destroyed and become a ruin. Rather, the real palace is to be found over there." At this, he pointed toward the graveyard. There, souls who have trusted in worldly riches come to ruin while the true lovers of God who renounce the temporary pleasures of this world find satisfaction in the divine palace and gardens of paradise.

A soldier who was standing nearby became incensed at these words and struck the saint on the face, hitting him so hard that he

---

27 Annemarie Schimmel, *Mystical Dimensions of Islam*, 37.
28 Al-Hujwiri, *Kashf Al-Mahjub*, 217.

almost fell down. Recognizing Ibrahim, some of the others in the crowd rebuked the soldier, crying, "You fool! What are you doing? Don't you recognize him? He is our former king who left the sultanate of this world to become the sultan of hearts. Even now, it is his son who sits on the royal throne." Hearing this, the soldier was mortified and threw himself at the feet of Hazrat Ibrahim Adham, begging forgiveness. Ibrahim lifted him up and said, "No, my son. No! It is I who need to be forgiven by you. For I am sure you must have injured your hand when you struck me." By this time, after years as a dervish, a selfless nature had completely replaced the old conditioning that had formerly belonged to the king.

From Ibrahim Adham a new dervish order was to come into being: the *Adhamiyya* tarikat. The great fourteenth century Turkish poet Yunus Emre mentions the former King of Balkh in one of his most popular mystic hymns *(Gönül Hayran):*

> *The heart is amazed by the movement*
> *of the hand of love;*
> *Heart melted at last by the radiant fire of love.*
> *Ibrahim Adham gave up crown and throne*
> *for the sake of love.*
> *The whole earth burst into flames*
> *from that holy spark of love.*

This is how it is with the lovers and saints who are mystically drawn into the divine unity by the great love of the Friend. The fire of love can melt a calloused heart and allow the Source of Love to remold it nearer to the divine desire. Under the effects of love, worldly kingdoms cease to hold any allure. Love can change one from a tyrant into a saint (or *waliyullah).*

In using the English word *saint,* by which the Arabic word *waliyullah* is often translated, we should note that the word may evoke certain Christian connotations involving canonization and veneration, and thus may not accurately reflect the Islamic or Sufi concept, which is rooted in Qur'anic usage. The meaning of *waliyullah* is two-fold: it means a master *(wali,* plural: *awliya),* in whom the divine dimension of the soul is awakened, ruling wisely over the carnal soul or ego; and secondly, it indicates a friend *(wali)* of the Divine *(Allah)*, one who has gone beyond the veils of separation between the self and the Divine Source, experiencing only one universal will and action operating in one's life. Thus, their prayers are one with the will of Allah and they are gifted with spiritual sight into the human heart. Though they still exist at some level as individual souls with a name and a form, they are inwardly empty of self, existing only as limbs of one vast divine tree or waves in the ocean of love.

Rab'ia al-'Adawwiya

Undoubtedly, one of the brightest lights among the lovers of Allah in the early period of Islamic Sufism was the enlightened lady of Basra, Rabi'a al-'Adawwiya (ca.717-801). She is unique in many ways, not only in her eminence as a woman ascetic of great spiritual renown in early Islam, but also inasmuch as she is a mystic who does not figure into the usual sheikh and disciple pattern of Sufism. Indeed she is counted as an associate of some of the great Sufis of Basra, such as 'Abdul-Wahid Zayd, Maliki Dinar, Sufyan Thawri (a disciple of Rabi'a), and probably Hasan al-Basri. (Some scholars have questioned whether Hasan and Rabi'a were contemporaries at all, but tradition favors the likelihood that they were indeed acquaintances in Basra.)

The narratives which chronicle Rabi'a's life are often framed as teaching stories, ending with a pointed punch line in which Rabi'a's realization trumps, often caustically, the limited religious perspectives of her contemporaries. How much these stories reflect her actual teaching style as opposed to the propensities of her biographers is now difficult to determine. Some of the stories may indeed represent fictional conversations as well. However, the uncompromising brandishing of the staff of truth against the sham of hypocrisy and the vain wiles of the ego—a trait which sparkles through Rabi 'a's personality in many of these tales—is certainly a time-honored hallmark of the deeply realized *jelali* dervish soul.

'Attar reports that every Friday, Hasan Basri gave a *khutba* (sermon) for the congregation who gathered for *Jum 'a* prayers, and many men of knowledge would attend. Each week, when Sheikh Hasan mounted the *minbar* he would gaze among the crowd to see if Hazrati Rabi 'a was there. He was reluctant to preach beyond the most basic levels if she was not present, giving as his reason: "That wine which we have made for the capacity of elephants cannot be poured into the breasts of ants." Similarly, when she came and his inspiration flowed and warmed the hearts of the congregation, he would sometimes turn toward Rabi 'a and say something like, "Ah, though concealed beneath a veil, all this passion comes forth from but an ember in your heart!" Indeed, though Rabi 'a was but a poor slave girl, orphaned at a tender age, her pure and passionate love for Allah alone grew like a giant tree until it broke through to a new level of Divine Love *(muhabbat)*, far surpassing the station of the celebrated male sheikhs of her time.

She dwelt in the station of humble contentment with whatever gifts she received from Allah and did not wish to be encumbered by anything which would divert her love away from the divine giver of the gift. From this perspective, she saw quickly through the various vanities and desires that plagued other would-be lovers of God around her. Maliki Dinar once visited Rabi'a in her bare dwelling place and offered to procure her a few basic amenities, but she insisted that the All-Knowing One knew best what she needed and what she did not need.

Sufyan al-Thawri came another day and, finding Rabi'a ill, suggested that she might pray for the alleviation of her suffering. "You know very well Who has willed this suffering," she answered, "and yet you want me to ask Him for the opposite of what He wills? You are a learned man, Sufyan; surely you know it is not right to speak like this. If I wish and my Lord does not wish, this would be infidelity. To be a servant of the Truth, one must only want what Allah wishes. If Allah Himself gives, that is a different matter." Having been silenced on this point, Sufyan said, "O mother, perhaps instead of speaking about your condition, you could speak about mine instead." Rabi'a told him, "You would be a good man, Sufyan, if you didn't love the world so." Puzzled, he asked, "How so?" She replied, "You love reciting *ahadith* (traditions of the Prophet)," implying that his ego had made ill-use of a good thing, turning it into a form of status-seeking. In exasperation, he cried, "O Lord, be content with me!" But Rabi'a answered him, still driving home her point, "Aren't you ashamed to seek the contentment of One with Whom you are not yourself content?"

Another famous teacher, Salih Qazwini, used to preach (in a manner reminiscent of Jesus): "Whoever knocks at the door constantly will soon find it opened." One day Rabi'a happened by, heard him say this and retorted, "How long will you go on preaching this way? Has the door ever been shut? Never! It is always open!" Salih humbly conceded the point.

One scholar came to Rabi'a for advice, saying: "For forty years now I have faithfully observed even the smallest requirements of the *shariat* (religious laws) and have not committed any sins. Is there anything more I need to insure myself of paradise?" Sensing the presumptuousness inherent in his ego-encapsulated piety,

Rabi'a did not mince words. "Your very existence itself is a sin greater than any you could possibly imagine."

Her answer is, of course, not intended to denigrate his essential being, but to awaken it from the veil of separation from his True Source. This clouded-over, luke-warm spiritual outlook causes him to perform prayers and devotions with a wage-earner mentality instead of with passion for the Source of Love. Certainly, this man's way of approaching religion is common, but for one at the spiritual station of Hazrati Rabi'a, such worship is tantamount to the sin of *shirk*—setting up partners (one's own ego-self or even paradise) beside the oneness of Allah. As Rabi'a elaborated to the sheikhs on another occasion, "He is a sorry servant who worships Allah from fear and terror, or from the desire of reward—though there are many of these. Surely Allah is worthy of worship devoid of any motive (of self-interest)." For the love of the lover to become pure, one must constantly cleanse the heart, turning away from everything which one sees as separate from Allah, and from every derivative goal (including the heavenly delights) which would tend to waylay one's love from the Essential Source Itself.

To make this point clear, Hazrati Rabi'a once went through the streets of Basra carrying a fiery torch and a pitcher of water. Some of the Sufis saw her and asked her, "O Lady of the Afterlife, where are you going like that and for what purpose?" She answered, "I am going to set fire to *janna* (the garden of paradise) and douse water on the flames of *jahannam* (hell) so that both of these veils may vanish altogether from before the lover's eyes and set their purpose clear! Then Allah's servants will be able to see and serve the Divine, devoid of any ulterior motives which would taint their view. Right now, you cannot find anyone who would continue to worship or obey their Lord if these two motivations were taken away." [29]

Someone asked Rabi'a about repentance, the initial step on the spiritual path. The person wanted some assurance that when one repents, Allah will accept it. Rabi'a answered, "How can anyone repent in the first place unless their Lord sees fit to put repentance

29 Aflaki, *Manaqib al- 'Arafin*, fol.114a

in their heart and thereafter accepts them?" And concerning those who carried on about their repentance, she pointedly observed, "It is hypocrisy to merely ask for forgiveness out loud. Though we repent, we need still another repentance to repent of repenting."

Once Rabi'a passed by Hasan Basri's house while the sheikh was leaning out his window, weeping. A drop fell on Rabi'a as she passed and, thinking it was rain, she looked up; then she saw Sheikh Hasan. "Master," she said, "this weeping is a sign of spiritual indulgence. Guard your tears, so that there may surge within you such an ocean that when you seek the heart within, you will find it only *in the keeping of an Omnipotent Sovereign* (Qur'an 54:55)."

Rabi'a was also known to weep extensively. In one of her famous sayings, she declares: "The lover of God will cry and weep until the lover finds rest in the Beloved's embrace." While weeping is characteristic of the lover who still feels the slightest veil of separation from his or her Lord, or feels compassion for the suffering of others, at the highest level of the soul *(an-nafs as-safiya),* the unified soul enters a sublime state of peace, beyond all sorrow. When Rabi'a was once queried about her own tears and lamentations, she confessed, "My deepest fear is separation, for I have become accustomed to Him. Is it not possible that at the time of death a voice will come saying, 'You are not worthy of Me?'"

It is related that Hazrati Rabi'a dug a grave for herself inside her own home. For forty years she stood by the grave's edge every morning and evening, and said, "Tomorrow you shall be here." Then she would engage in her devotions. 'Abda bint Abi Showal, a pious lady in Rabi'a's service, related that Rabi'a used to pray all night and only doze lightly before dawn. Then she would awaken and say in deep awe, "O soul, how long will you go on sleeping and waking? Very soon you will enter such a sleep that you will not awaken until the trumpet-call of the Day of Resurrection." She would also make this morning *dua*: "Lord, engage me in Your worship and remembrance so that no one may find occasion to engage me in anything else."

At night, she would climb on her rooftop and speak to God, saying, "O my Lord, the stars have all set and the world is asleep; behind barred gates princes slumber and sweethearts privately caress. Yet here, before Your face, I stand alone." Sometimes she would supplicate, saying: "O Allah, whatever You have apportioned to me of worldly goods, give them to Your enemies; whatever You have apportioned for me of the world to come, give to Your friends; but as for me, You alone are enough."

When Rabi'a was asked for some insight concerning love she replied, "There exists absolutely no separation between the Beloved and the lover." Further, she said, "If the rapture of divine love which I have realized was ever bestowed upon humanity, no heart would be exempt from its power." On another occasion she gave this teaching on the subject: "The lover of true knowledge seeks the heart of God. But once it has been granted to them, they immediately offer it back to God so that it remains with Him and is shrouded from human access in the divine mystery *(sirr)*." As a lover, she was also asked about her attitude toward Satan *(Shaitan)*. She replied, "My love for the All-Merciful leaves me no room for hostility toward Satan."[30]

Hasan Basri relates: "I spent a day and night with Rabi'a discussing the *tarikat* and the *hakikat*, yet it never once occurred to either of us that one of us was male and the other female. But when I left her, I discovered myself to be destitute, while I could see that she was utterly pure in her dedication."

Thereafter, Rabi'a sent three objects to Hasan: a piece of wax, a needle and a hair. These were accompanied by the exhortation: "Like the wax, light up the world while burning yourself up. Like the needle, always be engaged in spiritual work, while naked of

---

30 Javad Nurbakhsh, *Sufi Women*, 47.

outward dependency. And when you have done this, a thousand years will be like the hair's breath separating you from Allah."

A woman in America once asked Sheikh Muzaffer al-Jerrahi how it was that Rabi 'a remained unmarried all her life, despite the traditional stress in Islam on marriage among Muslims. He explained:

It is indeed *sunna* (the way of the Prophet) for every man and woman to enter into marriage, regardless of whether or not they are a saint, but it is harder for ladies such as Rabi 'a al- 'Adawiyya to find their equals—as one normally marries one's equal. For instance, many of the companions of the Prophet, including all of the first four caliphs, wanted to marry the Prophet's daughter, Hazrati Fatima, but in the end only Hazrat 'Ali was considered equal to marrying her. But in the case of Hazrati Rabi 'a, there was no equal in her time and that is why she did not get married. Even such a great saint as Hasan al-Basri desired to marry her, but was not able to.

When he proposed to her, she said, "I will ask you three questions and if you can answer them I will marry you: first, Am I going to die with pain?" Hasan admitted that he didn't know—only Allah knows. The second question was, "When the angels will come to my tomb to question me, will I be able to answer them correctly?" Again, Hasan said that only Allah knows. Rabi 'a said, "You have not been able to answer either of those questions. Nevertheless, I will ask you one more: "How many minds does a woman have and how many *nafs* (egos) does a woman have? And how many of each do men have?" Hasan replied, "That I can answer. Women have nine nafs and one mind while men have nine minds and one *nafs*." Rabi 'a laughed and said, "O Hasan Basri, you have nine minds which can't even control one *nafs* and you want to marry me?"

One day Rabi 'a prayed and prayed until she dozed off from fatigue. Just then, a thief entered her room and gathered what he could, including Rabi 'a's *chador* (a woman's cloak-covering). But when he tried to leave through the door the way was blocked as though a solid wall was there. He put down what he was stealing and then the door became passable; but when he picked them up again he still could not get through. Twice more he tried it and then heard a heavenly voice saying to him, "O thief, if My friend is asleep, her Friend is not."

Faced with a situation like that, what kind of man would be capable of marrying her? Perhaps if Hazrat 'Abdul Qadir Gaylani had been alive during Rabi'a's lifetime, he might have been appropriate for her. The messengers of Allah are totally pure and the *awliya* (saints; those who are near to Allah) are protected and cannot just do whatever they will [as far as marriage].

There was a woman in Baghdad at the time of 'Abdul Qadir Gaylani, who was somewhat of a saint, though a bit mentally disturbed. She never covered herself, and though they put clothes on her, she would tear them off and go out into the crowded streets in that condition, saying that it was hot and there was nobody around to see her anyway. But one day, after she had stripped nude in the market place, embarrassing everyone, she started to cry out, "Cover me, cover me! There's a man coming!" Some of them said, "What about us? Aren't we men?" But she cried, "No, no! A *man* is coming!" And about that time, around the corner came Hazrat 'Abdul Qadir Gaylani. So—one needs a man like that for Hazrati Rabi'a.

If Hazrati Rabi'a was the greatest woman saint among the poor, among the rich it was Hazrati Zubayda, the wife of the 'Abbasid Caliph, Harun ar-Rashid. Half of the civilized world belonged to the 'Abbasids at that time. Zubayda was given as a gift a beautiful bejewelled Qur'an which she loved and treasured. But one day she opened the book to that ayat which says, "You will never know My Divine Unity unless you give away what you love." She closed the book and called a poor person and gave it to them, saying, "I love this book so much. Here, please take it as a gift." Zubayda was also responsible for having a number of mosques and hospitals built.[31]

Rabi'a al-'Adawiyya died in Basra in 801 CE She reflects the heights of spiritual maturity to which a woman can rise and be recognized in Islam, a station unequaled by any of the men of her generation. Her life and teachings are a living demonstration of the collective breakthrough which occurred in the dervish heart; a breakthrough of pure mystic love and divine union of the soul with its Source, stripped of every veil which had formerly obscured the soul's loving absorption in the Divine Countenance.

'Abdullah ibn al-Mubarak

Another Sufi master of the time was 'Abdullah ibn al-Mubarak (736-797 CE), a celebrated hadith scholar born of a Turkish father and Persian mother. We will relate only one story from his life, important in showing how the scholar gained intimate practical knowledge of the levels of the soul. These levels are mentioned in the Qur'an and systematized in the tarikat. 'Abdullah knew of them in theory, but had yet to directly experience them through essential knowledge.

There are three kinds of knowledge. The first is *'ilm al-yakin*, which is the knowledge one gets from reading or hearing about something unfamiliar. (For example, one hears about making pilgrimage to the Ka'ba in Mecca and perhaps sees a picture of it.) The second kind of knowledge is *ayin al-yakin*, in which one goes, observes, and experiences for oneself what one had merely heard about. (For instance, one actually visits the Ka'ba, circumambulates it, touches it, smells its fragrance, and feels the atmosphere there.) Both of these kinds of knowledge are commonplace in our everyday experience of things; however the third kind of knowledge, *haqq*

31 Talk by Muzaffer Efendi at Spring Valley, NY. on May 8, 1982.

al-yakin, is more rare. It means to see or experience the truth—the inner depth—of what one observes. It is an insight, an unveiling of the essence of an object or being. (For instance, one perceives the true inner spirit of the Ka'ba, beyond its outward form.)

Once every three years, 'Abdullah ibn al-Mubarak used to travel on foot to Mecca to perform the *hajj*. One year, as he was making the return journey, he chanced to enter a somewhat deserted town along the way. The only person he saw in the town was a little boy around seven or eight years old, who was engaged in a rather odd form of play.

As 'Abdullah approached from afar, he observed that the child would gather up sand, earth and debris, shape it into a pile and laugh merrily to himself as he contemplated it. Then he would suddenly destroy it and burst into tears, weeping all the while as he spread the earthen pile out level again. Then he would repeat the whole process. As 'Abdullah drew near to the child, he debated within himself whether to speak to him, giving the customary salutation of *"As-salaamu 'aleikum*—peace be upon you." On one hand, he reasoned within himself: "He is the only being I see around here; should I salute him? But he is only a child—and a rather unbalanced one at that. Look at what he's doing there gathering up earth and laughing oddly. What could he possibly understand about salutations or how to return them? Perhaps I should just walk on by and ignore him."

"But on the other hand," another voice inside him countered, "the blessed Prophet used to salute the children, caress their heads, and talk with them in a friendly manner—and we are supposed to follow his *sunna*. So perhaps I should follow the Prophet's example and greet him with *salaams*; I have nothing to lose by it." So 'Abdullah walked up to the youngster and said, "The Peace of Allah be upon you, O child. *As-salaamu 'aleikum.*" The little boy lifted his head and gazed into 'Abdullah's face and then answered, *"W'aleikum as-salaam*, Ya 'Abdullah ibn al-Mubarak. May His peace be upon you also."

Amazed at the child's response, 'Abdullah blurted out, "How did you know my name? I'm a stranger in this town and nobody here knows me." The child answered, "O yes, I remember you. We were together in the universe of souls *('alam-i arwah)*. We were there shoulder to shoulder when Allah spoke to all the souls, saying, 'Am I not your Lord?' *(Alastu bi-Rabbikum?)*" When we answered, 'Yes,' *(bala)* Allah addressed you as 'Abdullah ibn al-Mubarak. Yes, I remember you clearly from then."

'Abdullah reflected on this for a moment. He knew that everything for the souls of all humanity had been established by Allah pre-eternally in the universe of souls, including each one's name, form and destiny. Clearly, he surmised, this child must have access to eternal knowledge and I should see what else he could explain to me. So he said to the boy: "There's something I'd like to ask you. Could you explain to me the difference between the animal soul *(ruhu haiwani)* and the human soul *(ruhu insani)?*"

The boy answered, "Well, when you were approaching me, you heard a voice in your mind saying, 'Don't bother to greet this child because he couldn't possibly understand about salutations.' That was the voice of your animal soul speaking to you. Then you had another thought which said, 'Follow the example of your Prophet and offer your salutations of peace to the child.' That was the voice of your human soul and sultan soul *(ruhu sultani)* which was calling upon you."

In recounting this episode later, 'Abdullah ibn al-Mubarak admitted that up until that point he had been unable to identify in himself where the animal soul and human souls were; but he learned it from this amazing child. He also asked the child the meaning of his ritual of gathering, then laughing, then destroying and crying which he had observed upon his approach. "Don't you see?" said the boy. "Since I'm only a child, I need to play. You can learn from my example and have your children play when its time to play. If they don't, they may play at the wrong time and wind up in trouble." 'Abdullah asked, "But what about your particular way of playing?"

The child explained, "Well, when I gather this soil together, I am experiencing how this body of flesh is built up from earthly elements. The flesh is made from whatever food and drink my father took in and absorbed, and from that essence, a sperm went into my mother's womb. And in this way the sustenance from the fields and rivers and everything around us came together so that, as it is said (in Qur'an), I was "formed out of clay." So I'm sitting here gathering together all these things into a heap to make a clay form, like the human body, which is a vehicle for the soul. It is a happy occasion when the material body is built up, so I laugh. But inevitably, that which is built up is destroyed. Death comes to the body and it is spread out and, in decomposing, returns to its original elements of earth. What can one do then but cry, faced with the destruction of such a marvelous gift? When I spread the earth back out I think of death and weep."

At that, recounts 'Abdullah ibn al-Mubarak, I kissed the hand of that child and asked his permission to teach. He says: I was greatly affected by the power of his spiritual glance; [32] from that time forth my spiritual stations *(makamat)* began to grow and grow.

THE WAY OF DIVINE INTOXICATION

AFTER THE TIME of the *tabi'un* (the first generation after the Prophet and his companions) and the following generation of ascetics, a new development in the history of Sufism emerges in Mesopotamia and Northern Africa, characterized by an orientation toward ecstasy. At least three figures stand out in this movement, the third coming a half century after the other two. They are: Dhu'n-Nun Misri (759-859 CE) in upper Egypt, Bayazid al-Bistami (d.874 CE) of Khurasan (Iran), and the Persian mystic and martyr, Mansur al-Hallaj (857-922 CE), whose ecstatic disposition led him to publicly divulge the divine secrets and undergo execution in Baghdad.

---

32 The potent spiritual glance of a master is known as *darshan* (Sanskrit), or *nazar* (Arabic).

Al-Bistami is credited with founding the Khurasanian ecstatic school of Sufism. He is called *Sayyid as-Sakirin*, the Master of the Drunken Ones, those who are intoxicated, not by alcohol, but by the inebriating wine of divine love. The counterbalance for the rapturous excesses of Sufism was already coalescing in al-Bistami's time, blossoming after his death in the famous Baghdad school of Pir Junayd. In contrast to al-Bistami, Junayd al-Baghdadi is known as *Sayyid as-Sahivin*, the Master of Sobriety, the one who exemplifies the "second sobriety," in which the station of God-intoxicated ecstasy[33] finds its mystical completion. Junayd's spiritual lineage comes through Hasan Basri and Imam 'Ali, while Bistami appears in the Naqshbandi silsila representing a spiritual link with the noted mystic Shi'ite imam, Ja'far as-Sadiq.

---

33 Spiritual ecstasy; Ar., *wajd,* Turk., *vecd,* generally associated with the fifth level of the *nafs.*

Dhu'n-Nun Misri

The Nubian mystic, Dhu'n-Nun Misri, is chronologically the first of the three masters of the ecstatic way. A wandering gnostic on the path of blame, Dhu'n-Nun was famous for his ecstatic utterances, known in Arabic as *shathiyat* (plural of *shath*). These sayings were primarily preserved through the efforts of his daughter, who was wise enough to recognize their value and write them down. Dhu'n-Nun was also schooled in the alchemical and arcane sciences of Egyptian mysticism and may have written some Hermetically-influenced works on the alchemy of spiritual transformation; but if so, they have been lost to posterity. Dhu'n-Nun was one of the last persons to possess a knowledge of Egyptian hieroglyphics before the rediscovery and deciphering of the Rosetta stone during the nineteenth century.

With Dhu'n-Nun's generation, we begin to see the cross-fertilization of mystical ideas from other esoteric traditions, such as Neo-Platonic, Hermetic, Anchorite, Magian and Hindu mysticism, to mention but a few. The very same truth that is found in the Qur'an, appears as well in other authentic traditions before and after the revelations received by the Prophet Muhammad (peace and blessings be upon him). According to the authentic Islamic understanding, which is always universal in scope, what shines forth as clear truth from the other spiritual traditions neither rivals nor conflicts with the truth found in the Qur'an, but simply confirms this same essential truth through other channels of mystical expression. According to the Qur'an (5:47-51), this process of multiple religious systems occurs naturally as part of the divine prerogative—the Qur'an being, in it own assessment, the most clear and unchanged summation of the perennial message of divine unity. The Islamic masters of *tasawwuf* in this period continued to adhere faithfully to the tenants of Qur'an and *sunna*; but, as ardent explorers and empirical scientists of their tradition, were moved to expand the conventional parameters of the inner mystical life as far as possible by allowing their souls to be ignited in the all-consuming fire of divine love *(muhabbat)*. They were unfolding the implicit ramifications of a Qur'anic wisdom tradition which had only begun to be tapped by the highly austere ascetic approach of their immediate predecessors.

The name Dhu'n-Nun was a surname meaning "he with the fish;" his given name was Abu'l-Faiz Thawban ibn Ibrahim al-Misri. He was considered an important mystic in his time, but despite his avowed principal of not accepting any doctrines which ran contrary to the Qur'an, he was regarded by many as a heretic. Sadly, he was not fully appreciated until after his death because most of his contemporaries could not understand the rapturous language which poured forth from his soul. Caliph Mutawakkil had Dhu'n-Nun arrested and brought in chains to Baghdad in 829 CE. He was incarcerated along with many other prominent teachers and scholars who disagreed with the state's official theological decree (a doctrine, later repealed, which stated that the Qur'an was a created work rather than an eternally pre-existent expression of Divine Truth). Upon hearing Dhu'n-Nun's eloquent explanation of his doctrine, the Caliph was so moved that he immediately released the gnostic from prison.

After the Prophet himself, Dhu'n-Nun was one of the beings most responsible for opening the station of *marifat* in Islam and making clear the distinction between mere discursive, learned knowledge *('ilm)* and the intuitive gnostic wisdom of the *'arif* (knower of Truth). He affirms a mystic knowing which is potentially available to all, but understood and assimilated only by the intimate friends and lovers of Allah. In this respect, he has been compared to the second century Egyptian Church Father, Clement of Alexandria, who was first among the Orthodox to bring out the gnostic dimensions of Christianity. Dhu'n-Nun stressed mental prayer and meditation *(fikra)* as a key to unlock the door that brings one into the Divine Presence of the King. He was also one of the earliest ecstatic Sufi poets and perhaps the first to use the metaphor of the *wine of love*, which became so popular with the later Persian mystic poets. Dhu'n-Nun says: "Drink the wine of His love for you, so that He may intoxicate you with your love for Him." Like

Hazrati Rabi'a, he relates to Allah as the Beloved, but is prudent enough to say: "Dear God, in public I call you 'My Lord,' but in private I call you 'Beloved'." Carried on wings of ecstatic love, he prays:

> O Allah, include us among those whose spirits have soared to Your kingdom; for whom You unveil Your Majesty; who swim in the flood of certainty, drawn up by love's whirlwind, by the degrees of nearness to Your Glory, whose good intentions and obedience have severed all affinity with deceit and made the lovers overflow with gratitude for Your Divine Grace, O Most Merciful One.[34]

According to Al-Kalabadhi, when Dhu'n-Nun was asked, "What is the end of the path for the knower of Allah?" he cryptically replied, "When he is as he was where he was before he was." The essential principal of the *marifat*—that the gnostic who realizes the Truth actually becomes the Divine Truth—was central to Dhu'n-Nun's understanding and figured strongly in his preaching. He says:

> The *'arif* (gnostic) becomes more humble every hour, for every hour is drawing him nearer to Allah. The gnostics see without knowledge, without sight, without information received, and without observation, without description, without veiling and without veil. They are not themselves, but in so far as they exist at all they exist in Allah. Their movements are caused by Allah, and their words are the divine words which are uttered by their tongues, and their sight is the divine sight which has entered into their eyes.[35]

In concluding this saying, Dhu'n-Nun validates the thrust of his words by referring back to the words of the Prophet himself, quoting one of his most famous *hadith qudsi*, a saying which can be taken as the quintessential divine exegesis of the station

---

34 Yafi'i, *Nashr*, ii.335.
35 Schimmel, *Mystical Dimensions of Islam*, 43.

of *marifat*: "Allah Most High reveals: 'When I love a servant, I become the ear by which they hear, the eye by which they see, the tongue by which they speak, and the hand by which they grasp.'"

Where the ascetic tendency was to deprecate the world as a snare or distraction from the transcendence of the Divine Reality, Dhu'n-Nun's poetry sets the tone for the future mystic poets of Islam. He extols the beauty of nature, psalm-like, as an expression of what can be called the Cosmic Qur'an, the sacred manuscript of nature, written as *ayat* with the divine pen, and always reminding the creation of its Creator:

> *O Allah, Never do I hear the voices of the animals in the field or the rustle of the trees, the splashing of the waters or the song of the birds, the whistling of the wind or the rumble of the thunder, but I sense in them a testimony of Your Unity, and a proof of Your incomparability, that You are the All-Prevailing, the All-Knowing, the All-True.*[36]

When Dhu'n-Nun passed away, people of various religions, including Christians and Jews, attended his funeral. Many of the witnesses were amazed by the saint's final gesture from the coffin when he raised, then lowered his index finger (as Muslims do during daily prayers when they are affirming the *shahada* of divine unity). This occurred during the call to prayer, as the hafiz chanted: *"Ashadu-an La ilaha illallah."* They checked Dhu'n-Nun's hand afterwards and found it stiff with rigor mortis. Some of them accepted Islam as a result of this sign, while many others realized that they had misjudged this *waliyullah* while he was living among them.

---

36 Ibid, 46.

Abu Yazid Bistami

Abu Yazid Tayfur ibn Isa al-Bistami, also known as Bayazid al-Bistami (d.874 CE), was the founder of the *Tayfuriyya* tarikat, whose doctrine was rapture *(ghalabat)* and intoxication *(sakr)* by means of *fana* (self-annihilation in the divine unity). Bayazid was born in the town of Bistam in northern Persia (Iran) and is buried there. He came from a Zoroastrian family and, according to as-Sulami, he studied under Abu 'Ali as-Sindi and from him learned the mystical doctrine of unity and the nature of Reality. The implication, which Zaehner brings out in his *Hindu and Muslim Mysticism*, is that as-Sindi was from Sind (lower Indus Valley) and that Bayazid may have traveled to India and there learned the Vedantic approach to non-dual Reality; this, in turn, may have influenced his interpretation of *tawhid* toward a more monistic understanding based on the negation of *maya*. In other words, by the central phrase of unity in Islam, *La ilaha illallah,* Bistami might have understood: "Nothing real exists except Allah (and that Reality is none other than Yourself—*Tat twam asi.*" Although this is certainly plausible, we cannot be totally certain of

the Hindu influence and needn't search outside of Islam to explain the passionate way of unification which came through Bistami. Bayazid himself left no writings which would inform us one way or the other.

There does exist a brief description of three pilgrimages made by Bistami to the Ka'ba, which allows a revealing glimpse into the nature of his realization of unity. When he first went to Mecca he was disappointed, seeing the Ka'ba as only a building made of stones, similar to many other stone buildings. The next time he made *hajj*, he saw not only the Ka'ba but the Lord of the Ka'ba as well; however, he still did not consider this to be the real unification. Going a third time, he saw only the Lord of the Ka'ba, and a voice in his heart whispered, "O Bayazid, if you didn't see yourself, you would not be a polytheist *(mushrik)*, even if you saw the whole universe; but by seeing yourself, you remain a polytheist who is blind to the whole universe." At that, he recounts, "I repented and repented of my own repentance, and again repented—this time of seeing my own existence."

Later, when someone came knocking on his door saying he had come there searching for Bayazid, the sheikh called out to him, "I too am in search of Bayazid." When this remark was reported to Dhu'n-Nun, he commented, "God have mercy on my brother Abu Yazid! He is lost in the company of those who are lost in God." Indeed it is said that Bayazid was so absorbed in Allah and forgetful of self that he could never even remember the name of his servant of twenty years. Every time he would be informed of his servant's name—the label for his ego-persona—Bistami would immediately forget it.

On still another occasion, Bayazid was traveling to Mecca for the *hajj* when he encountered a man on the road who asked him if he was bound for Mecca, and how much money he had. When Bayazid replied that he had two hundred dirhams and was indeed headed toward Mecca to make the *hajj*, the man asked for the money as alms, saying, "I am a man with a family. You can circle around me seven times and that will be your pilgrimage." Bistami agreed to this, circled around the man and then returned home.

Bayazid regarded asceticism as an early stage of the way. He said: "The gnostic is concerned with what he hopes, the ascetic with what he eats. Blessed is he who is concerned with one thing only, and whose heart is not distracted by what his eyes behold and his ears hear." For the whole emphasis on *self* (*I* must renounce the world, *I* must repent, *I* must seek Allah, etc.) can be seen as part of an ingenious pattern of subterfuge by which the conventional ego-self manages to retain center-stage and to even congratulate itself for fostering any glimpse of Reality which does manage to break through. Bayazid explains how he initially formulated the terms of his spiritual quest: to seek Allah, to know Allah and to love Allah. Elsewhere he boldly describes it in terms of his being the "blacksmith of his self," making himself into a pure mirror to reflect Reality. Later, he realized that he had been all wrong in his appraisal of the situation—it was, in fact, the very opposite of what he supposed: from the beginning, Allah was the One Who was seeking, knowing and loving him.

In the course of his spiritual trail-blazing, Bayazid helped develop and expand upon the doctrine of *fana* (disappearing in Allah) and *baqa* (subsisting in Allah), with emphasis on the former. Of his loss of selfhood, he said: "I shed my *nafs* as a serpent sheds its skin; then, when I regarded my essence it became apparent that I, myself, was He... How great is My glory!"[37] Though some were alarmed by such claims, the authorities and guardians of the *shariat* in his time generally dismissed Bayazid's eccentric claims as the harmless ravings of a disturbed person, who was better ignored than arrested. Some of Bistami's daring mystic accounts reveal certain imperfections in his attainment of this unification founded on the cessation of the ego. However, his overall direction is certainly in keeping with the words of the noble Prophet Muhammad, who said, "Die before you die," *(Mutu kabla anta mu'tu)* and set forth the mysterious mystical paradox: "I am He and He is I, save that I am I, and He is He." *(Ana huwa, wa huwa ana, ghayra ana ana, wa huwa huwa.)*

As Bayazid pressed on through the gate of *fana* and into the Palace of Unity, he penetrated still further into the divine mystery of non-dual Reality, a secret level of realization which is normally couched in protective metaphorical allusions (as in Qur'an) and best remains unspoken in the conventional language of the individualized consciousness. Without this etiquette of subtle linguistic allusion and silence, the level of the sublime mystery, the secret of the *ruhu sirr*, would be exposed directly to the glare of every kind of pedestrian misunderstanding. But ecstasy has a way of loosening tongues, and the bright Sun of divine truth

---

37 Sahjali, *Shatahat al-Sufiyya,* 77.

THE GARDEN OF MYSTIC LOVE

cannot forever remained veiled by the mundane perspectives of those who dwell in the world of shadows.

Bayazid reports that, during one of his unitive experiences, he "flew through the field of Eternity and encountered the Tree of Oneness," and, looking back on the conventional world of separation, he clearly saw "that it was all a cheat." In fact, in his railings against the prevalent acceptance of the hoax of *maya*, Bistami once went so far as to say: "Ah, God will deceive you in the marketplace of this world, and in the next you will also find yourself in the marketplace and discover that you are forever the slave of the market." Bistami was not one to be satisfied in this world or the next with less than the soul's ultimate unification with its own Essential Source. To this end, he retired to the caves of Northern Iran and endured great privations and intense soul-searching, endeavoring to strip his *nafs* of every vestige of duplicity and separation which veiled him from the divine source of being.

Here Bayazid conveys the results of his journey toward divine mystic union: "For thirty years Allah Most High was my mirror. Now I am my own mirror; that which I was, I am no more, for 'I' and 'God' represent polytheism, denying the divine unity. Since I am no more, Allah Most High is His own mirror. Having become free of self, I looked and I saw clearly that lover and beloved and love are one. Praise be unto Me! *(Subhani!)* How Great is My majesty!" In this state of *fana*, not only has Bistami's personal self disappeared, but with it has vanished the conventional religious language of the servant who says, *"Subhan Allah—How great is God's glory."* In its place, we are given to understand that the One Being is exulting in a joyous act of Self-discovery through the medium of His own creation.

Evidently, many of these *shathiyat* were uttered by Bistami in spite of himself and without his cognizance or later remembrance of what he had said. Jelaluddin Rumi recounts a somewhat allegorized tale in his *Masnavi*, which recounts how Sheikh Abu Yazid Bistami once scandalized his disciples by crying out in their midst, "Under my garment there is nothing but God!" Later, when they apprised their master of what he had said in his ecstatic condition, he disavowed any knowledge of having uttered it and urged them to run him through with their swords if he ever began to say such things again. When he began once again to speak in this manner, the disciples stabbed at their teacher but only succeeded in wounding themselves wherever their blades penetrated Bistami's robes.

We should note here the Islamic legal position concerning such sayings. One who is enrapt is not morally responsible for what they have uttered under the influence of ecstasy. He or she is canonically excusable *(ma'dhur)* as long as they do not condone such statements once they have been brought back to their senses. But if they continue to uphold and approve of what appears to be a blasphemous statement while in their normal state, they are subject to the law, even if they are believed to be a saint. An enraptured Sheikh Bayazid made many outrageous statements, such as, "My banner is greater than the banner of Muhammad!" Similarly, when he heard the verse from the Qur'an (85:12): "Surely the Lord's assault is terrible," he answered, "By my life! My assault is more terrible than His!" But as Pir Abu Najib as-Suhrawardi later observed: to put these *shathiyat* in context, one has to see them against the background of the boasting contests *(mufakharah)* of the ancient pre-Islamic Arabs, in which each side made exaggerated claims in order to outdo the other. This tradition continued in the Prophet's time among poets such as Hassan Ibn Thabit, who triumphed on behalf of Hazrati Muhammad over the Banu Darim tribe in a boasting-match.

In Bistami's case, there were also extenuating circumstances in the *malamat* direction which sometimes accounted for his audacious words to people. He did not want to be an intermediary who might serve as a veil for others; so, for example, once when he was being followed by a crowd who sought his company, he said, "O Lord! I pray that you do not veil the people from Yourself by Yourself!" Then, after leading them in the morning prayers, he turned and said to them, "I am I, there is no god but I; therefore worship me!" And when the people heard this, they decided he had gone mad and left him, just as he had hoped.[38]

---

38 Carl Ernst, *Words of Ecstasy in Sufism*, 45.

Fariduddin Attar's *Tadhkirat al-Auliya* records a lengthy account of Bistami's mystical ascent *(mi'raj)* to the divine throne, after the manner of the Prophet Muhammad. At its climax, Bistami comes face to face with the Divine Source of Being. He perceives his own dark selfhood shrinking meanly into oblivion as a result of the encounter with the light of Divine Glory. Bistami himself relates:

After I uttered many praises to Allah, He gave me wings of majesty, so that I flew in the arenas of His glory and beheld the wonders of His handiwork. Perceiving my weakness and recognizing my need, Allah strengthened me with His own strength and arrayed me with His own adornment. He laid the crown of munificence on my head, and opened unto me the door of the palace of Unity. . . . And Allah said to me, "Oh I." And I replied: "O Lord, do not delude me in my ego." Then Allah responded, "O thou," and I was distraught, through the agonies of separation. Then Allah looked upon me for a moment with His Eye of Power and annihilated me completely in His Essence. I saw that I existed through Him and I remained without soul or body like one who is dead until He revived me with His Life and said unto me, "O thou." And, with no vestige of separation left in my awareness, the response of the One Being emerged from my own lips, affirming, "Oh I."

. . . When Allah thus perceived that my attributes were annihilated in His attributes, He bestowed on me a name of His own presence and addressed me with His own Selfhood. Singleness became manifest; all duality vanished.

. . . And He spoke again, saying: "My creatures desire to behold you." I answered, "But I do not wish to see them. Yet, if it is Your will, I will not oppose it, but will only ask of You: Adorn me in Your Unity, and attire me with Your I-ness, and exalt me to Your Oneness, so that when Your creatures see me and gaze upon Your handiwork, they will see only You, the Divine Artist, and my self shall be completely absent." Then I traversed four thousand wildernesses and reached the end. When I gazed, I saw myself at the beginning of the degree of the prophets. And I went on in that infinity so long that at last I said, "No one has ever reached higher than this. Loftier than this no station can be." But when I looked well, I saw that my head was at the sole of the foot of a prophet. Then I realized that the end of the state of the saints is but the beginning of the states of the prophets . . .

. . . Then bewildered with awe and confusion, I desired to be able to see but the tent-peg of the pavilion of Muhammad, the *Rasul* of Allah, but I had not the boldness to attain this. ... And the divine command came, "To be delivered of every trace of 'thouness,' follow after Our beloved, Muhammad of Arabia. Anoint your eye with the dust of his foot and continue following after him."[39]

It is said that Abu Yazid attained propinquity to the Divine Presence seventy times and he lived to be over seventy years old. He relates that in each station to which he was admitted Allah offered him a kingdom, but in every case he declined, as his true desire was not to desire. Someone asked Bistami, "What is the throne?" He replied, "It is I." They asked, "What is the footstool and the Tablet and the Pen?" Bayazid still answered, "It is I". They said, "Allah has servants such as Abraham, Moses and Jesus and angelic servants such as Gabriel, Michael and Seraphiel." Bayazid repeated, "All of these are I. Whoever has become effaced in Allah and has attained the Reality of all that is, all is Allah."[40]

After all that has been related, the words of Abu Yazid on his death bed may come as a surprise, but they are really the measure of his total sincerity. He said, "O Allah, if I said one day, 'Glory be to me, how great is my dignity,' then today I am but a Magian infidel. (But now) I cut the *zunnar*, and testify, *Ashadu an La ilaha illallah, wa ashadu anna Muhammadan rasulullah.* (I bear witness that there is no god but God and Muhammad is His messenger.)"

In conclusion, we will ask the question which Bistami once put to Yahya ibn Mu'adh: "What do you say of one who, if all

39 'Attar, *Muslim Saints and Mystics,* 105-10.
40 Ibid, 123-24.

the oceans in the world were filled with the wine of love, would drink them all and still cry for more to quench his thirst?" Among the Sufis, the answer to this question—the consensus of opinion about Bistami—was mixed. Junayd, on one hand, acknowledged Bistami's high station by saying: "Abu Yazid holds the same rank among us as Gabriel among the angels;" but, on the other hand, he felt that, by remaining in his state of God-intoxication, Bistami had not reached the final goal of the seeker. Junayd felt that, in the end, no amount of excesses, abnormal states, craziness *(madzubiat)* or spiritual trances would ever serve to release anyone from the bondage of self and the corruption of the phenomenal world.

Certainly, there existed a theological difference of opinion between the *Tayfuri* school and the *Junaydiyya* revolving around the interpretation of the mystic's experience of God-consciousness. We will return shortly to consider in more detail Pir Junayd al-Baghdadi and his sophisticated doctrine of divine unification, but for now will simply point out some of the theological implications of the Drunken School of mystical unification as it fits within the context of Islamic exotericism.

The Qur'an speaks against any doctrine of *hulul* (incarnation of the Divine in human form) in the sense of avatars, pagan god-men and goddess-women, or the way in which the Christian Church has often conceived of Jesus as being God incarnated in temporal human form. Likewise, *pantheism*[41] is not considered compatible with ideas of divine transcendence, inasmuch as this philosophy ultimately equates the Perfect Transcendent Source as being identical with the corruptible physical creation. Still less acceptable would be the belief that Allah is limited to, or even trapped within His creation, perhaps through some process of *henotrophy*.[42]

What the Qur'an does affirm is that the souls have been brought forth from the Essence of the One Primal Source, Allah, who has breathed the divine spirit of life into Adam and his progeny, existentiated the physical universe for the benefit of these created life forms, and will ultimately call the entire creation to return to

---

41 Pantheism: maintaining that "All is God".

42 Henotrophy: the concept that physical creation is transcendent spirit which has become "congealed" into solid matter so that the Divine is now actually limited by natural laws.

its Eternal Source, where all of life will be recreated on a higher plane of being. The created realm has come into being without struggle or entropy, proceeding simply from the divine thought or command, "Be *(kun)!*" and from this, the universe exists and is continually sustained, moment by moment, by the power of the Omnipotent, Omnipresent Source. This formless, transcendent Source does not exist inside nor outside of the created realm; it is neither separate nor remote from the creation, nor is it in any way limited by the finite worlds which have emanated from it. A very important *hadith qudsi* explains the situation through the divine saying: "I was a hidden treasure and I desired to be known, so I created the worlds (that I might know Myself through their experience)." Thus, in Islamic mysticism, we can speak of human beings—who are by nature an expression of the hidden treasure of the Divine Essence, yet veiled from a full realization of their divine origin—awakening into a conscious participation in this One Reality. However, this understanding of Reality would preclude the possibility that a mortal human being, as a result of encountering the Divine Source, could change their nature and become deified, shedding altogether the perishable aspects of their human nature.

It is unlikely that Abu Yazid was actually advocating a metamorphosis from "non-divine" to divine; but as he was not a careful theological hairsplitter, some might have misunderstood this as his doctrine. To compound the situation, some Persian converts to Islam and members of Shi'ite sects were indeed, during that era, attempting to import deifying trends of thought into the esoteric schools of Islam. This aroused a growing suspicion among the Islamic orthodoxy of where these ecstatics "were coming from" and where they were headed theologically. As a major spokesperson for Sufism, Junayd was anxious to clarify the matter in such a way that the ecstatic extravagances would be trimmed without relinquishing the soul's legitimate recognition of its divine inheritance. To this end, he carefully explicated the mystic experience of unification so as to acceptably reflect the deep teachings of the Qur'an while also "grounding" the far-flung theological flights of the ecstatic Sufis. Junayd believed that these inebriated ones had become unbalanced in the *hakikat* (or highest sphere) of Divine Truth and needed to integrate their experience with the mature sobriety of the *marifat*, which he considered to be the further step on the mystic path. To a great extent, he succeeded in this quest, since it is said that Junayd was accepted by all the authorities in Islam, mystics and non-mystics alike, without ever being touched by the shadow of heresy.

Bistami's *Tayfuriyya* sect became known as a school of *wujud* (being or existence), in which the experience of unity involves transcending one's limited self in order to discover that one's very nature is none other than the divine nature—the supposed individual self being ultimately unreal. By contrast, the *Junaydiyya* established itself as a school of *shuhud* (witness). Here, there is no question of relinquishing one's created human nature, or the last veil of servanthood, while one is in the body; rather, one's will becomes unified with the Divine Will and one enters into the Divine Consciousness, awakening to the realization that "everything you see is the Act of the One." This subtle difference of approach was succinctly earmarked when al-Hallaj proclaimed, "I am the Divine (Truth)—*Ana'l Haqq,*" and Junayd reportedly responded: "No. It is through Divine Reality that you exist."

We have examined the lives of many of the earliest Sufi masters up until the formation of the first major school of mysticism in Baghdad. We now turn to that school and its founding teachers. This early line of Sufi sheikhs, in a direct line of spiritual transmission from the Prophet Muhammad and Hazrat 'Ali, constitutes the beginning of the *silsila* of a number of mystic orders, such as the Halveti-Jerrahi, a lineage that includes the first major pir of the Halveti-Jerrahi line, Hazrat Junayd al-Baghdadi. The beginning of this noble chain of transmission is listed below:

ALLAH

Gabriel

Muhammad (d.632)

'Ali ibn Abi Talib (d.661)

Hasan al-Basri (d.728)

Habib al-Ajami (d.773)

Da'ud at-Ta'i (d.777)

Ma'ruf al-Karkhi (d.815)

Sari as-Saqati (d.871)

Pir Junayd al-Baghdadi (d.910)

HABIB AL-AJAMI

HABIB AL-AJAMI was an illustrious Persian student of the renowned mystic, Hasan Basri. Habib was raised in the Zoroastrian faith in Basra and made his living as a usurer. He was a very unpopular figure among the people of Basra because of his daily dunning of clients who were essentially paupers. Even if his clients were destitute, he would still demand something from them. Finally one day, a collection from a poor woman went so terribly that Habib himself became revolted with his accursed way of life: Habib had forced the woman to make him some soup, as she had nothing else to give; but it turned dark, like blood, in the pot. Full of remorse, Habib wandered off to a nearby mosque and chanced to hear Hasan al-Basri preaching and extolling the virtue of absolute reliance upon the One True Sustainer, Allah. Habib was deeply affected and immediately took *shahada* as a Muslim. He renounced usury and relinquished all his assets to his former debtors, inwardly vowing to rely exclusively upon Allah for his sustenance. Then he retired to a hermitage to study and pray.

However, Habib still had a wife and children to provide for, and they were naturally worried at the prospect of Habib having no job or resources with which to feed them. Not wanting his wife to worry or to think badly of their new chosen religion, Habib assured her that he had a new and better job which would certainly produce wages by the end of the week. Meanwhile, Habib spent the rest of the week going to the hermitage and praying fervently that Allah would accept his *islam* and save him from shame by somehow providing for his family during this time of transition. He had given away everything as an act of repentance and absolute trust in God in response to Hasan's sermon, which he believed was Allah's personal call to him; perhaps later he could find another livelihood, but just now he was determined to turn everything over to Allah. He would not doubt for a moment that the Abundant Source of Life is responsive to those who ask, with complete faith, for what they truly need.

When the end of the week came, Habib was still waiting at the hermitage, empty-handed, knowing that his children at home were crying with hunger. Habib walked home with a heavy heart, wondering what to do next and what he could tell his wife and children. But when he approached the house, he began to smell delicious food cooking and, when he entered the house, his wife embraced him and exclaimed, "O husband, whoever you are working for, he is a generous master. See what he has sent by the hand of a handsome young man who came to our door today with a sheep, a load of flour and other provision, including a purse of 300 silver dirhams! He told me to tell you this: 'You increase your output and we will increase your wages.'"

After this, Habib turned his face completely away from worldly pursuits and toward the service of Allah. As his sainthood increased, people began to come to him for help. One old woman came to Habib saying that her son had been missing for some time and that she longed for him to return. Habib recited a prayer and instructed her to give what little money she had as *sadaqa* (alms) to the poor. When she had done so, he sent her home, saying, "Begone. Your son has returned to you." She found him at home when she returned.

Like many masters, including Hasan Basri, Habib was endowed with the power of bilocution. Once he was seen in Basra (Iraq) on the eighth day of *Dhul-Hajj* and on the ninth day was sighted at Mt. Arafat in Southern Arabia.[43] Yet however gifted he was in the

43 'Attar, *Tadhirat al-Auliya,* 36.

spiritual arena, coming from a Persian background, Habib found it very difficult to read and pronounce the Qur'an in Arabic, and thus earned the nickname "the barbarian."

One day, Hasan Basri came to visit Habib's cell just after Habib had made the *adhan* for prayers. Knowing Habib's propensity towards mistakes and his poor command of the Arabic language used in salat, Sheikh Hasan politely abstained from joining (i.e., following) Habib in his ritual prayers, and visited with him after Habib had finished making his individual salat. That night Hasan dreamed that he was in the Divine Presence and he asked, "O Lord, in what does your good pleasure consist?" He was answered, "You found My good pleasure but did not know its value. If you had said your prayers after Habib yesterday evening, and if the righteousness of his intention had restrained you from taking offense at his pronunciation, I would have been well pleased with you."

A number of stories in the tradition illustrate the point that what Sheikh Hasan knew and taught, Habib, with his tremendous faith, heard and turned into a reality to a degree which surprised even his teacher. We conclude with such a story which also reflects the mood of political events of that time: The notorious Ummayad general Hajjaj was rounding up important people in Basra and wanted to arrest Hasan. Having no desire to fall into Hajjaj's hands, Hasan fled to Habib's hermitage and hid himself in Habib's room. The officers of Hajjaj came there searching for Hasan and, finding only Habib, demanded to know if he had seen his teacher, Hasan. Habib told them, with complete honesty, that he had. "Then where is he?" they asked menacingly. Habib calmly answered, "He is right in there, in my cell." The guards went in and searched everywhere but couldn't find Hasan. They returned to Habib and, thinking that he was making fun of them, called him a liar and even physically abused him, but still he maintained that he was telling them the truth. They searched several more times; seven times they practically laid their hands on Hasan but were simply unable to see him. Finally, they gave up and stormed out of the place.

Hasan emerged from the back room, relieved not to have been captured, and said to Habib, "I realize that it was owing to your benedictions that Allah did not deliver me to those wicked men, but was it necessary to actually point out your teacher to them?" Habib replied, "O Master, it was not so much on account of my benedictions that they failed to see you, but through the blessedness of my having spoken the truth. Had I lied, we would have both been arrested." Hasan further inquired, "And what did you recite that they did not see me?" Habib replied, "I recited (from the Qur'an) the throne verse, *Ayat al-kursi* (2:255) ten times; then ten times the verse (2:285-6), *Amana rasulu . . .*; and ten times *Surat al-Ihklas* (112), and finally I prayed, "O God, I have committed Hasan to You; may You watch over him."[44]

In time Habib, became revered as the founding pir of the *Habibiyya*, an order from which eight other significant orders later emerged. From Pir Habib al-Ajami, the mystic mantle of succession was passed on to Da'ud at-Ta'i of Kufa; then, from Da'ud to Ma'ruf al-Karkhi of Baghdad, who founded the *Karkhiyya*. From Ma'ruf, it passed to Hasan Sari as-Saqati, who founded the *Saqatiyya*. From Sheikh Sari, the succession went to his maternal nephew, Junayd, who founded the *Junaydiyya*, from which the Halveti-Jerrahi Order, as well as many other important turuq *(Qadiriyya, Rifa'iyya, Badawiyya, Dusukiyya,* etc.) trace their spiritual lineage. The other five orders coming from Pir Habib are the *Tayfuriyya* (the Bistamis); the *Guzruniyya* (from Pir Abu Ishaq Gazruni, fourth in line after al-Junayd); the *Tartawsiyya* (from Pir Abu'l-Farah Tartawsi, who stands midway between Pir Junayd and Pir 'Abdul Qadir Gaylani in the Qadiri line); the *Suhrawardiyya* (from Pir Abu Najib Suhrawardi, who is also included in the Halveti-Jerrahi line); and finally the *Kubrawiyya* or *Firdawsiyya* (from Abu Najib's successor, Najmuddin Kubra).

At the same time as Hasan al-Basri was training Habib al-Ajami, he was also instructing 'Abdul Wahid ibn Zayd, who, like Pir Habib, also stands at the head of a number of great Sufi lines, having directly taught Fuzayl ibn Iyad, who was one of the

---

44 Al-Hujwiri, *Kashf al-Mahjub,* 88-89.

The Rise of Sufism

teachers of Ibrahim Adham. Both of these pirs, whose lives we have previously examined, were contemporaries of Pir Habib's successor, Da'ud at-Ta'i, to whom we now turn.

DA'UD AT-TA'I

DA'UD AT-TA'I was not only a student of Habib al-Ajami, but also undertook initial studies with the famous jurist Abu Hanifa, after which he was converted to the ascetic life by Habib ar-Ra'i, a noted companion of Salman al-Farsi. Da'ud was drawn to the mystical path at a time when the world had lost all attraction for him. Something in his nature made him acutely aware of the brevity of life and the inevitability of decay and death, and though he read and studied with the best scholars of his time, nothing seemed to heal his grief. He was once seen running to the congregational prayers. "What's the hurry?" someone asked him. He replied that there was an army at the gate of the city waiting for him. "What army?" the person exclaimed. Da'ud answered, "The men of the tombs."

Finally Imam Abu Hanifa steered him toward the tarikat and the ascetic path. After receiving *bayat* (initiation into the path), Da'ud cast all of his books into the Euphrates River and went into retirement, cutting himself off from society. Having never married, he was free from any obligations to others; however, he had a mother who was still living and had received a goodly inheritance of twenty dinars. Rather than giving it all away, he entered into a covenant with his Lord in which he promised not to repair anything in this world, but only to be granted permission to consume this money slowly until it ran out, at which time he would die. Thus the mansion which he owned, with its many apartments, gradually decayed around him. When one area of the building would deteriorate and collapse in ruins, Da'ud would move to another area. This went on for twenty years until the whole building had gradually collapsed, except for the portico, and Da'ud's money had

— 115 —

dwindled to a small supply. During this time he taught disciples, including Ma'ruf al-Karkhi, and associated with theologians such as Muhammad ibn Hasan. Da'ud's reputation extended beyond Kufa even to Baghdad.

The caliph, Harun ar-Rashid, came with the qadi, Abu Yusuf, to visit Da'ud during the last phase of the saint's life. Only through the intercession of his mother did Da'ud reluctantly admit them and preach to them. The caliph was moved to tears and offered to leave some money, but Da'ud refused explaining his covenant. Not long after this, Abu Yusuf stood for prayers at the palace and announced that Da'ud at-Ta'i had died. "How do you know this?" the caliph asked Abu Yusuf explained that after their visit, he had learned how much money Da'ud had left and had calculated how many days remained before his inheritance ran out. Indeed, just as Da'ud had prayed, he died the very evening his money ran out. The portico, the last remaining structure of his house, also caved in on that same fateful evening.[45]

Ma'ruf al-Karkhi said of him: "I never saw anyone who held worldly goods in less account than Da'ud Ta'i; the world and its people had no value whatsoever in his eyes, and yet he used to regard the dervishes *(fuqara)* as perfect, although they were corrupt."[46]

MA'RUF AL-KARKHI

MA'RUF AL-KARKHI was a Persian student of Da'ud at-Ta'i and became one of the principal sheikhs of his time, noted for his generosity and devoutness. He lived in Baghdad during the time of Harun ar-Rashid in the Karkh quarter of the city. His parents are thought to have been Elkhasaite Christians or Sabians—they may even have been Mandaeans (an ancient gnostic sect which honors John the Baptist and stresses ritual ablutions). The schoolmasters

---

45 Attar, *Tadhirat al-Auliya,* 138-42.
46 Al-Hujwiri, *Kashf al- Mahjub,* 110.

where they sent Ma'ruf tried to teach him that "God is the third of three," but he instinctively rebelled against this and maintained God's oneness, even in the face of beatings. Finally, he ran away and took shahada as a Muslim with the eighth Shi'ite Imam, 'Ali ibn Musa ar-Riza, who held Ma'ruf in high esteem. When his parents learned this, they too converted to Islam and were reconciled with Ma'ruf. By this time, he had placed himself under the spiritual direction of Da'ud at-Ta'i and was undertaking many austerities. His stations blossomed and his fame began to spread rapidly; soon, he was accepting pupils to whom he expounded gnostic ideas of great profundity.

Among his aphorisms is a definition of Sufism as "the apprehension of divine realities and the renunciation of human possessions." He also said: "The friends of Allah are known by three signs: their thought is of Allah, their dwelling is with Allah, their business is in Allah." He taught that heaven and hell and everything in between "is contained in the hand of God. When you love Him, He will make you forget all these; and when you become intimate with Him, He will protect you from all of these." Ma'ruf also instructed some of his disciples, such as his nephew Ya'qub, to invoke his name in their prayers whenever they desired something from Allah.

Whenever food was offered as a gift to Ma'ruf, he would accept it and eat it. When someone noted that Ma'ruf's Sufi brother, Bishr ibn al-Harith, customarily refused such food offerings, Ma'ruf replied: "Abstaining causes my brother's hands to be tied, while gnosis causes my hands to be stretched forth. I am only a guest in the house of my Lord. When he feeds me, I eat; when He does not, I have to be patient. I have neither objection nor choice."[47]

One of the most famous stories about Ma'ruf involves a gang of drunken youths who were playing instruments, dancing and singing and abusively harassing Ma'ruf and his disciples as they walked down to the Tigris River. The disciples became incensed with their behavior and entreated their master to call down the curse of God upon these lawless revellers, so they would drown and the

---

47 *Qut al-Qulub*, quoted in A.H.Abdel-Kader, *The Life of Al-Junayd*, 15-16.

world would be rid of them. Ma'ruf told his disciples to lift their hands in supplication and then he prayed: "O Allah, as You have given them a happy life in this world, may You grant them as well a happy life in the world to come." The disciples were astonished and said, "Master! What kind of prayer is this? Is there some secret hidden in it?" Ma'ruf answered them, "The One with Whom I am speaking knows its secret. Wait for a moment and you will even now see its mystery revealed." The youths had become silent and were staring at the sheikh. Suddenly they began pouring out their wine and breaking their lutes, then came before the sheikh and repented. After this, these same youth began to lead upright lives and found joy in the spiritual path, several of them even becoming sheikhs. Ma'ruf told his disciples who had originally suggested the prayer, "You see, your desire has been fulfilled completely, without anyone drowning or suffering." For the fulfillment of the sheikh's prayer—that the youths might find joy in the hereafter—it was necessary for them to change the priorities in their life in such a manner as to make this possible.

Ma'ruf's end came when a crowd of Shi'ites were one day jostling at the door of Imam ar-Riza, and broke the sheikh's rib, causing him to fall very ill. His khalifa, Sari as-Saqati, asked Sheikh Ma'ruf to give him his last testament. The master replied, "When I die, take my shirt and give it as alms. I wish to go out of this world naked, even as I came naked from my mother's womb." Jews, Christians and Muslims alike attended Pir Ma'ruf's funeral and all of them claimed him as one of their own.[48]

After his death, 'Ali ibn al-Muwaffaq dreamed that he saw someone in paradise at the Pavilion of the Throne, staring without blinking at Allah Most High. He asked, "Who is this?" and was told, "This is Ma'ruf al-Karkhi who worships Allah, not through fear of hell nor desire for paradise, but only for love of Him; thus he is allowed to gaze upon the Divine Countenance until the Day of Resurrection."

48 'Attar, *Tadhirat al-Auliya,* 161-65.

SARI AS-SAQATI

FROM MA'RUF, the spiritual mantle was passed to his khalifa, Sari as-Saqati, who lived in Baghdad during the first period of the 'Abbasid dynasty. Sari used to say: "Whatever I have learned is from the blessing of my association with Ma'ruf." Hujwiri credits Sari with being the first of those who devoted their attention to the arrangement of stations *(makamat,* i.e., the seven levels of the *nafs)* and to the explanation of spiritual states *(ahwal).* The historian as-Sulami said of him: "Sari was the first in Baghdad to teach unification *(tawhid)* through the way of mysticism, and the first to teach the knowledge of Reality *(Haqq);* he was also the leader of the Baghdadis in the symbolic utterances *(isharat)."* *Isharat* was a special esoteric system of code words which Sari and his *Saqatiyya* school, which included Junayd, invented for the purpose of concealing their doctrine from the uninitiated. At a time when Sufis such as Sari were developing their doctrines and pursuing the knowledge of tawhid to dangerous heights, this mystic terminology of *isharat* served as a protection against other more conservative factions who might become adversarial if they chanced upon explicit formulations of the Sufi's doctrine of unity.

There were many factions in Baghdad at this time, of whom we shall only mention a few. There was the Persian as-Saqati, whom we may consider as the founder of the Sufi school of Baghdad, the master of most of the contemporary Sufi sheikhs of Iraq, and the head of the advanced wing of research into *tawhid* (Sari is sometimes credited with being the first to use the word *tawhid* in the sense of mystic union between the soul and its Lord). There was also the Arabian Sufi master, Muhasibi—with whom Junayd studied for a time—representing the conservative wing of the tarikat, which was concerned more with moral issues than mystical states. Finally, there was Imam Ahmad ibn Hanbal, who founded the most conservative branch of the four major schools of Islamic jurisprudence (the imam closest in view to the modern

Wahhabis of Saudi Arabia). Ibn Hanbal appears to have opposed
Sari, even though Sari was held in high esteem among a majority
of the leaders, governors, generals, and scholars of his time, as
well as the public at large.

Sari as-Saqati lived to be 98 years old. His full name was Abu'l
Hasan Sari ibn Mughallis as-Saqati; he was called *saqati* because of
his profession as a merchant or haggling tradesman *(saqat farosh)*
in the Baghdad bazaar, where he dealt in spices and seasonings
and sold other odds and ends. Sari marked the beginning of his
spiritual career to the day when the renowned *tabi'un* Habib ar-
Ra'i passed by his shop and gave him something to give to the
poor. "May Allah be good to you," Habib told him, and from that
moment, says Sari, the world lost its attraction for him.

The next day Sheikh Ma'ruf al-Karkhi came along, bringing
with him an orphan child, whom he asked Sari to clothe. When
Sari did so, Ma'ruf blessed him, saying: "May Allah make the
world hateful to your heart and give you rest from this work."
This, Sari says, completed his detachment. A further story comes
from Sari's final period as a shopkeeper in the Bazaar. Sari had
become very scrupulous in his sales so that he never marked up
any merchandise more than five percent, even when there was the
chance to take advantage of a shortage elsewhere. Sari would close
his shop and draw the curtains for prayers throughout the day.
One day when he had just reopened after salat, a man came from
Mount Lokam to bring Sari salaams (greetings of peace) from his
sheikh in Mount Lokam. Sari returned the salaams, adding, "He
dwells in the mountains, where one has to exert very little effort.
A man ought to be able to live in the midst of the market and be
so preoccupied with Allah that not for a single instant is he absent
from the Divine Presence."[49]

Then one day a fire raged through the bazaar and someone
informed Sari that his shop had been lost. He replied, "Then I am
freed of the care of it." When he subsequently found that all the
shops around his had burned, except his own, he maintained his
attitude of detachment toward it and gave all he possessed to the

---

49 Ibid, 167.

poor, devoting himself exclusively to the study of Sufism, studying with Sheikh Ma'ruf. In this way, he advanced and, in time, became the first mystic to preach the Sufi truths of unity in Baghdad. He trained other students who gradually formed the school known as the *Arbab at-Tawhid* (the Masters of Unification), which included such prominent Sufi teachers as Junayd, Shibli, and Nuri. As he grew older, Sheikh Sari withdrew from the public eye and spent his time with a few select pupils, the most famous being his nephew, Junayd. Like Socrates, Sari left nothing in writing, but taught using a question and answer format, which Junayd—his Plato—worked out, transforming the structure of Sufism into a system which he both taught and recorded for posterity.

We conclude with two of Sari's extant sayings: "If Allah were revealed to the people of *jahannam* (hell), sinful believers would never think of *janna* (paradise), since the sight of Allah would so fill them with joy that they would feel no pain."[50] Along similar lines, he also prayed to Allah: "We deem all torments more desirable than to be veiled from You. When Your beauty is revealed to our hearts, we take no thought of affliction."[51]

PIR JUNAYD AL-BAGHDADI

ABU'L QASIM IBN MUHAMMAD JUNAYD was destined to become one of the great founding pirs of Sufism, known as the *Sheikh at-Tariqa* (Master of the mystic way), the *"Sultan al-'Arifin"* (King of the knowers of Allah) and *Sayyid at-Ta'ifa* (Lord of the crowd, or chief of the mystical organizations). Like his father, Junayd was a merchant of glass bottles; he was physically stout and vigorous. As a young man, Junayd studied with the Shafi'ite canonist Abu Thawr Kalbi and the prominent Sufi master Harith al-Muhasibi, and finally was initiated into the mystic way by his maternal uncle, Sheikh Sari as-Saqati. Hazrat Sari exhibited a fondness for

50 Subhan, *Sufism, Its Saints and Shrines,* 169.
51 Al-Hujwiri, *Kashf al-Mahjub,* 110.

— *121* —

his serious and thoughtful nephew and saw great potential in him even as a young child. He took Junayd with him on pilgrimage when he was but seven years old and there, in an assembly of some four hundred sheikhs in the Mosque of the Sanctuary, Sheikh Sari urged his young nephew to join in the discussions. Junayd's

Khadhimain Mosque near Baghdad

mature contributions impressed everyone, prompting his uncle to tell him that his tongue would soon show itself to be his special gift from Allah, a compliment that brought tears to Junayd's eyes.

Hazrat Junayd returned to Baghdad and took up glass selling in a shop. Every day he would draw down the blinds and perform four hundred *raka'at* of prayer. Later, he altered this routine, abandoning the shop and worshiping at a room on the porch of Sheikh Sari's house. He would continue this practice for forty years; during thirty of those years, it is said that he stood and repeated the name of majesty, *Allah*, all night until the *fajr* prayers at dawn.

Junayd studied with a number of great scholars, became a *hafiz*, and developed a profound grasp of orthodox theology and traditions. Sheikh Sari approved of such a sturdy scholastic foundation for Junayd but warned him against too much speculative reasoning. He told Junayd: "May Allah make you a (well-grounded) traditionalist who becomes a Sufi, not a Sufi who becomes a traditionalist."[52] After years of spiritual maturation, Sheikh Sari began to urge Junayd to preach, but Junayd deferred, insisting that it was improper for him to do so while his master was yet alive and actively preaching.

Gradually, it came about that as many as thirty of Allah's saints had implored the reticent Junayd to preach to the people, without yet convincing him. Then the Prophet himself appeared to Junayd in a dream and ordered him to preach. At this, Junayd acquiesced, and in so doing, it occurred to him that perhaps the reason for his receiving this direct message from the holy Prophet was that he had now surpassed his own teacher. But when he saw his sheikh the next day, before Junayd had a chance to utter even a word, Sari said to him: "You would not speak when I urged you to or when the disciples or other sheikhs of Baghdad asked you, but now that the Prophet has commanded you, you must speak." Remembering his former presumption, Junayd responded, "God forgive me! How did you know I saw the Prophet in a dream?" Sheikh Sari replied, "Allah Himself came to me in a dream and said, 'I have sent the Rasulullah to tell Junayd to preach from the pulpit.'" Humbled, Junayd replied, "I will preach then; but only on the condition that it be to no more than forty persons."[53] (Some traditions give an even smaller number, saying that Junayd would only accept a select group of twenty disciples at any one time.)

Junayd was to teach for the next thirty years. At times, there were complaints against his public preaching and Junayd would stop for a while, only to resume again later. At one point, tragedy struck his home when Junayd's son was accused of a crime and subsequently beheaded. Then thirteen years after the passing of Hazrat Sari as-Saqati, many of the leading Sufis were brought to court on charges of heretical doctrines by a Hanbalite named Ghulam al-Khalil. At that time, Junayd broke his ties with the accused Sufis and returned to the garb of a Shafi'ite jurist. Nevertheless, he later succeeded Abu Ya'qub Zayyat as director of the Sufi convent of Shuniz, and at this time, according to some traditions, received Mansur al-Hallaj

52 Makki, *Qut l-Qulub,* Vol.2, 35.
53 'Attar, *Tadhirat al-Auliya,* 201-4.

as a novice. Like his uncle Sari, Junayd lived to an advanced age (around 90 years); he was also buried in his uncle's tomb, a *mazar* that still exists in Iraq today.

During his career, Junayd translated Bistami's ecstatic accounts from the Persian and made a commentary on them *(Sharh Shathiyat Abi Yazid al-Bistami)*. He also transmitted many of Sheikh Sari's formulas, at times adopting a more conservative vein like his friend Muhasibi, and toning down his own master's sayings when they bordered on *hulul* (divine incarnationism). This was especially true after other disciples of Sari (such as Abu'l Husayn an-Nuri) developed a strong tendency toward *hululi* doctrines, and were accused of heresy by the orthodox. What has primarily survived of Junayd's sparse corpus of writings are some letters (fragments of several of his *Rasa'il*) and an extensive assortment of his sayings and teachings transmitted by others, such as as-Sarraj in his *Kitab al-Luma*. Always cautious and circumspect, Junayd never intended for his esoteric teachings to reach a wide public audience; one tradition relates that he went so far as to request that all his writings be buried with him.

We will examine some of the teachings of Hazrat Junayd, but first, a few stories, variously attributed to him, which reveal the sanctity of his station beyond the level of mere intellectual acuity.

One day a criminal was being publicly executed in Baghdad, a man who, after committing many crimes, had been apprehended and sentenced to die by the courts. He was to be hanged in the public square, as was the custom of the time, so that people would witness and learn from it. Hazrat Junayd happened to be passing by the square and saw that an execution was about to take place. His gaze fell upon the convicted man and he felt great compassion and mercy for this fellow human being, wishing with his whole being that the man would have been able to lead a good and moral life. Then the executioner hanged the man until dead. (According to one tradition related by Attar, Hazrat Junayd kissed the dead man's feet, saying, "A thousand pardons upon him. He worked at his trade so perfectly that he gave his life for it.")

That night many a sheikh and waliyullah in Baghdad dreamed

about that man; not one, but forty people dreamed about him. Each one of them saw this criminal dwelling in Allah's paradise, and was amazed by it. They said to him: "We know that we condemned you to die and that you were a terrible criminal who made the whole society suffer. How did you possibly merit to enter paradise?" The hanged man answered, "Indeed I was a terrible criminal, and I have paid the penalty for my crimes in terms of worldly justice. But a lover of Allah—a beloved of Allah—looked upon me with mercy and compassion, and for the sake of this divine closeness, Allah has forgiven me and accepted me in his paradise."

Another story[54] concerns a young dervish who took hand with Junayd, a student whom Junayd particularly loved because of his spiritual gifts and realization. Many of the other disciples, having been with Junayd for years, were jealous of the master's affection for this seemingly immature neophyte. Now, such a feeling of jealousy for the affections of the sheikh is considered permissible; it is called *gayret* and implies the need for extra effort or perseverance on the part of the one who is jealous. The sheikh knew and understood the feelings of the other dervishes in this circumstance, but kept a discreet silence about it.

Then one day, with the intention of administering a lesson to all the dervishes, Hazrat Junayd had twenty live fowls brought in. He asked each of the dervishes to take one of the birds to a hidden location, where absolutely no one could see them, and there, slaughter the fowl and bring it back to the tekke for a feast that was being prepared. All of them went forth, found a deserted place, and brought back their prepared fowl, except the young dervish who was the master's favorite. He returned still holding the live bird and looking perplexed. When the rest of them saw that he couldn't even accomplish this simple task, they thought, "Now, maybe our master will realize how incompetent this young dervish really is." When the sheikh asked him why he had not been able to follow instructions and slay the fowl where no one could see him, the young dervish sighed and explained that he had tried in vain to find a truly deserted location, but no matter where he went, he felt he

---

54 As recounted orally by Muzaffer al-Jerrahi. The story has sometimes been attributed to other Sufi masters, such as Abdul Qadir Gaylani.

was in the divine presence and never alone. Hazrat Junayd turned to the others and said, "You see the measure of his understanding. Now, do you see why I love him so?"

Junayd did not encourage his dervishes or fellow Sufis in the direction of outward ecstacies, crying out or swooning. One day, Abu Bakr ash-Shibli—himself a well-known Sufi of Junayd's circle—was among those in a congregation listening to Junayd preach on the mysteries of divine unity. Suddenly Shibli was inspired to cry out, "Allah!" (as Sufis often do). Junayd remarked, "If Allah is absent, to mention the absent One is a sign of absence, whereas Allah is never absent. And since Allah is, in fact, present, to call out His name right in the midst of contemplating His presence is a little rude."[55]

Junayd had another ecstatic dervish who was prone to crying out, so he warned the man that he could not continue to attend their meetings unless he was able to control and "ground" his ecstasy in a mature way. The dervish agreed to comply and, though it was difficult for him, he succeeded for a time. Then one day, a number of great sheikhs of Baghdad came to be with Junayd at their meeting and everyone began to feel the intensity of love and knowledge that was being generated through this encounter. Suddenly that passionate dervish lover reached the limits of his restraint and, crying out in ecstacy, breathed his last and collapsed in the midst of them.

If nothing else, this shows the difficulty of holding back ecstasy, once one has quaffed the inebriating wine of divine love. Junayd aspired to help them assimilate it and so become strong, knowledgeable, useful, functioning reservoirs of divine awareness. To give an analogy, it is not unlike the story (related by Muzaffer Efendi) of a sheikh who once came upon many large casks of wine and stopped, in awe, to consider them. His disciples asked, "Master, why are you gazing at these barrels of wine, which, after all, are *haram* (unlawful)?" He answered, "I was just contemplating how much wine these barrels contain and how many, many persons could become intoxicated from this wine; yet these barrels have no difficulty containing it all."

---

55 Ibid, 206.

The teaching of Hazrati Pir Junayd al-Baghdadi is characterized by an attitude of sobriety *(sahw),* a perspective in which divine knowledge or gnosis is stabilized within the soul during this earthly life. Proceeding from mystic realization to divine participation, those who sojourn on the mystic path not only lose themselves in an encounter with Truth at the level of Ultimate Reality *(hakikat),* but go on to the next step of transformation at the level of *marifat,* where this knowledge of the divine is grounded in the very fiber of their being. In this way, they achieve a state of "essential union" in the One, and live from this advanced station of God-realization in a graceful and natural way, without becoming isolated or estranged from the rest of society. While encouraging the integration of mystical states and stations into the everyday life of the Sufi, Junayd similarly discouraged unbalanced eccentricities and spiritual excesses, justified as spontaneous expressions of divine intoxication *(sakr).*

Perhaps here we should recall the precise meaning of the word *ecstasy,* derived from the Greek *ekstasis,* meaning "to be beside oneself" or "joyfully carried beyond oneself." A further spiritual ramification of the term would be: "to stand outside of the conventional self," blissfully freed from one's conditioned assumptions about oneself and the world. If one has accepted a certain set of values and restraints regarding one's identity and place in society, and then, through mystic insight, suddenly realizes the relative unreality of that perspective—or, like Bistami, perceives that "this is all a cheat"—how will they handle this bewildering realization? Will they enter a rather awkward spiritual adolescence in which they say things to shock others and rudely awaken those who are enjoying their sleep, or deliberately provoke the suspicions of the guardians of the religious law? Or will they have the inner strength to quietly contain and integrate their realization, patiently working to help others who are not yet inwardly free, just as a parent would help a child (sometimes humoring them, but without condescension)?

Although Junayd certainly recognized the value of the ecstatic states and unveilings achieved by Bistami, Dhu'n-Nun, and Nuri (Junayd is even credited with some ecstatic utterances of his own), he had no desire to allow the deep truths of Islamic mysticism to be marginalized and repudiated by the main body of Muslims on account of the indulgences of a few daring provocateurs and misguided libertines. Several aphorisms, attributed to Junayd or his followers, attest to Junayd's emphasis on cultivating spiritual maturity, a doctrine sometimes called "the second sobriety." In a succinct statement, Junayd says: "Ecstasy is for novices; sobriety is for the elect." In a similar vein, Hujwiri quotes an unnamed Junaydi sheikh as saying: "Intoxication is a playground for children and sobriety a field of struggle for mature human beings."

Of course, some of the ecstatics for whom this dose of cold water was intended, begged to disagree, believing that this condition of "sobriety beyond inebriation" represented a mere regression from their God-intoxicated state which would solidify not the divine attributes, but only the veils of human attributes which they were trying to transcend. Notwithstanding this difference in temperament between the two perspectives (and the suspicion of all ecstasy among the *ulama*), Junayd's view eventually carried enough weight and authority to gain credible acceptance among the majority of both mainstream Muslims and Sufi mystics.

He insisted that the conditions of bewilderment and craziness typically associated with *fana-fi'llah* were not the end goal of the path but only a necessary stage along the way, a passing phase in which Allah's overwhelming qualities spill over and annihilate the worshiper's personal self. Viewed in its full context, the process can be seen as an unfolding of the divine intention, meant to temporarily obliterate the individuality of the ripened seeker. The final aim of the process is to restore the original, unveiled power of the soul, fully integrating one's earthly consciousness with the eternal consciousness of the One Being, beyond time and the illusion of separate selfhood. The primordial condition of the soul, prior to its involvement in the created realms, exists as a pure expression of divine will. In the second sobriety, the transforming initiative of the divine volition finds its completion. Allah victoriously overwhelms the self, reassumes command of the psyche, and replaces the individual's separate, limited consciousness with a timeless, pristine awareness. Seen in this way, *fana* and *baqa* are never separate. As Junayd says in his *Risala*, in the final stage of the path, the worshiper returns to his "original state, and one is as one was before one existed."

Here, Junayd's theory of *mithaq* (the primordial divine covenant) may help to clarify his teaching on this subject. Many commentators have posited an influence of Neo-Platonic thinking upon Junayd's doctrine of the soul, as the teachings of Plotinus were very popular at that time. The Qur'an explains (7:166-7) that, in the *'alam-i arwah*, the universe of souls, as it existed timelessly prior to, and beyond the creation of the physical universe, "Your Lord brought forth souls who were destined to descend from the loins of the sons of Adam, and asked them to witness (to the Truth) about themselves, saying, *'Alestu bi-Rabbikum?* Am I not Your Lord?' They all answered, *'Bala!* Yes! we testify to the truth of this.'" As Hazrati Junayd interprets this verse, "Allah spoke to them at a time when they did not exist, except so far as they existed in the Divine Being...When He called them and they answered quickly, their answer was a gracious and generous gift from Him; it was His answer on their behalf when He granted them their being... He spoke to them when they had no formal existence;" their existence was exclusively spiritual and was aware only of Allah's spirit—which "in no way postulates their being aware of their own existence."

Thus, as Junayd says in one of his letters, there are two types of existence: the first is our perfect prototypical divine existence in Allah, which is completely real and which survives death through its eternal nature, while the other type of existence is our relatively unreal, "secondary," derived existence as created beings. The first type of existence "only Allah knows and is cognizant of," while the second is characterized by the consciousness of limited, human attributes. Thus Junayd says that "in essence, *tasawwuf* is an attribute of Allah, but by image, it is an attribute of humanity." This is to say that essentially Sufi mysticism is not a limited path invented by human beings (nor is it a process initiated strictly from the human side). Rather, it is a divine gift, an act of our primordial divine nature awakening in us. We are real inasmuch as we are conscious of existing by means of the divine consciousness and action. As one reaches the goal of *tasawwuf*, one's normal human existence does not continue (*fana*) but awakens to its existence in Allah *(baqa)*, completely absorbed in the Divine Being. This is the real *tawhid* (unification) and goal of *La ilaha illallah*.

"It is for this reason," adds Junayd, "that when Allah granted existence to His worshipers, He caused, as it were, His desire to flow over them according to His will. And in view of that, we said that Allah has obliterated what appears to the worshiper, and when He has overwhelmed him, Allah shows Himself as the most overpowering, the perfect conqueror, the completely victorious... [As a result] one's physical being continues while one's individuality has departed." In this state of *baqa*, only the divine will and action remain. In another letter *(Risala, No.10)*, Junayd describes the transition from the intoxicated state of *fana*, in which one is bewildered in one's loss of conventional identity, to the further stage of lucidity and authenticity characteristic of the second sobriety:

> Then, after he has not been, he is where he had been (eternally, before creation). He is himself, after he has not been really himself. He is present in himself and in Allah, after having been present in Allah and absent in himself. This is because he has left the intoxication of Allah's overwhelming *(ghalaba)* and come to the clarity of sobriety *(sahw)*, and contemplation is once more restored to him, so that he can put everything in its right place and assess it correctly.

Junayd left several well-known aphorisms on mysticism and divine union. He said: "*Tasawwuf* is that Allah should make you die from yourself and should make you live in Him."[56] Elsewhere, he explained: "*Tasawwuf* is to be (united) with Allah without attachment to anything else." And of *tawhid*, he said, "Unification is the separation of the temporal from the eternal." The latter definition, which has been handed down as a classic formulation of the goal of Sufism, defines the path of mystic union in terms of a purification of the contingent, transient aspects of creation, which

---

56 Junayd, *Qushayri*, 126.

have originated in time, revealing the Eternal Essence which is the perfect and unlimited expression of the divine life.

Junayd's Four Stages of Tawhid (Unity)

In one of Junayd's letters, he offers an explanation of the meaning of divine unity, citing four stages of understanding what *tawhid* really is. The first level, which is the most common understanding, involves a verbal attestation that God is one and that no other deities exist except Allah—that nothing other than Allah is worthy of worship. In point of fact, however, this belief is accompanied by "the retention of hopes and fears in forces other than Allah." This simple *tawhid—la ilaha illallah—*is all that is required of the believer in Islam; however, if one really grasps the complete power of *tawhid*, these other things (which seem to be other than Allah) will certainly disappear, just as the stars disappear when the sun shines.

The second stage of *tawhid*, the understanding of those well-versed in formal religious knowledge, again consists of attesting the divine oneness beyond any companions, equals or opposites. In this case, however, it is accompanied by a rigorous external performance of the positive commands and the avoidance of the forbidden. One who is at the second stage has become outwardly virtuous and law-abiding (upholding the *shariat)* at a level far surpassing what is possible for one at the first stage, but both are still motivated by hopes, fears and desires (which are still not realized as integral components in the realm of Allah's oneness).

The third stage, the first of the two esoteric levels of *tawhid*, again involves an attestation of divine oneness as well as moral virtue, but now it is an internalized virtue of the heart, devoid of hopes and fears associated with forces other than Allah. One sees that everything comes from Allah. At this level, one is in the Divine Presence but still aware of one's separate individuality.

In the fourth and final stage, the real unification, even the consciousness of individuality *(shabah)* has disappeared, as has all sense of separation; likewise, all intermediaries between self and Lord have disappeared. At the fourth stage, one "is lost to sense and action because Allah fulfills in one what He has willed through one." One's will has become one with Allah's will, so that when the person wills, he or she no longer experiences it as a separate act of personal will—there is only one undivided will animating the individual. Again, the model in prophetic experience is the Qur'anic verse (8:17) which points out to Muhammad how, at the Battle of Badr, when "he willed" to throw a handful of gravel and sand at the approaching enemy: *"you did not throw when you threw, but Allah threw."* This principle is fundamental to the understanding of the Junaydi philosophy of *shuhud* (consciousness)—that in unification, the will of the witness becomes one with the greater will which transpires through them, so that ultimately, "everything one sees is the Act of the One." From the perspective of the true *muwahhid* (person of unity), there are no separate persons (much less victims) taking orders from somewhere above; there is only one seamless expression of Reality acting on the stage of Earth.

By way of example, using the *shuhud* interpretation of divine union, Jesus' famous statement of unity in the Gospel of John[57] could be translated "I and my Father are *of one accord,"*as indeed George Lamsa has rendered it in his translation from the original Aramaic *Peshitta* (Gospel). In contrast to the *Tayfuriyya* philosophy of *wujud* (in which one's very being or nature is discovered to be divine), Junayd maintains that the worshiper's human nature cannot become identical with God's Being *(ittihad)*. Rather, he says, in achieving unification, the part of us which is human retains its finite human qualities; likewise, what is physical remains physical. These are our contingent aspects, which have been set in motion with our pre-eternal response, *bala*. Meanwhile, what is infinite stays infinite; though the *muwahhid* may experience a shift of identity from awareness of a seemingly separate, finite self to identifying with his or her unlimited Source, it is simply the eternal divine consciousness in one awakening to that which it has always been, beyond time and space. Such is

---

57 "I and my Father are one." John 10:30.

Hazrat Junayd's explanation of divine unity; it has the advantage of presenting mystic union in a legitimate Islamic context which effectively bypasses any heretical *hululi* associations—*hulul* (the idea of divine incarnation) being a concept which the Qur'an speaks against and which would be instinctively avoided by all Sunni Muslims. Even the daring al-Hallaj avoided the term *hulul* in his Qur'anic commentaries.

As mentioned earlier, Junayd did not advertise the higher teachings among the people of Baghdad, but discreetly taught only a very limited number of disciples. Like his master, Hazrat Sari as-Saqati, he wrote letters in the special esoteric code of *isharat*, so that his words would be camouflaged in the event that it would fall into the hands of someone other than one to whom it was addressed, and be misunderstood. Such a thing did happen with one of Junayd's letters, and he regretted it very much. When his student Shibli wrote him a daring mystic letter, Junayd scolded him for being too explicit. He explained, "One must be kind to these people and careful of what one says and talk to them in a manner which they understand...and omit that which they cannot understand." Junayd felt that the knowledge of the Divine was so vast that even in their own circle, they were able to drink but a drop of that infinite ocean. With what they did receive concerning the nature of divinity, some Sufis of the time held that such inner knowledge should never be revealed publicly to the uninitiated, lest prophecy and knowledge itself dry up.

The Political Climate of Baghdad in Junayd's time

Besides spiritual considerations, we must also take into account the tense political situation that existed in Baghdad during the time of Junayd, which resulted in some of the leading Sufis being brought before the caliph on a variety of charges. Certainly in that period, those under 'Abbasid rule faced real political dangers if suspected of espousing spiritual doctrines consonant with the revolutionary Shi'ite Isma'ili sect or any of their activist offshoots, such as the Qarmathian insurrectionists in southern Iraq.

The Qarmathians, as part of their strategy to undermine and replace the existing government, taught the spiritualization of the *hajj* along with the abandonment of the material pilgrimage sites in Mecca, a sphere of 'Abbasid guardianship. To this end, the Qarmathians actually took over Arabia in 930 CE, sacked Mecca, and symbolically removed and hid the black stone for several decades. The dualist gnostic doctrines of the Manichean type in Persia often mingled freely with the more extreme Shi'ite precepts which deified Hazrat 'Ali and various imams descended from his progeny. The Sunni 'Abbasids considered all such teachings highly objectionable (though they accepted 'Ali and the Twelve Imams as wise and noble Muslims apart from these more extravagant claims).

These and other dissident heterodox sects posed a very real threat to the political stability of the 'Abbasid dynasty during Junayd's time, a period when the caliphate was already in a weakened and vulnerable position, financially destablized and embroiled in political intrigue. There were many reasons for this, some stemming back to the civil war which took place in the early ninth century, when rival 'Abbasid factions supported two different sons of the late Caliph Harun ar-Rashid, al-Amin and al-Ma'mun, in their bloody bid for succession to the caliphate. There were also strongly-supported Shi'ite claims for installing a legitimate heir of the Prophet, through 'Ali and Fatima or other 'Alid descendants. (In an attempt to appease the Shi'a and assure their financial backing, the 'Abbasids, at one point, allowed a moderate Zaydi Shi'ite to exercise a limited reign as caliph.) The caliphate lost a further measure of its already diminished moral and spiritual authority when Caliph al-Ma'mun adopted the Mu'tazilite philosophy, with a *mihnah* or inquisition to enforce it—a highly-contested policy which was later rescinded.

Turkish army guards were employed to physically shore up the weakened position of the caliph, but these protectors soon became more powerful than their leader. Caliph al-Mutawwakil (847-861 CE) and four other successors were murdered by their own Turkish guards. One after another, various grand wazirs *(viziers)* to the caliph built up their fortunes and power through corrupt political means only to be eliminated and replaced by other ambitious aspirants to that powerful position which ranked second only to the monarch himself. The caliphs were sometimes able to use such ruthless men against each other for their own advantage, but, over time, such practices had an extremely degenerating effect on the institution of the caliphate.

In 869 CE, a contingent of black slaves from East Africa (the *Zanj)* began a decade-long revolt against their 'Abbasid masters in Iraq. They captured parts of Arabia and sacked Basra before their rebellion could be put down by the caliph's troops, further calling into question the authority and military strength of the caliph. By 969 CE, North Africa had slipped from 'Abbasid control, with Egypt coming under the rule of a rival Fatimid caliph. Having succeeded in installing an 'Alid claimant to the caliphate upon the Egyptian throne, the Isma'ili-based Fatimids dominated Africa for several centuries thereafter (909-1171 CE). In 929 CE, in Spain, still another leader assumed the title of caliph—the Umayyad ruler, 'Abdul Rahman.

In Baghdad, the 'Abbasid Caliph, al-Qahr and several of his successors around the time of al-Junayd's passing (910 CE) were blinded with hot needles and deposed by the Turkish guards to wander the streets of Baghdad like beggars. Then, in December 945 CE, Ahmad ibn-Buwayh, the chieftain of the Turkic Daylamites, a Shi'ite faction from the shores of the Caspian, conquered Baghdad, scattered the Turkish guard and assumed full power, establishing a Buwayhid (or Buyid) rule which was to last more than a century. The Buyids also controlled Persia and brought certain benevolent Persian influences to Iraq. In the religious arena, they introduced Shi'ite practices such as the observance of *Ashura*—the public mourning over the martyrdom of Imam Husayn on the tenth of *Muharram.* The Buyids decentralized the government and relegated the Sunni caliphs to figurehead status, thus preserving the 'Abbasid caliphate as a titular institution, whose nominal existence lasted until its final demise at the hands of the Mongol invaders in 1258 CE.

Calligraphy in Tawqi script honoring Imam Ali

The Shi'i Perspective

For those who are generally unfamiliar with the significance of Shi'ite Islam, a brief explanation may be helpful. Today, approximately eighty to ninety percent of the one and a half billion Muslims on the planet are Sunni Muslims (including most Sufi turuq). They represent the majority party who accept the legitimate successorship from the Prophet to Abu Bakr to 'Umar, to 'Uthman, to 'Ali. Sunnis generally agree upon the following: a certain body of authentic ahadith, following the *sunna* (established precedents) of the Prophet, four major schools *(madhhab)* of deductive jurisprudence *(fiqh)*, individual reason and judgment *(ijtihad)*, and community consensus *(ijma)* in cases where there are no clear precedents established in Qur'an or *sunna*. Shi'ites, on the other hand, form about ten percent of the world's Muslim population. Both Sunnis and Shi'ites fully accept the validity of the entire Qur'an, although interpretations may occasionally vary; furthermore, the Shi'ites have preserved many mystical pro-'Alid traditions which are not accepted by Sunni scholars.[58]

---

58 We should add that there are, or have been historically, many other smaller sects and

The Shi'a initially separated from the main body of Muslims over the matter of Hazrat 'Ali ibn Abi Talib's right to be the first caliph, based on statements made by the Prophet, such as: "'Ali is to me as Aaron was to Moses." Political considerations aside, the older Abu Bakr was probably favored by those who ratified him as the first caliph on account of his more seasoned status as a community elder, as opposed to the more youthful, idealistic and exacting figure of Hazrat 'Ali. 'Ali waited patiently for two decades before being allowed to assume full leadership of the community of the Prophet—an *umma* which by that time had become highly factional and difficult to rule.

The Shi'a rejected the legitimacy of the first three caliphs and those who succeeded 'Ali, especially Mu'awiya. This occurred despite the fact that the Prophet had praised the good qualities of these men (perhaps even including Mu'awiya) and had, in the weeks before passing from this world, chosen Abu Bakr to lead the prayers in his own place. Like Hazrat 'Umar and Hazrat 'Uthman, Imam 'Ali was assassinated at the hands of political enemies. However, it was the massacre of his second son, Husayn, and his followers at Karbala that forever set the tone of martyrdom and hiddenness of the true divine knowledge which came to characterize the Shi'ite world-view. Each of the successive surviving imams from the progeny of 'Ali and Fatima, and thus the line of the Prophet himself, were subsequently considered by Shi'ite sympathizers as bearers of the divine light of wisdom. The Shi'a regarded each of these imams as being the illumined spiritual world leader of his time and the true heir to the caliphate, an office which too often resided in the hands of decadent Sunni dynasties who had little idea of the true mystic heights inherent in Islam.

Three major Shi'ite sects emerged, the primary one being known as the "Twelver" sect. The Twelvers follow the teaching that, after the death of the eleventh imam—believed poisoned at the instigation of the Sunni caliph (873 CE)—the twelfth imam, a seven year old boy named Muhammad, disappeared from the Great

---

philosophical schools of thought in Islam besides these two major ones, such as the Mu'tazilites and Kharijites. The Prophet, in fact, foresaw at least 72 sects which would, in various ways, differ from his main Sunna.

Mosque of Samarra. At that time, he is thought to have gained immortal life in the spiritual realms, from whence he continues to guide his people. It is believed that, in the future, this "Hidden Imam" will return as the *Mahdi* to restore the world.

Besides "Twelvers" (Imamites), there are other Shi'i sects such as the "Fivers" *(Zaydis)* and "Seveners," the latter believing in the true successorship and divinity of the seventh imam, Isma'il ibn Jafar (as opposed to his brother Musa al-Kazim, whom the Twelvers accept). The Seveners are called Isma'ilis and even today have adherents in India, Central Asia and East Africa. Closely affiliated with the Isma'ilis were the Fatimids, who in 909 CE, took over Tunisia and shortly thereafter set up a Shi'ite caliph of alleged 'Alid descent on the throne of Egypt, in Cairo. Unlike the more moderate Twelvers, the Isma'ilis and their offshoot, the Fatimids, were ardent political activists who sought universal Shi'ite rule in the present, instead of focusing on the return of a hidden spiritual imam in the future.

Slightly later, in Syria, there would emerge from the ranks of their underground the notorious *Hashishiyyun*, a *Nizari* Isma'ili faction founded by Hasan as-Sabbah—a cult better known in the West as the *Assassins*. They were given to political assassinations, hashish-use, *jinn* contact, scientific learning, and the preservation of secret dualistic gnostic doctrines. These eventually culminated in a ritual feast of the end times, in which they drank intoxicants during Ramadan and declared that the "fetters of the Islamic law *(shariat)*" had been destroyed by "the ruler of the universe" (meaning their secret imam). A later leader reinstated the shariat and repudiated their strange doctrines in favor of Sunnite Islam.

For the most part, Shi'ite Islam has prevailed to the present in Iran, the spiritual home of Zoroastrianism and Manicheism, two rival religious traditions which also exerted influence upon various Islamic sects during 'Abbasid times. The religions of Zarathustra and Mani, as they were then practiced in Persia, were based upon a dualistic doctrine, involving a belief in a god of evil who exists independently of a good god—an idea which was the very antithesis of the divine unity (or "monotheism") upon which Islam is based.

Around 890 CE, Hamdun Qarmat, an Iraqi peasant and "Sevener," read in the stars that the 'Abbasid dynasty would soon come under Shi'ite rule. In response, he organized an underground revolutionary movement to help overthrow the 'Abbasid government. His Qarmathian sect combined various elements such as the Zoroastrian worship of the "Supreme Light," worship of the divinity of the seventh imam, ideas culled from gnostic dualism of the Manichean variety, and even featured ritual *agape* "love-feasts" where the Qarmathians consumed "the bread of paradise."

While such syncretic movements were rivaling for political ascendancy, other Shi'ite-influenced ideas were unobtrusively entering the mystic mainstream of Sunnite Islam, especially the Sufi turuq. For instance, the wise Qur'anic commentaries and teachings of the sixth imam, Ja'far as-Sadiq, were well received and respected by the Sunnis. Sheikh Sahl at-Tustari (d.896 CE), one of the teachers of al-Hallaj, introduced the interpretation that the first light of eternity was a column of pure radiance, the Muhammadan Light, or *Nuri Muhammadi*, which is the fountainhead of prophecy, the primordial light of all souls and indeed, the light behind everything in creation, including the Prophet Muhammad of Arabia. This noble teaching has to this day remained an accepted staple of Islamic mysticism. After all, the Prophet had himself taught that behind the light of this world is the divine light (*an-Nur*), and had prayed, "O Allah! May You put light in my heart, light in my eyes . . . light all around me...light in my hair, light in my body, light in my soul . . . and magnify Your light therein."

Shi'ite teaching emphasized the divine light's capacity to illumine the soul with the radiance of gnostic knowledge. Although their approach differed, the Sunnis also accepted the light of knowledge—especially self-knowledge—as a core aim of Islam. The common tradition of these two branches shared the Verse of Light, *ayat an-Nur,*[59] and various admonitions given by the Prophet, such as: "Seek knowledge, even if you must go to China to find it," and, "He who knows himself, knows his Lord." However, the Sunni turuq have found it politically prudent to downplay

---

59 Qur'an 24:35.

THE GARDEN OF MYSTIC LOVE

and veil any appearance of Shi'ite sympathies in cases where the teaching of the Sufi turuq has similarity with Shi'ite ideas (such as intercession of saints and *qutbs*—as it might superficially resemble the divinization of the Shi'ite imams—or any special veneration of Imam 'Ali). This has especially been true since the inception of the Safavid Empire in Persia (1501-1732 CE).

Besides Shi'ism and Persian dualism, we should also mention the ideology known as Libertinism (*ibaha*), a philosophy of license and freedom which Ibn al-Jawzi (a Hanbali jurist and Sufi of the thirteenth century CE) actually listed as a deviant Islamic sect in his work, *Tablis al-Iblis*. As an example, Ibn al-Jawzi cites a near contemporary scholar named Ibn Tahir al-Maqdisi, who advocated gazing upon beautiful men and women as commendable subjects of adoration, with a strong element of sexual innuendo. Other libertine propensities include the indulgent principle, "Whatever we wish to do, Allah is generous and will forgive." Also: "Those who reach high states are beyond performing prayers and other requirements of the shariat;" and "since everything is predetermined, we needn't concern ourselves with religious duties."[60]

Significantly, none of the great classical Sufis masters ever advocated such permissive libertine policies, such as licentiousness or even leaving the performance of religious duties behind when one has entered higher spiritual states. A famous story to this point, relates how a great light appeared to the famous Sufi Pir 'Abdul Qadir Gaylani and informed him that, because of his sanctity and high station, Allah was absolving him of the duties of prayer and fasting. The sheikh, aware that even the Prophet himself never excused himself from prayers or fasting during Ramadan, instinctively recoiled from this dubious message and recited the formula of taking refuge in Allah from the influence of the accursed *Shaitan*. Immediately, in response to his prayer, the light was forced to reveal itself in its true form: a devious dark being masquerading as a bright angelic messenger.

Having discussed various sects and philosophies, let us return to Baghdad, late in the life of Hazrati Junayd. We have sketched

---

60 Ernst, *Words of Ecstasy in Sufism,* 118-19.

the political environment of Junayd's time to provide perspective on the tense conditions which then prevailed in Baghdad. All these factors contributed to an atmosphere in which the 'Abbasid government was swift to act on accusations of political conspiracy or doctrinal heresy, which in many cases were linked.

It would be a mistake to imagine all of the orthodox Islamic scholars and jurists of the time as fanatically opposed to the teachings of the tarikat. For instance, when the renowned jurist, Ibn Hanbal, critically attacked one of Junayd's teachers, Harith al-Muhasibi, over the matter of his having adopted innovative terminology from the Mu'tazilites, it was not part of a general attack on mysticism. In fact, Ibn Hanbal and the other major jurists are all on record as having said very positive things about the Sufis.

We must not, then, facilely assume that stern theological intolerance of mystical ideas among the *ulama* formed the sole basis for any charges leveled against the Sufis. Rather, it is toward court intrigue and the prevalent political rivalry of that turbulent era that we must look in many of these cases. Indeed, there was a whole educational range of learning which was considered acceptable by the 'Abbasids—often taught by Nestorian Christian tutors. This included the Hellenistic influenced philosophy known as *falsafa*, a secular approach to knowledge which had grown out of the Mu'tazilite rationalism which Caliph Ma'mum had formerly championed. During an era when the West had not yet rediscovered the Greek philosophers, Aristotle's rationalistic ideas were influencing young Islamic scholars to regard love as a madness which turns wise men into fools.

A Charge of Heresy
Against the Sufis of Baghdad

Sometime around 885 CE, Ghulam al-Khalil, a strict Hanbali who had close ties with Caliph al-Muwaffaq (through the regent's mother, Ashar), impetuously raised a charge of *zandaqa* (heresy) against many of the leading Sufis of Baghdad, based on the word of one disgruntled informer. Among those named were Junayd and a number of other members of his school, including Nuri, Abu Hamza, Raqqam, Shahham and Sumnun. Hazrat Junayd, who until this time had enjoyed an excellent reputation among the people of Baghdad, escaped going to court when he described himself simply as a Shafi'ite jurist; but even the very fact of such an accusation apparently tainted his character in the eyes of some, and Junayd withdrew from public life for a time.

The story behind the trial is an interesting one. In Junayd's absence, it pivoted around another renowned Sufi sheikh, Abu'l Husayn ibn Muhammad an-Nuri, whose name, Nuri, was given to him because of the radiance which emanated from his presence during his *sohbet*s (spiritual teaching), illuminating even darkened rooms. His ecstatic words and mystic poems, as Sarraj said, came forth from him as though "ladled from a great ocean." Several of his short musical odes have survived, as well as a work entitled *Maqamat al-Qulub* (The Stations of the Heart), in which he speaks of seven citadels within the garden of the heart.

An intimate friend of Junayd, Hazrat Nuri was a fellow student of Junayd's master, Sari as-Saqati. Like Sheikh Sari, Nuri stressed the idea that Allah instills *ishq (ashk),* or divine desire in the human soul. In this way, he moved toward the Hallajian thesis of divine union through love, becoming the first to openly preach the notion of pure love *(mahabba)*. Though given to ecstatic states, he made a point of upholding the shariat. After Nuri passed away, Junayd desired to be buried next to him (although this did not occur), lamenting, "Since the death of Nuri, no one has spoken about the essential Truth." [61]

Meanwhile, Ghulam al-Khalil held very strict ideas which forbade any innovative *(bida)* interpretations or new terminology which was not explicitly used by the Prophet. When he learned that Nuri had said, "I love Allah *(a`shuqu)* and Allah loves me *(ya`shuqani)*," he was incensed and interpreted these words of

61 Qushayri, *Risala,* 25.

love at the lowest level of depraved passion, believing that Allah was high above earthly sentiments of passion and that a respectful Muslim should worship the transcendent God with proper awe and humility. It is may be difficult for us in modern times to imagine how scandalous this idea seemed to those of Khalil's mind-set; but what Nuri, Junayd and the others had in mind was not anthropomorphic love, as might be conceived between two physical bodies. They were relating to that ecstasy and longing which fills the lover's heart with passion to always be immersed in the presence of Allah Most Exalted, blessed by divine nearness and acceptance.

Actually, the Qur'an (5:59) does explicitly say of Allah, "He loves them and they love Him." *(Yuhibbuhum wa yuhibbunahu.)* However, the word *ishq* (desire or passionate love), which Khalil found objectionable, is not used. Nuri defended his own linguistic usage, explaining that "passionate love *(ishq)* is not greater than serene love *(mahabba)*, except that the passionate lover *(ashik)* is kept away, while the serene lover *(muhibb)* enjoys His love."[62] But Khalil felt that, left unchecked, the use of such sensuous words and preoccupations among the Sufis would soon lead to libertine excesses, such as free love and adultery, ultimately corrupting the purity of Allah's religion.

About this same time, a dear colleague of Junayd's, Abu'l Hasan Sumnun, a handsome sheikh whose tender poems on the subject of divine love earned him the nickname *al-Muhibb* ("the lover"), abruptly dismissed a woman disciple from his Sufi circle when it became apparent that she had become infatuated with him. Feeling hurt and rejected, she went to Junayd and asked him, "What do you think of a man who was my way to Allah, but then Allah vanished and the man remained?" Junayd understood what she meant and knew that she had harbored hopes of marrying Sheikh Sumnun, but refrained from commenting.

Having received no satisfaction from Junayd, the woman next went to Sumnun's adversary, Khalil, and complained of improper behavior, insinuating that the passionate teachings

---

62 Sarraj, *Pages,* 5.

propagated in the Sufi circles led to the excitement of earthly love for the sheikhs rather than pure love for Allah.

This was all Khalil needed to hear. He took his distorted cache of hearsay evidence straight to the caliph, demanding the immediate arrest and execution of a number of prominent Sufis, all of whom, he claimed, were involved in similar scandalous pursuits. Among Khalil's trumped-up charges against the sheikhs were: accusations of license *(ibaha)*, incarnationism *(hulul)*, heresy *(zandaqa)*, and perhaps even teaching reincarnation. As Dr. 'Ali Hassan 'Abdul-Kader says in his *Life & Personality of Junayd*,[63] "It seems that the accusation against the Sufi School of Baghdad confused theological objections to their teachings with objections to their behavior."

Khalil was successful in procuring the desired arrest warrants from the caliph (al-Muwaffaq, who was actually reigning viceregent for his brother, al-Mu'tamid, the titular caliph). The arrest notice called for their immediate execution, without so much as a trial. Sumnun, Nuri, Raqqam and the other alleged *zindiqs* (heretics) were rounded up and brought to the caliph's palace, where they were lined up before the executioner. But when the headsman approached the first of them, Raqqam, Hazrat Nuri stepped in front him and cheerfully asked to be beheaded first. The executioner was amazed and said, "Young man, the sword is not a thing that people desire to meet so eagerly as you have welcomed it; and your turn has not yet arrived." Nuri answered him: "True, but my doctrine is based on preference. Life is the most precious thing in the world; I wish to sacrifice for my brother's sake the few moments that remain. In my opinion, one moment of this world is better than a thousand years of the next world, because this is the place of service and that is the place of nearness, and nearness is gained by service."

When the headsman heard Nuri's beautiful explanation and felt the serene quality of divine submission *(islam)* in his being, he halted the execution and sent word to the caliph. The caliph, in turn, summoned the chief *qadi* (judge), a Maliki scholar named

---

63 Abdel-Kader, *Life & Personality of Junayd*, 39.

Abu'l 'Abbas ibn 'Ali, to examine them on their doctrine. The Sufis were taken to the qadi's house where they answered his questions perfectly and he gradually became satisfied that there was nothing abnormal nor heretical in their practice of the shariat. Then Sheikh Nuri spoke up, saying, "O Qadi, you have asked us all these questions but none that were really to the point, for Allah has servants who see and hear by Him, who eat and drink and sit through Him, and live through Him, abiding in divine contemplation. If they were cut off from contemplating Him, they would cry out in anguish." At this, the qadi was moved to tears and reported back to the caliph, "If these people are *zindiqs*, there are no monotheists on earth!"[64]

In the end, all of those charged were spared and released—some even claimed it was due to the caliph's special affection for the Sufis. When the caliph released them, he tried to offer them a boon, as an gesture of compensation. They replied, "The only boon we ask of you is that you would forget about us, and neither make us your favorites nor banish us from your court, for your favor and disfavor are all the same to us." Though they were acquitted with honor, the very fact that heresy charges were leveled against them had an adverse effect on public opinion of the Sufis. As a result, the Sufi circles in Baghdad withdrew and became ever more cautious in protecting their secrets.

Though this constitutes one version of the trial, there exist further stories concerning the questioning of Hazrat Nuri, which may or may not allude to the same occasion. Once, Nuri, in the name of Allah, broke open all the vials of wine that were being delivered to the palace for the caliph. The caliph was highly annoyed at first, but became contrite when Nuri was dragged before him and explained that he did it on behalf of the caliph's soul.

During one of his trials, Nuri was grilled about an incident in which he had allegedly behaved like an atheist. It was reported that Nuri, upon hearing a *mu'azzin* give the call to prayer, cried out in reply, "A curse and deadly poison!" Then, when he heard a dog bark, he responded with the formula with which one normally

---

64 Al-Hujwiri, *Kashf al-Mahjub*, 190-1.

beseeches one's Lord during pilgrimage, saying: "*Labbayk!* Here am I, Lord! Blessings to You!"

Hazrat Nuri told his accusers he would be happy to explain the significance of his actions. The *mu'azzin,* who was giving the call to prayer, was chanting it hypocritically—for the sake of a mere pittance of a salary, rather than for the sake of Allah—while the dog's bark was deemed a more acceptable invocation to Allah, in accord with the Qur'anic verse:[65] "There is nothing that does not glorify Him with His praise, although you do not understand their glorification." They accepted his explanation, but queried, "Why did you once say, 'Last night I was in my house with Allah?'" Nuri countered that not only he, but all of them, even now this moment, were with Allah; as the Qur'an says (50:15): "We are closer to man than his jugular vein." At this, the caliph extended his hand of protection and asked Nuri to speak to them further about divine intimacy. He did so, and after he had pointed out many truths which they had never before considered, the caliph and those present wept and praised Nuri.

In the end, Nuri voluntarily went into exile, moving to the city of Raqqa, which lay several hundred miles to the north in Syria, only to return years later in a somewhat deteriorated condition. He eventually died, for the sake of love, from infection after having cut his feet while walking barefoot outdoors during an ecstatic state. Divine love, whose intoxicating kiss had rendered him oblivious to the pain, subsequently embraced the soul of Nuri as his physical body passed away.

Mansur al-Hallaj

We now come to the most eminent, yet controversial champion of mystic love and unification, the martyr of divine love, the one who offered his head for the sake of Truth, Husayn ibn Mansur al-Hallaj, may his secrets be kept. Mansur was born into a Persian

---

65 Qur'an 17:46.

family of cotton-carders. The word *hallaj* means "carder"—thus, Mansur's name. He was called *mansur al-aswad*; in his case, it carried an additional significance, meaning "the carder (reader, opener) of people's innermost hearts."

Al-Hallaj studied with a number of Sufi sheikhs including Sahl at-Tustari, Amr ibn 'Uthman al-Makki, and finally Junayd. Hallaj went to Junayd for arbitration when Sheikh Makki violently turned against him after Mansur, in spite of Makki's expressed disapproval, married the daughter of a rival sheikh. According to some accounts, Mansur studied for a time with Junayd but, unsatisfied with some of Junayd's conservative metaphysics, finally left and struck out on his own, breaking all ties with the traditionalist Sufis—or as Hujwiri has it, he was banned by all the sheikhs.

Why could Hallaj find no lasting satisfaction with the Sufi sheikhs of his time, much less the mainstream exotericism of the 'Abbasid scholars? The reasons are complex and not to be found in any straightforward rejection of the shariat on Hallaj's part. Mansur had a profound love for the Prophet and his sunna; he made hajj several times and stayed for years in Mecca, but no matter how much he fasted or made extra prayers (like Junayd, Hallaj made as many as 400 *raka'at* a day), he never felt it was enough. At the same time, he clearly sensed the inadequacy of the type of categorical thinking to which his contemporaries clung, a theological rationalism which tended to interpret divine love as incompatible with divine transcendence.

While al-Hallaj found the shariat a worthy outward expression of the deep prophetic inner experience of divine realization, he believed the worshiper must also strive to realize the matching inner experience behind the form in order to render it truly authentic for oneself. He understood the limitations of external rites as a means of inner transformation of the heart, since the ego and the heart can become hardened and tyrannical through inculcating a rigid, legalistic approach to the life of the spirit. Thus al-Hallaj prayed on behalf of one of his own disciples, "May Allah veil you from the exterior of the religious law, and may He reveal to you the reality of infidelity. For the exterior of the religious law is a hidden idolatry, while the reality of infidelity is a manifest gnosis."[66]

This saying, though outwardly scandalous, is simply Hallaj's own commentary on the Prophet's saying, "I take refuge with You (Allah) from hidden idolatry *(shirk khafi)*." Slavish adherence to the outward forms of religious duties can easily turn idolatrous when the spirit of the law is neglected; however, one needn't abandon external forms to avoid subtle idolatry, but simply appreciate them as finite tools given for the enrichment of the soul. When the worshiper utters *Allahu akbar* during salat, it is in part an acknowledgment that the Divine Reality is far beyond confinement to any single human form of praise.

When someone asked Mansur to which *madhhab* (school of jurisprudence) he belonged, he replied, "*Madhhab* is for you. I follow the *madhhab* of my Lord."[67] Actually, his practice was to take the hardest portions of each of the major schools and practice that. But because, as a universalist, he tried to communicate with everyone—speaking to the Shi'ites using their vocabulary, the Mu'tazilites in theirs, and to Sunnites in theirs—he was cynically accused of pretending to belong to whatever sect he happened to encounter.

Below, Hujwiri relates a meeting which supposedly took place between Hallaj and Junayd. Contrary to the testimony of Mansur's son, Hamd, this account implies that Mansur was never (even briefly) accepted into Junayd's circle:

> I have read in the Anecdotes (of Khuldi) that when Husayn ibn Mansur al-Hallaj, in his rapture, broke off relations with Amr ibn 'Uthman al-Makki, and came over to Junayd, Junayd asked him, "Why have you come?" Husayn answered, "To join your community with you as sheikh." Junayd replied, "I do not live in community with *majanin* (madmen). Community life requires balanced sanity; if that is lacking, the result is such behavior as yours in regard to Sahl at-Tustari and Amr." Husayn countered, "But master, sobriety and intoxication are two human aspects of the

66 Ernst, *Words of Ecstasy*, 3.
67 Ibid, 124.

mystic, which veil him from his Lord as long as they are not both annihilated." Junayd replied, "O son of Mansur, your definition of sobriety and intoxication is not correct; the former denotes soundness of one's spiritual state in relation to Allah—which cannot be acquired through human effort—while the latter signifies extremes of desire and love. O son of Mansur, in your words I see much indiscreet curiosity as well as some useless expressions."[68]

The dialogue contrasts the Hallajian thesis with the Junaydi. Hallaj believed that through human effort and cooperation with divine grace, the Living Truth Itself is unveiled in one's being, causing all intermediaries, rites and spiritual states to fade in importance. By contrast, Junayd held that it is Allah alone—the Eternal Transcendent Source of the soul—who activates these spiritual states and rites in us, beyond human participation or effort.

An alternative dialogue between these two has Mansur coming and knocking at the door of Junayd. When Junayd asks, "Who is there?" Mansur answers, "(I am) the Truth! *(Ana'l-Haqq)*" Junayd replies, "You shouldn't say 'the Truth,' but rather: 'I come on behalf of the Truth.' What gibbet will you stain with your blood?" Attar adds a reply for Hallaj, "The day when I redden the gibbet with my blood, you will be wearing the cloak of the formalists." Attar even asserts that this came to pass, but according to the accepted historical dates, Junayd passed away some eleven years before Hallaj's execution. However, Attar is correct in principle to point out that many of the "formalist" Sufis of the time did renounce Hallaj, judging his behavior to be at fault, at least according to the exterior level.

Within the fragmentary accounts of Hallaj's life, there exists much legendary material as well as a strong tendency to put predictions of martyrdom in the mouth of Hallaj and others, many of which are suspect from the point of view of form criticism. Still another tradition, perhaps more likely (as it seems to be supported by Hamd), reproduces this last-quoted conversation as occurring

---

68 Al-Hujwiri, *Kashf al-Mahjub,* 189.

instead between al-Hallaj and his famous Sufi compatriot, Shibli; so that the famous phrase, *Ana'l Haqq*, "I am the Absolute Truth (i.e., God)," is uttered to Shibli in a public mosque where the latter was preaching. Among those mentioned in the early traditions, the most likely to have originally cursed Hallaj and predicted for him a bad end was Sheikh Amr al-Makki, who had turned hostile to Mansur in part because Mansur alleged that he was capable of receiving inspiration similar to the Qur'an.

After breaking with Junayd, al-Hallaj quit wearing the Sufi *khirka* (cloak) and returned to his native Persia to spread his own teaching. He subsequently journeyed to the East, through Central Asia as far as Hindustan, preaching to whomever could receive it that great love which leads to divine union (*ittihad*). Always a popular charismatic teacher and healer, Mansur drew people wherever he went and even made friends in high places; but he also seemed to attract opponents just as readily, especially when he would allegedly produce miracles such as materializing gold or out-of-season fruit for people with the aid of the *jinn*. He would move on whenever detractors began to accuse him of practicing magic and Hindu conjuror's tricks. But, notwithstanding the controversy he created, he also won the hearts of many with his direct ecstatic teachings on divine love.

His son, Hamd, relates that, after his father's return from his mysterious travels, they would receive letters from exotic places in the East calling al-Hallaj "the Great Helper" and "the Nourisher." Such titles would seem to give weight to the rumors that Hallaj was being proclaimed among the Shi'ites as the Mahdi, or herald of the Mahdi, who is expected to appear in the last days to restore the world to righteousness.

Mansur was given to producing "new hadith," introduced with an *isnad*, not of human transmitters of the saying back to the time of the Prophet, but in grand Qur'anic style, offering such natural witnesses as: "By the desert at dawn, the flash of lightening, the green grass growing," or "the last *Ju-jube* tree, the great Angel, the well-guarded tablet...the ruby of light, the crescent of Yemen."

In one of these sayings, apparently referring to the *'abdal*[69] or "substitutes" who were mentioned by the Prophet Muhammad, Allah is quoted by Hallaj as saying: "There are 360 divine glances during each day and night. In each glance, Allah brings closer to Himself the spirit of His loved ones, and replaces him with one of His servants. And with His looking at His loved one, He gives mercy to 70,000 of those who profess friendship for that friend." Another "new hadith" begins, "From the quintessence of the balance of the year 902, from the age of the announcer of the year seven of the call, from the friend of nearness," which some see as a reference to the extremist Shi'ite uprising in the year 902. CE.[70]

When he was finally arrested, Hallaj's executioners were to contend, however absurdly, that he was a secret Qarmathian agent, a key figure in a popular social revolution to overthrow the 'Abbasid government. Even Louis Massignon, in his monumental work, *The Passion of al-Hallaj,* dismisses the charges as insupportable circumstantial allegations, trumped-up for political expediency; yet others, such as Julian Baldick, have argued that Massignon is missing the obvious. As a rule, such slanderous reports are not even dignified with a mention in Eastern Sufi texts. What little evidence still exists is fragmentary and inconclusive, as most of Hallaj's works and trial transcripts were purposely destroyed.

Certainly, the Baghdadi Sufis did not welcome the glare of such charges and the spectacle of a public execution of a fellow mystic. Their interpretation was generally to the effect that Mansur publicly divulged the great secret of the lovers, about which one who knows should remain silent. One later Sufi tradition has it that, though what Mansur said *(Ana'l Haqq)* was inwardly true, he was executed on earth and his entry into paradise delayed for several hundred years as chastisement for having inappropriately revealed the inner secrets in public.

Other Sufis would say, as Mansur himself would have certainly understood, that through Hallaj's state of union with divine love, Allah caused him to "tear the veils" and disappear (even bodily)

---

69 The *'abdal* are saints in the spiritual hierarchy (including qutbs) whose positions are always replaced by other saints as soon as they pass away.
70 Julian Baldick, *Mystical Islam,* 48.

in his Beloved, drinking to the dregs the cup of love's agony, yet triumphantly serving as a true non-dual witness to divine unity. It was Hallaj who, after all, first spoke of the moth who is so attracted by the fiery light of the candle that, in a state of ecstatic, burning love—beyond all reason and discussion—he dives into it, extinguishing himself completely in the light of its essence. In his *Kitab al-Tawasin*, Hallaj also spoke of Pharaoh's unjustified claim to divinity, saying (on behalf of Allah): "Pharaoh saw only himself and lost Me [saying, 'I am God']; Husayn (al-Hallaj) saw only Me and lost himself [saying, 'I am the Truth']." In this regard, Hallaj has inevitably been compared with Christ who said, "I am the way, the truth, and the life." There is even a controversial saying, quoted by Husayn ibn Hamdan, in which Mansur is supposed to have said, "Go tell my friends that I have set sail on the sea and my boat is smashed. It is in the confession of the Cross that I will die; I no longer care to go to Mecca nor Medina!"

During his preaching, he once cried out three times: "O people save me from Allah!" and then added, "For He has robbed me from myself, and He does not return me to myself! I am not capable of witnessing to Him the respect due to His presence, for I am afraid of His forsaking me, leaving me deserted, abandoned and outlawed!" He also, more than once, during his public preaching to the Arabs, is said to have urged the people to kill him, saying that Allah had made the shedding of his blood lawful for them, that they would gain merit thereby and he peace of mind, dying as a martyr. But the people only wept and desisted at such promptings, seeing only a pious man and lover of Allah and Qur'an before them.

Then, at the door of the mosque in Suq al-Qati'a, he stood and spoke, saying: "O people! When Truth has taken hold of a heart, He empties it of all but Himself! When Allah attaches Himself to a man, He kills in him all else but Himself! When he loves one of His faithful, He incites the others to hate him, in order that His servant may draw near Him so as to assent to Him!"[71]

---

71 Massignon, *Hallaj, Martyr and Mystic,* 142-47.

Another ode of this kind has been preserved:[72]

> *Kill me now, O my faithful friends,*
> *For in my being killed is my life,*
> *My death would be to go on living,*
> *And my life would be to die.*
> *To me, removal of myself*
> *Would be the noblest gift to give*
> *And my survival in my flesh*
> *The ugliest offence, because*
> *My life has tired out my soul*
> *Among its fading artifacts.*
> *So kill me, set aflame*
> *My dried out bones*
> *And when you pass by my remains*
> *In their deserted grave,*
> *You will perceive the secret of my Friend*
> *In the inmost folds of what survives.*

One of the keys to understanding Mansur's quandary has been preserved in his *Kitab al-Tawasin*, where Mansur recounts, in a seeming allegory to his own situation, the monotheistic dilemma of *Iblis* (Satan or Shaitan). According to the Qur'an, Iblis was staunchly faithful to Allah's command, "Worship none but Me." But when Allah created Adam, he asked Iblis and the angels to bow down before this dark body of clay. The angels were obedient to the divine command and bowed before Adam, or humanity. (According to a common Sufi exegesis, the angels were not only obedient, but understood that Allah had placed his exalted spirit in man, and thus, without any real breech of monotheism, were able to bow before God's representative in human form, who was in no way separate from Allah.) Iblis, however, refused to bow before physical man, claiming that, despite this new divine edict (a *koan* if you will), he had already previously sworn to bow only before Allah and not Allah's temporal creation; so he disobeyed Allah and refused to bow—in effect, denying the divinity in humanity.

---

72 Herbert Mason, *The Death of Al-Hallaj*, xiv.

But did the Shaitan actually disobey or did he secretly obey Allah's real intention through disobedience to the second command? This is a major theme of Mansur's *Kitab*, where he points out that, in this regard, Shaitan became "more monotheist than Allah Himself." There are at least two rather intriguing ramifications to this Qur'anic episode. The first is that the well-intentioned traditional worshiper who denies the divinity in humanity in order to uphold the monotheistic transcendence of God, finds that they are inadvertently in agreement with Iblis on this issue.

The other closely related secret implication, which is drawn out by Hallaj, requires going beneath the surface of the usual exoteric explanation that it was spiritual pride which caused Iblis' disobedience to Allah's command to worship Hazrat Adam. This involves an esoteric understanding of Iblis as the misunderstood prototype of the lover of God who, out of selfless devotion and love, is willing to be blamed for apparently disobeying certain divine commands in order to obey and serve an even more primal and hidden facet of the divine will, even though the world may misunderstand, hate, and punish him for it—all out of their belief that they too are righteously serving God's interests.

Though Mansur and Iblis were both considered rebels against God by the authorities, Hallaj differed significantly from Iblis, even in his desire to be martyred as a seeming heretic; for he fervently continued his religious duties and prayerful prostrations to Allah, while yet seeking to obey the divine summons to unity. In light of the actuality of divine unity, al-Hallaj considered Iblis's labors at teaching duality to be ultimately futile, saying, "the only one who separates each of you is Iblis."[73]

Any serious reflection on the dilemma that brought Mansur to the gallows, begs the question: "What was the real divine intention with al-Hallaj? That, in awakening to the divinity within himself, he—or the divine source in him—would proclaim, "I am the Truth?" Or, as Junayd quietly queried: "What should he have said, "I am the false?" Would his overly zealous enemies have preferred that Hallaj truncate the full meaning of the Islamic

73 Massignon, 223.

affirmation of unity and proclaim that he was separate and distinct from Allah's Oneness? Despite such plain Qur'anic testimony as, "We are nearer to man than his jugular vein," the most common exoteric understanding of the Qur'an among Muslims is that they are enjoined to uphold God's utter transcendence, even at the cost of denying the inherent divinity in Allah's creation, including humanity. (With the exception of the doctrine of Christ's exclusive divinity, the same could also be said about exoteric Christianity and Judaism in reference to their own scriptures.)

The well-known danger, of course, lies in the temptation to confuse the levels in one's being in such a way as to surreptitiously allow the ego—the shadow of the real human being—to falsely claim divinity for itself. The best safeguard against such imprudent spiritual error, as exoteric religion has always known, is for the conventional self to be taught the absolute otherness of God. Yet, the truly God-realized mystic, whose limited self has "died before death, soon comes to understand that this is not a helpful or even totally accurate spiritual teaching at the level of *hakikat*, where there are no discreet entities and nothing exists except the Absolute Truth.

In the words of the modern Sufi master, Hazrat Inayat Khan: "If God . . . were so far away as to be in the seventh heaven then it would be most unfortunate for man to be kept far away from the very life and the very reason of his being."[74] In contrast to such subtle understatement, Hallaj expresses his assessment in bold terms, comparing the whole situation to a man who is thrown into the water with his hands tied behind his back, while Allah warns him, "Be careful not to get wet."

In his *Diwan*, Hallaj asks, "Is it You or I? That would be two gods in me; far, far be it from You to assert duality! The "He-ness" that is Yours is in my nothingness forever; my 'all' added to Your 'All' would be a double disguise...Between You and me there is an 'I am' that battles me, so take away, by Your grace, this 'I am' from in between." In still another verse from this same Diwan, he writes, "Your spirit was mixed in my spirit, just like wine and

---

74 Inayat Khan, *The Unity of Religious Ideals*, 14.

water, and if something touches You, it touches me, for You are I in every state." [75]

Whether people blamed him or praised him was not important to al-Hallaj, who once drew a figure containing four concentric circles to illustrate this point. He said:

> The denier remains in the outermost circle. He denies my state since he cannot see me, he accuses me with zandaqa [heresy or blasphemy], and accuses me of evil. The inhabitant of the second circle thinks I am a divine master ('alim rabbani). And he who attains to the third circle reckons that I am in my heart's desires. But he who attains to circle of reality forgets, and is hidden from my sight. [76]

As we have mentioned, in the years before his arrest, al-Hallaj was an itinerant preacher of love traveling far and wide and meeting with people of many religious persuasions. After many years of travels and three pilgrimages to Mecca, he finally returned to live with his family in Baghdad. According to Ibn Hajj, one day, while Hallaj was staying in Tustar, a group of Sufis came to him asking for alms. He took them with him to a Zoroastrian fire temple where they witnessed inside the sacred flame, which tradition says cannot be extinguished except by Jesus, son of Mary, at the end of time. When Hallaj approached it and extended his sleeve, the flame died out. The custodian was dumbfounded and, believing the Last Judgment had arrived, began to cry out, "O God! Now all the fire-altars from the East to the West are extinguished! Who could relight them? According to our scripture, only the one who extinguished them." And he wept before al-Hallaj, who reassured him, "If you have something to give these sheikhs, I will relight it." When the man emptied the fire temple's alms box and gave it to them, Mansur extended his sleeve again toward the fire and it reignited. [77]

---

75 Ernst, 27-28.
76 Ibid, 145.
77 Massignon, *Al-Hallaj, Martyr & Mystic,* 62.

On another occasion, one of Mansur's disciples, 'Abdullah ibn Tahir Azdi, was quarreling with a Jew in the market of Baghdad and blurted out at him, "Dog!" Just then Mansur passed by, scowled at 'Abdullah and said, "Don't make your dog bark so!" Hallaj hurried away, whereupon 'Abdullah quit the argument and followed him to Hallaj's house, where he apologized. "My son," Mansur replied, "all of the religious faiths arise from God Most High. He assigned to each group a creed, not of their own choice, but of His choice imposed upon them. When one reproaches another for belonging to an erroneous faith, it is because one presupposes that he has chosen it of himself, which is the heresy of the (Mu'tazilite) *Qadariyya*, who are (according to the hadith of Ibn 'Abbas) the "Zoroastrians of this Community." I would have you know that Judaism, Christianity, Islam and the other religious denominations may be different names and contrasting appellations, but that their Goal, Himself, suffers neither difference nor contrast." Then he recited the following verse:

> *I have pondered as to how to give religious faiths an*
> *   experimental definition*
> *And I formulate it as a single Principle with many*
> *   branches.*
> *Do not demand therefore that your companion in*
> *   discussion adopt this or that confessional denomination.*
> *That would prevent him from arriving at honest union*
> *   (with you and with God).*
> *It is up to the Principle Himself to come to this man,*
> *And to clarify in him all of the supreme meanings:*
> *Then this man will understand (everything).*[78]

By the time Mansur was finally arrested in 913 CE, he had built up quite a popular following, and political tensions with the Qarmathians were high in Baghdad, where Qarmathian-inspired riots had taken place in the streets against the caliph. Hallaj was placed on an arrest list and barely escaped from Baghdad, only to be captured later in Sus, where he was returned to Baghdad on a

---

78 Ibid, 104.

camel with a placard around his neck falsely labeling him: "The Apostle of the Qarmathians." According to Hallaj's son, Hamd, his father's arrest had nothing to do with heresy or Qarmathianism, but was an opportunity seized by the old corrupt tax-farmer, Hamid, to become wazir by arresting and besmirching the friend of the present wazir, Ibn Isa (a sympathizer of Hallaj, as was the queen mother, Shaghab).

A Zahirite[79] jurist named Ibn Da'ud, a Mu'tazilite-educated rationalist who was revolted by what he considered foolish talk of loving God, took a special dislike to Hallaj and sought the death penalty against him. However, a more impartial and renowned Shafi'ite jurist named Ibn Surayj found Hallaj's mystic sayings obscure, but not heretical; he judged them as falling within the category of *sarira*, the inward conscience of every soul whose truth will only be revealed on Judgment Day. On this subject, the Prophet is quoted as saying, "Differences of opinion are a (divine) blessing for my community." Ibn Surayj knew that Hallaj was a devout Muslim, a hafiz who often fasted and prayed all night, and thus refused to sign a *fatwa* pronouncing Hallaj an unbeliever *(kafir)*, nor would he authorize the death penalty against him. As long as Hallaj continued to make the confession of faith, *the shahada*, as he fervently did, there was no way to execute him as an apostate. As a result, Ibn Isa was able to recommended the minimum sentence for Hallaj, a flogging on the pillory which was to serve as a warning. As long as Ibn Surayj lived (until 918 CE, the same year Hamid became wazir), no one took further action against Hallaj and no other Shafi'ite or Hanbalite would think of speaking against Hallaj.

In the end, Mansur was not released after his flogging but was imprisoned indefinitely on the palace grounds. One of his friends in the palace, Nasr, the chamberlain, obtained the caliph's permission to build a special cell for Hallaj, from which he was, for years, able to preach to the other prisoners, visit with his disciples, his family, and even the queen mother. On one occasion Mansur even healed Caliph Muqtadir of an illness, thus winning his favor for a time.

---

79 The Zahirite school recognized the Qur'an and Hadith as the only legitimate sources of jurisprudence.

At other times Mansur was kept in carefully guarded isolation and wore chains. Despite his heavy manacles, Mansur performed 1000 rak'a daily during the eight years of his incarceration. When asked why one who claimed to be God felt the need to pray in this way, Hallaj answered, "Because we know what we are worthy of."[80]

The authorities were divided on the subject of Mansur's guilt, and his friends in high places were able to forestall his trial for nearly a decade. When it became almost impossible to visit him, Ibn Ata, a fellow student of Junayd and devoted friend and follower of Hallaj, sent word to his prison cell saying, "Master, ask pardon for the words you have spoken, that you may be set free." When Hallaj sent back word that "the one who said this should ask pardon," Ibn Ata wept and said, "We are not even a fraction of Hallaj."

Finally, in 922 CE, things came to a head. A former Sufi named Awariji wrote a book denouncing Hallaj as a fake miracle worker and the weak-willed Caliph Muqtadir, despite his mother's royal protests, gave in to the demands of his grand-wazir, Hamid, who fervently advocated a trial to finally condemn Hallaj. When the trial at last began, Hallaj's Hanbalite Sufi friend, Ibn Ata, aroused the common people to march in the streets for four days, protesting the royal persecution of Hallaj. The Hanbalite march soon degenerated into a riot. Ibn Ata was arrested, but he refused to be intimidated by the corrupt wazir and his henchmen who had initiated this political witch-hunt. When asked whether he agreed with various questionable sayings of Hallaj, Ibn Ata boldly answered in the affirmative. He, in turn, accused Hamid of launching attacks against noble helpers of the people in order to deflect attention from his own involvement in oppressing the poor, seizing people's property and having them killed. Outraged at his response, Hamid kicked Ibn Ata in the teeth. Then he ordered the guards to beat Ibn Ata to death with his own shoes.

By this time, Hamid had collected all of Mansur's confiscated writings and was able to begin wrapping up the trial, with a guilty verdict virtually assured. A Hallajian letter was produced

---

80 Ibid (quoted by 'Attar), 220.

which began, "From the Compassionate, the Merciful to so-and-so..." They claimed that in writing it, Hallaj was claiming divine omnipotence. Hallaj agreed that he had written the letter, but denied that he was claiming personal divinity or omnipotence for himself, saying: "No! This is what we call, among ourselves, essential union! (Persian: *ayn-i jam*) Of this mystical state we say: who is it but Allah who writes, since I and my hand are but His instruments?"

They produced another letter—which they chose to take literally—in which Hallaj had encouraged a follower "to destroy the Ka'ba, or temple (of his body) that it would be rebuilt in Wisdom and thus partake in the *sajda* and *rak'a* (prostration and bowing) of the true worshipers."[81] Finally, they produced a passage in which Hallaj recommended to those unable to make the pilgrimage to Mecca, that they build a substitute model of the Ka'ba in a special room and make circumambulations around it on the appropriate days, concluding with a feast in which they fed and clothed orphans. Hallaj explained that he was simply conveying a suggestion which Hasan Basri had put forward in his *Book of Sincerity*.

"Lies!" Mansur's accusers shouted, insisting instead that this was a subversive Qarmathian doctrine being advocated by the prophet-pretender and Mahdi claimant, al-Hallaj—all part of a very real Shi'ite-extremist movement designed to abolish the rite of pilgrimage to the holy places, change the religion, and overthrow the 'Abbasid government.

The caliph, fearful of a revolt which would destroy the state, began to lean toward a guilty verdict against Hallaj. His wazir, Hamid, promised him that if any evil consequences befell the caliph as a result of Hallaj's execution, he, himself would accept the blame and could be put to death. With this reassurance, the caliph accepted the signed *fatwa* that Hamid handed him and consented to Hallaj's execution.

When the *fatwa* had been signed in court, spuriously condemning Hallaj for this interpretation concerning the hajj, the accused spoke

---

81 Massignon, 262.

up, protesting this travesty and proclaiming his religion as Sunni Islam, founded on the sunna of the Prophet and his heirs from Abu Bakr to Abu 'Ubayda ibn al-Jarrah. "Allah!" Mansur cried, and repeated several times: "Allah will answer for my blood."

The authentic spirit of Hallaj's teaching about the hajj is preserved in a fragment from his works on the "perishableness of intermediaries":

> As long as you remain attached to this physical enclosure [of the Ka'ba], you will remain separated from Allah. But when you have really detached yourself from it, then you will reach the One who built it and established it; then, meditating on the temple (destroyed) in yourself, you will possess the real presence of its (Divine) Founder.

Mansur is said to have recited the following:[82]

> *O you who censure me for loving Him,*
> *how much you crush me,*
> *If you could only see the One I mean,*
> *you would no longer censure me.*
> *People make the pilgrimage;*
> *I am going on a (spiritual) pilgrimage to my Host;*
> *While they offer animals in sacrifice,*
> *I offer my heart and my blood . . .*

The night before his execution, al-Hallaj was visited by his son, Hamd. Mansur made two *raka'at* of prayer, and when he had finished, began to repeat to himself, "Illusion, illusion..." for much of the night. Then after a long silence, he cried out, "Truth, Truth *(Haqq, Haqq)*" and standing up, wrapped in his mantle, he entered into ecstatic prayer, saying:

> Here we are, your ecstatic witness. We are seeking refuge in the (pre-eternal) splendor of Your glory, in order that You show (finally) what You wanted to fashion and achieve, O

---

82 Ibid, 268, 264-65.

You who are God in heaven and on earth . . . How is it that You, who bestowed Your own "I" upon this present witness and used me to "proclaim Myself to me,". . . now wish me to be seized, imprisoned, judged, executed and hanged on the gibbet, my ashes scattered to the winds and to the waves which will play with them? If only because their smallest particle . . . assures to the glorious body (temple) of my transfiguration a more imposing foundation than that of immovable mountains.[83]

On the morning of his execution, al-Hallaj was taken to the esplanade, near the Khurasani gate, and scourged with at least five hundred lashes of the whip, part of Hamid's cruel punishment orders. An enormous crowd of police, well-wishers, enemies, as well as the curious of Baghdad and surrounding regions, gathered to witness the execution. There are many conflicting accounts of the details of the execution, some offering legendary embellishments which, if not precisely factual, at least give some idea of the triumphant spirit with which Hallaj faced his own martyrdom.

It is said that when he was led out to the execution site, Mansur laughed and danced in his chains and then recited a mystical ode, which included the words: "He who invites me, and cannot be called guilty of injustice, has invited me to drink poison which bestows eternal life, a cup from which He Himself has drunk, thus treating me as a host treats his guest. How can I refuse?" He kissed the wood of the gallows and ascended the steps, saying to some who were taunting him in the crowd, "The ascension of true men is the top of the gallows."[84] When he saw his relative and fellow Sufi, Abu Bakr Shibli, among the crowd, Hallaj asked him for a prayer rug and, facing Mecca, made two final *raka'at* of salat and then uttered a *du'a* thanking Allah for having clothed Mansur's own temporality (or human nature, *nasut)* in the disguise of His eternity *(lahut,* or divine nature). He then prayed for the forgiveness of his enemies, saying, "If You had revealed to them what You have revealed to me, they would not do what they are doing, and if You had concealed

83 Ibid, 283.
84 'Attar, *Tadhkirat al-Auliya,* 269.

from me what You have concealed from them, I would not be able to undergo the ordeal that I am enduring. Praise be to You in whatsoever You do and will." Then he concluded with his own verse: "Kill me, O faithful friends for in my death is my life . . ." [85]

Al-Hallaj was silent during his scourging, except to occasionally call out what he was seeing inwardly. At the four hundredth lash of the whip, Mansur experienced a prophetic vision of the capture of (what would become) Istanbul by the Muslim armies; he cried out: "Now Constantinople is taken." After the flagellation ended, Mansur's hands and feet were alternately cut off. According to Attar[86], he smiled and said, "With these feet I made an earthly journey; other feet I have which even now are journeying through both the worlds. Hack off those feet, if you are able!" Then, with the bloodied stumps of his hands, he rubbed his face, as an ablution, saying: "When one prays two *raka'at* in love, the ablution is not perfect unless performed with blood."

The Martyrdom of Al-Hallaj

Then he was hoisted into the air with ropes, upon the gibbet, a kind of cross, and as the evening was approaching, the final decapitation was postponed until the next morning, so that the wazir Hamid could be present and publicly read the charges and *fatwas* concerning Hallaj's guilt to the people. That evening, there

85 Massignon, 284-85.
86 'Attar, 269-70.

were riotous commotions throughout the city as looters roamed the streets, setting fire to shops.

As Mansur hung on the cross toward dark, some of them tried to force Shibli to curse him. He pulled free of them and then, seeing a friend, Fatima Naysaburiya, agreed to send her with a message to al-Hallaj. "Go to Hallaj," he said, "and tell him that Allah gave him access to one of His secrets, but he made it public; therefore Allah has made him taste the blade. But then ask him; 'What is Sufism?'" When she conveyed the message, Hallaj disagreed that *he* had divulged Allah's secret and pointed out that when the prophets suffered it was never interpreted as a divine punishment. As for the nature of Sufism (or in some versions the question takes the form, "What is the highest form of mysticism?"), Mansur replied, "Its exterior is what you see; its interior remains hidden to men; its beginning you are witnessing today, its end you will see tomorrow." When Shibli heard this answer, he acknowledged, "Husayn ibn Mansur is right. Sufism is spiritual sacrifice; pay no attention to the 'follies' of mystics."

Another tradition has Shibli personally approach the gallows and call out to Hallaj a quote from the Qur'an[87]: "Did we not forbid you to receive any guest, whether man or angel?" By this, he perhaps meant, "Do you receive Allah as a guest and in so doing publicly divulge His secret to those who are on the level of the coarse people of Sodom who uttered this verse to Lot when he housed the angels?" Hallaj was silent, knowing that the following verses in the Qur'an reveal the answer—how, at sunrise, the cry of the angels, the guests of Lot, overtook the city, and stones rained upon the accursed inhabitants who had threatened Lot.

The next morning Hamid came and read the verdict, and affirmed before the crowd that the caliph was personally absolved of responsibility in this case. "This is for the salvation of Islam," he said. "Let his blood fall on our necks!" This was the blood of yet another martyr named Husayn, slaughtered by fellow adherents of the faith. Hallaj, still alive on the cross, but much weakened by the loss of blood, was lowered to receive his final

---

87 Qur'an 15:70.

decapitating deathblow. At that time, Hallaj spoke his last words: "It is sufficient for the mystic when Allah alone testifies to His unity." Sulami says he also recited verse 42:18 of the Qur'an, after which he said nothing more: "Those who do not believe in the Hour seek to hasten it; but those who believe await it with a reverential fear, for they know that it is the Truth."[88]

Hallaj's body was burned and his ashes cast from a minaret into the Tigris, spreading the fragrance of sacrificial love and the remembrance of Divine Truth in all directions. Though Hallaj was accused by the authorities of teaching a *hulul* doctrine (that he had claimed to be a divine incarnation in the flesh), many prominent Sufi masters since his time have defended him against this charge and honored him as a great *waliyullah* who genuinely passed away in Truth. Jalaluddin Rumi, for instance, frequently mentioned Hallaj in favorable terms in his *Masnavi*, and was of the opinion that the authorities lacked just cause in condemning Hallaj. Though no formal Hallajian tarikat lineage ever developed, due in part to the scandal associated with his execution, Fariduddin Attar took Hallaj as a spiritual guide as a result of a dream, and even today, especially in the Persian and Turkish traditions, Hallaj enjoys an exalted reputation as the supreme martyr of love among the mystics. The Bektashi order of dervishes connect their central rite of *bayat* (initiation) with the *dar-i Mansur*, the "gallows of Mansur."

The late Sheikh Muzaffer[89] sums up the traditional perspective of the Halveti-Jerrahis by praising Mansur as a saint, while issuing a cautionary warning to those who might too facilely imitate Hallaj's famous words, without truly sharing his spiritual state of *fana-fi'llah*:

> Some wrongly equate themselves with al-Hallaj, who said: "I am the Truth *(Ana'l Haqq),*" when they are actually echoing Pharaoh's words: "I am your Lord Most High *(Ana Rabbukumu'l A'la).*" Mansur al-Hallaj did say: "I am the Truth," but he was *made* to say it. He never gave up his ritual

---

88 Massignon, 287-89.
89 M.Ozak, *Irshad,* 500.

prayer and fasting. If he really was the Truth, meaning God, then Who was praying to Whom? In fact, he was inebriated, not by any ordinary drink, but by the wine of divine unity.

Many Orientalists have seen in Al-Hallaj a Christ-like figure among the Muslims. He comes preaching love and religious tolerance, proclaiming the divinity in the human heart. He speaks as one with divine authority. When faced with execution, he asks forgiveness for his enemies and understands his death as the will of God. His death is a scandal. In chains, he goes willingly to his fate, a martyr of love, witnessing the Truth which is never allowed to be fully acknowledged in society. Though it is a tempting analogy for Westerners, it is not an insight born from the perspective of authentic Islamic Sufism. Not only does Islam eschew any doctrine of vicarious atonement, but according to the Qur'an, Jesus ascended to God untouched by martyrdom, making it most unlikely that Al-Hallaj would have conceived of himself in such terms. For Sufis, Hallaj is seen primarily as the exemplar of the fourth level, the level of *Haqq* (Divine Truth).

After Mansur's time, discretion would be the watchword of many Sufis, yet the Hallajian spirit continues to represent the true heart of the dervish way. The divine calls to every soul, exhorting it to awaken and discover the great secret: beyond all names, forms and seeming limitations in this world, "I am the True!"

The martyrdom of al-Hallaj represents the culmination of the saga of divine love and mystic union in that period, his blood sealing the end of an era. As for the other disciples of Hazrat Junayd, including those in the Halveti-Jerrahi silsila, starting with Sheikh Manshudu'n Nuri, they are somewhat less distinguished than their predecessors; however, some of them were responsible for producing valuable records of that which they had received from their sheikhs. Though the Sufis at first retreated from the public eye in the wake Mansur's execution, in time, a number of the great mystic orders blossomed forth from the fertile seed of Junayd and his Baghdadi circle of disciples. These include: the Qadiriyya, the Rifa 'iyya (through Junayd and Shibli), the Suhrawardiyya and the Dusukiyya (whose silsila shares the first five successors after

Junayd with the Halveti-Jerrahis). Other ecstatics, such as Niffari (d.965 CE) continued to boldly affirm the immanent presence of the Transcendent Source, saying, "Why do you imagine Allah up there in the heavens—He is right here!"

Mansur on the gallows (The Walters Art Museu, Baltimore.)

Though perhaps the most celebrated, Mansur was not to be the only mystic martyr among the masters of Sufism. Among others, over the course of the following centuries, the famous Persian illuminist mystic, Shahabuddin Yahya Suhrawardi (1154-1191 CE), Ayn al-Qudat Hamadani (d.1131 CE—not to be confused with his famous contemporary of Naqshbandi fame, Yusuf Hamadani), and the Hurufi poet 'Imaduddin Nesimi, who considered himself another Mansur, were all executed by Islamic authorities, the latter flayed alive in Aleppo in 1417 CE. It is worth quoting one of Nesimi's mystic odes, *Yandim Yakildim,* a renowned neva ilahi which is still popular in Turkey and frequently sung during dhikr ceremonies.

> *I burst into the flames of Love;*
> *I became drunk on the mystery of Love,*
> *Intoxicated from the realm of "Am I not (Your Lord)?"*
> *In service, O my Master,*
> *I am merged with the Sultan of Love.*
> *The secret of* Ana'l Haqq *has come alive in me;*
> *I have become Mansur in the paradise of Love.*
> *Sayyid Nesimi has abandoned all inward constraints,*
> *His body, consumed in the radiance of Love.*

SECTION THREE

*The Middle Period:
The Formation of
the Great Sufi Orders*

CHALLENGE OF THE WEST:
THE CRUSADES

IF HAZRAT JUNAYD AL-BAGHDADI stands out in the ninth and early tenth century as the central pir of tarikat in the capital city of the 'Abbasid-ruled Islamic civilization, no murshid of equivalent stature took up the mantle of Sufism in the century following his death. Rather, the Muslim world of the tenth and early eleventh century (CE) was characterized by political factionalism and change, coupled with a growing tendency toward consolidation and organization among the mystics of Islam.

Ultimately, from this environment of political upheaval and transfer of dynastic power emerged the first two full-fledged fraternal orders of Sufism in the twelfth century, the *Qadiriyya* and the *Suhrawardiyya*. These two principal turuq arose in Iraq at approximately the same time, blossoming later into international organizations after the death of their respective founders, Pir 'Abdul Qadir Gaylani [Jilani] (1078-1166 CE) and Pir Abu-Najib Suhrawardi (1097-1168 CE), both of whom lived and taught in Baghdad. The latter, Abu Najib, figures as a major pir (or founder of an order) in the Halveti-Jerrahi line, while the former, 'Abdul Qadir, is a direct ancestor of the pir who stands at the very beginning of the Khalwati (Halveti) line, Pir Ibrahim Zahid Gaylani (d.1304 CE)—may the secrets of these noble pirs be preserved. We will return to them after briefly examining a few major developments which occurred during the interval between their time and that of Hazrat Junayd.

The second half of the tenth century through the eleventh century was a time of Shi'ite domination in Islamic lands, a period which witnessed the gradual disintegration of the Sunnite 'Abbasid caliphate. By 945 CE, Baghdad had come under the control of the Shi'ite Buyid Dynasty, while Central Arabia had been taken over by the Qarmathians. Northern Syria came under the rule of the Hamdanite Shi'ites, while the Fatimid Dynasty was able to hold and govern Egypt for the next two centuries (969-1171 CE). Meanwhile in Spain, the Great Mosque of Cordova was being built by the Ummayad caliph, luxuriously suggesting the atmosphere of paradise on earth, in a Western Islamic setting famous for its vast libraries and stunning Andalusian architecture.

In 1055 CE, the army of the Seljuk Turks—composed of Central Asian Sunnis who had already been engaged in the military service of the 'Abbasid Empire—succeeded in securing a bloodless transfer of power in Baghdad to their Anatolian leader, Toghrul Beg, who assumed for the first time the title of sultan. The Seljuk Dynasty in Iraq would last until 1194 and would play a major part in the Sunnite re-appropriation of Islamic power from the hands of the Shi'a. The Seljuks also represented the first major foray of Turkish civilization into the governance of the Islamic world, a role they were to play henceforth with increasing regularity. This culminated in more than four centuries of Middle-Eastern Islamic rule by the sultanate of the Ottoman Empire, its longevity rivaled only by the Safavid Dynasty in Shi'ite Persia—the last remaining bastion of concentrated Shi'ite power after the demise of the Fatimids.

Though the Fatimid reign in Egypt was one of great splendor and opulence, rich in art, poetry, and learning, it had, at one point, the misfortune to be governed by a half-mad caliph, al-Hakim (996-1021 CE), who modeled himself on the character of Nero and happened to be a nephew of the Orthodox Patriarch of Jerusalem. In 1009 CE, tyrannically ignoring the objections of the Muslim populace, he commenced upon a series of degrading acts against the Christian and Jewish citizens, forbidding their pilgrimages and all music, commanding the uprooting of all vineyards in Egypt, declaring his own divinity and finally ordering the destruction of all the churches and synagogues throughout the empire, except the Church of the Holy Nativity in Bethlehem.

Like Caligula and other powerful, yet insane, emperors who have ventured far beyond the limits of their own subject's threshold of toleration, Hakim was murdered, and replaced by a saner successor.[90] However, the Druze sect, forming in Lebanon, accepted al-Hakim's claim of divinity and revered him as the last imam, while the Nizari Isma'ilis shortly thereafter recognized another imam, Nizar, and founded the group which came to be known as the Assassins, dedicated to the destruction of all Sunnite rule.

Unfortunately, Caliph al-Hakim's thoroughly un-Islamic destruction of various historic churches in the Holy land included the Church of the Holy Sepulcher in Jerusalem, a fact which did not escape the notice of the Papal See in Rome. Access to Christian pilgrims was soon restored, but in 1079 CE, the Seljuk armies conquered Damascus, then Antioch and Aleppo in 1085, renewing Christian anxieties about access to Jerusalem. In 1096, Pope Urban II traveled to Claremont in France and proposed the idea of an armed pilgrimage to recapture Jerusalem and various other holy sites, promising land, booty and spiritual redemption

Saladin, Sultan of Egypt

for all who fought the Muslims and Jews for the sake of European Christendom.

Initially, the fragmented Muslim governments of the region were slow to react to the invasion from the West. In 1099 CE, the Crusaders took Jerusalem, converted the Muslim holy sites[91] into churches and rebuilt such sacred sites as the Church of the Holy Sepulcher, putting them under the protection of the Order of the Knights Templar. The mostly French force held the city for nearly a century until the formidable Kurdish Sunnite general and future Ayyubid Sultan of Egypt, Saladin (1138-1193 CE), overthrew the Fatimids in 1171 and recaptured Jerusalem from the Franks in 1187.

---

90 Payne, *History of Islam,* 208.
91 Sites such as the Dome of the Rock and al-Aqsa Mosque.

In 1192, Richard the Lion-Hearted arrived, took Acre, and secured a truce with Saladin (Salah ad-Din Yusuf ibn Aiyuh), beginning a period of Crusader fame for the two opposing commanders, whose rules of conduct in battle were governed by similar codes of chivalry.[92] Once, when King Richard was sick with a fever, Saladin sent his men with snow from the mountains near Damascus to cool King Richard's tent. Among the Muslims and Sufis, the ways of spiritual chivalry are known as *futuwwah*, and are based on noble precedents from the time of the Prophet Muhammad and Hazrat 'Ali. This chivalrous code was especially favored by one of the last of the 'Abbasid caliphs, al-Nasir (who ruled from 1180-1225 CE), who

Richard, King of England

was assisted in his court by the great Sufi sheikh, Shahabuddin Abu-Hafs 'Umar as-Suhrawardi.

Until the time of the Crusades, there had been little overt religious conflict between the East and the West, or between Muslims and Jews or Christians. This was partially due to isolation, but also, no doubt, because of the Qur'anically based Islamic respect for the People of the Book, who were normally allowed to practice their religion in peace throughout Islamic lands, safe from persecution. Centuries before the founding of the United States, the Qur'an sanctioned religious pluralism (at least of the Abrahamic faiths) and even allowed Christians and Jews to judge themselves according to their own religious laws.

The Christian saint, Francis of Assisi (1182-1226 CE), went to the Crusades in Egypt and visited at length with the Saracean Sultan, Malik al-Kamil, and was treated with great honor and cordiality. Each of them emerged with a feeling of great mutual respect. The Sultan entreated Francis to return again and issued him safe conduct, with permission to preach to the Sultan's own

---

92 Lapidus, *A History of Islamic Societies*, 349-53.

subjects. Francis returned to the Christian camp and in vain attempted to dissuade them from attacking the Muslims. Had they taken his advice, the Crusaders would have not been driven back as they were, with heavy loss of lives.[93]

St. Francis of Assisi before Sultan Malik al-Kamil

Though the capture of Jerusalem by the Crusaders in 1099 resulted in an almost total annihilation of its residents, when the Muslims reclaimed it, they followed the example of the Prophet Muhammad's peaceful return to Mecca, and gave clemency to the general populace of Jerusalem. (Later, the Crusaders would briefly recapture Jerusalem, but by 1291 CE, it would slip from their hands for the last time.)

Having lost this holy city of Peace in the Third Crusade, the Fourth Crusade concentrated upon Constantinople and its sacred sites. Tragically, this generated a trail of carnage in which thousands of Jews in villages along the way were mercilessly

93 Idries Shah, *The Sufis,* 261-62.

slaughtered, culminating in a blood-bath at Constantinople— complete with barbarian raping, looting and burning—visited by Western European Crusaders primarily upon the Eastern Orthodox Christians who lived there. Their apparent fault lay in wearing Middle-Eastern style robes and professing rites which differed from their fellow European "Christian" brethren. Though such atrocities in the name of religion were a sad reality of the Crusades—and certainly neither side can be considered blameless in their political ambitions—the impact of the conflict on the larger Muslim world was not very great. It simply caused intermittent migrations of various populations in a time already rife with political conflicts and takeovers.

Crusader siege at Corinth.

It should be understood that one reason the Muslims were slow to react to the Crusader's invasion was that the idea of *jihad* against Christian armies did not automatically spring into every Muslim mind, as modern Westerners might assume. It was the Crusaders themselves who defined the armed pilgrimage in terms of a holy war, and when Saladin recaptured Jerusalem, the triumphant Sunni Muslims were as much pleased to have ousted the former Shi'i government of the Fatimids as they were the European invaders.

During this period, a number of writers on the mystic path penned biographies of the early Sufis and their mystical schools, as well as manuals of discipline and expositions of the newly-coalesced science of *tasawwuf*. Some of the more important Sufi contributions to this literary trend include: *Kitab al-Luma Fi't-Tasawwuf* by Sarraj (d.988 CE), *Kitab at-Ta'arruf* by al-Kalabadhi (d.990), *Qut al-Qulub* (Food of Hearts) by Abu Talib al-Makki (d.996), *Kitab al-Futuwwah* (The Way of Sufi Chivalry)[94] and *Tabaqat as-Sufiyya* (The Classes of Sufis) by Sulami (d.1021). Other notable works on *tasawwuf* during the eleventh century include: *Hilayat al-Auliya* (The Ornaments of the Saints) by al-Isfahani, the *Risala* of Qushayri (d.1074), *Manazil as-Sa'irin (The Stations on the Way)by 'Abdullah-i Ansari,* and *Kashf al-Mahjub* (Unveiling of the Hidden) by 'Ali al-Hujwiri (d.1071).

Hujwiri's book, which is the oldest Persian treatise on Sufism, includes a list of twelve major schools of the Sufis, as they existed in his time, just before the golden era which witnessed the arising of so many great pirs and mystic orders in the twelfth and thirteenth centuries CE. He lists twelve sects, two of which are condemned—the Hululis and the Hallajians—and ten which are approved. The remaining ten sects are: the Muhasibis, the Qassaris, the Tayfuris, the Junaydis, the Nuris, the Sahlis, the Hakimis, the Kharrazis, the Khafifis and the Sayyaris. These represent mainly schools of thought in early Sufism, associated with particular teachers, rather than full-blown mystic orders with rules of conduct, *usuls* (sacred litanies), *silsilas* (chain of transmission), *ijazets* (diplomas) and *tekkes* or *khanqahs* (Sufi lodges), as will develop over the course of the next few centuries.

We should also take into account the cross-fertilization of mystical Jewish and Islamic thought which transpired during the late Middle Ages. This occurred when a number of Jewish mystics began to realize that Sufism had preserved and developed many aspects of the teachings on mystic union and the inner life, teachings—representing authentic fruits of the Abrahamic tradition—which had been seriously neglected in mainstream Rabbinic Judaism.

---

94 *The Way of Sufi Chivalry* has been translated into English in recent years by Sheikh Tosun Bayrak al-Jerrahi.

During its formative years, historical Islam was influenced and enriched in a number of ways by Jewish tradition. The Qur'an refers often to the noble Prophets of Israel, alludes to stories contained in Jewish midrash, values the kosher dietary system and proclaims Islam as a pristine expression of the Abrahamic tradition (of which Judaism is another expression). Even the original *kibla*, the direction of prayer for the Prophet Muhammad and his followers, was, for a number of years, Jerusalem. The model of Western asceticism and meditation adopted by the early Sufis was anticipated by the Jews at Qumran who left us the Dead Sea Scrolls centuries before the Islamic era. Jewish Kabbalists had early on given the teaching that the holy scriptures could be read on four levels of understanding—*Assiyah* (action), *B'riah* (feeling), *Yetzirah* (knowledge), and *Azilut* (being)—which appears to antedate the Sufi teaching of the four worlds.[95] Like spiritual wealth long ago deposited in a bank, the investments were now maturing with interest. The Sufi way, in fact, held a great deal of attraction for many seekers traveling the road of Jewish mysticism.

Jewish writers soon began to translate Sufi works into Hebrew, some writing their own Sufi-inspired treatises in Arabic (often using Hebrew characters). One such writer was Bahya Ibn Paquda, from eleventh century Spain, whose works include: *Duties of the Heart* and *Doctrines of the Soul*. These were translated into Hebrew in the twelfth century by Rabbi Judah ibn Tibbon. Abraham ibn Hasdai's twelfth century Hebrew translation and modification of Abu Hamid al-Ghazali's Arabic Sufi text, *The Balance of Religious Practice*, is typical of the tendency among some Jewish translators to insert Biblical quotes of a similar kind in place of Qur'anic quotes, thus making the teachings more familiar and acceptable to Jewish readers.

Another recently discovered Judeo-Arabic work of note is *Al-Maqala al-Hawdiyya* (The Treatise of the Pool) by Obadya

---

95 There is, of course, no clear-cut evidence to demonstrate influence of one tradition upon the other. One could just as readily maintain that each mystical path independently drew from the same higher source of revelation. The corresponding four worlds in Sufism are: *shariat, tarikat, marifat* and *hakikat* (however, Sufis tend to reverse the order of *hakikat* and *marifat*. cf. Appendix II). Hinduism also has its own teaching of four levels of yoga: *hatha* or *karma yoga, bhakti yoga, gyana (jnana) yoga,* and *raja yoga.*

Maimonides, the grandson of the famous Jewish thinker, Moses Maimonides (1135-1204 CE). Maimonides (Moses ben Maimon), who was Saladin's physician, is best known for his great philosophic work, *The Guide for the Perplexed,* with its Aristotlelean approach to Judaism. Though known primarily as a rationalist, Maimonides did not hesitate to urge mystic practice as a door to direct spiritual

experience. Facing persecution and forced conversion in Spain, Maimonides moved to Egypt where several of his descendants became open exponents of Sufi practice, most prominently his son, Rabbi Avraham ben HaRambam. Rabbi Avraham was the leader of a mystical brotherhood incorporating Sufi teachings into the practices of Judaism. In answer to mainstream Jewish critics who predicatbly

Moses Maimonides

frowned upon this sort of syncretism, Avraham wrote: "You are aware of the ways of the ancient saints of Israel, which are not, or but little practiced among our contemporaries. They have now become the practice of the Sufis of Islam—on account of the iniquities of Israel . . . Do not regard as unseemly our comparison of the Prophets to the Sufis, for the latter imitate the prophets of Israel and walk in their footsteps, not the prophets in theirs . . ."[96]

Another descendent of the same family in Cairo, David Ben Joshua Maimonides, wrote a work entitled *Guide to Detachment,* which equates spiritual stages mentioned in the Jewish *Pirkei Avot* with stations of the Sufi path, substitutes Jewish for Muslim scriptures, and utilizes the Jewish terms *Hasid* and *Hasidism* as a fitting alternative for the words *Sufi* and *Sufism.* Hasidism, in later Eastern Europe would become the Jewish kabbalistic mystical movement perhaps most similar in Western religious history to Sufism and the dervish brotherhoods of the Near East.

---

96 *High Ways to Perfection,* translated by S. Rosenblatt, cited in Paul Fenton's "Judaeo-Arabic Mystical Writings of the XIIIth-XIVth Centuries", in Golb, Judaeo-Arabic Studies (1997).

A remarkable early kabbalist and author, Avraham ben Shmuel Abulafia of Malta (1240-after 1291 CE), is thought to have adopted the head movements from Sufi dhikrs into his letter visualization practices. In his fervor to bring down the walls between Judaism, Christianity and Islam, Avraham sought an audience with Pope Nicolas III, but only attracted a death sentence from the pontiff. His sentence was miraculously commuted when the pope died just as the execution fire was being lit. Avraham was released and lived out his days, writing a number of books on Kabbala and philosophy.

ABU'L-KHAYR

ABU SA'ID IBN ABU'L-KHAYR (967-1049 CE) was the first Sufi to draw up a preliminary monastic-like rule for his dervishes. An ecstatic Khurasanian mystic, Abu'l-Khayr, began his training with Sheikh Sulami with rigorous, even extravagant ascetic practices, saying "Allah" for seven years while hanging upside-down in a well for long periods of time. By age forty, he became illumined and, abandoning his former austerities, began to enjoy life, hosting great banquets and even becoming corpulent, joyfully

 surrounded by those who had been attracted to follow him. Abu'l-Khayr became famous for his ecstatic sayings: "Beneath this robe there is none but Allah" *(Ma fi'l-jubbati illa'llah)* and "All is He." He also helped establish the use of music and ritual movement among the dervishes, the use of which had formerly been viewed with a fair amount of skepticism as to its permissibility. He subsequently

founded what could be called a convent, though this was not a true order or tarikat organization.

IMAM ABU HAMID AL-GHAZALI

ANOTHER IMPORTANT FIGURE in the next generation of this era was the renowned theological scholar and philosopher, turned mystic, Imam Abu Hamid Muhammad al-Ghazali (1058-1111 CE), who was born in Tus, Persia, shortly after the Turkish Seljuk takeover of Baghdad. Al-Ghazali began his career as an Ash'arite theologian and jurist with a teaching post at the *Nizamiyya*, one of the most prestigious colleges *(madaris)* in Baghdad. He built up a scholarly reputation as one of the greatest jurists and imams of his time, a paragon of Islamic orthodoxy who was of great use to the Turkish Sultanate through his well-reasoned refutations of the schismatic doctrines of the rival Fatimids and Isma'ilis (especially the Assassins of Alamut).

Several years into his career as a Shafi'ite teacher of law and polemics, Abu Hamid began to realize the limits of the study of canon law and book learning as a path to Allah. Also, as he confessed in his autobiographical work, *Deliverance from Error*, "I examined my motive in my work of teaching, and realized that it was not a pure desire for the things of God, but that the impulse moving me was the desire for an influential position and public recognition."[97]

He underwent a crisis in his spiritual life that left him with a temporary speech impediment, making it difficult for him to carry on in his profession. We might say this was Allah's way of guiding his soul beyond a merely mental commitment to Islam. Turning his professorial post over to his brother, Ahmad, Abu Hamid retired to Damascus, and after a period of solitude and intense purification, began to travel throughout the East, investigating Sufism and visiting various places of

---

97 Williams, *Islam,* 197.

pilgrimage such as Mecca, Medina, Jerusalem and Hebron.

Two interesting stories concerning this period of his wanderings have come down to us. In one instance, Abu Hamid was traveling on a journey between Jurjan and Tus with a number of books and manuscripts among his belongings when some highwaymen stopped him and robbed him of his possessions. When he realized that the robbers were taking his satchel full of valuable books and personal notes, al-Ghazali anxiously followed them and asked the bandit chief if he might keep the books, since they were, after all, of no use to the illiterate highwaymen. The bandit chief at first refused him, warning him to keep away or die; but al-Ghazali persisted, explaining that he had "left his country in order to hear, write, and obtain the knowledge contained in those books." The chief laughed contemptuously at this, retorting, "How can you claim that you obtained their knowledge when we took it away from you and left you devoid of knowledge!"[98] Then the bandit turned and ordered his men to leave the books with the scholar. Al-Ghazali took the bandit's words as a divinely inspired message and resolved thereafter to memorize and internalize these deep teachings instead of depending on their written expression.

On still another occasion during his wanderings, Abu Hamid entered a mosque just as the local imam was concluding his Friday *khutba*. He happened to have been quoting al-Ghazali and concluded his sermon with the high-flown words, "Thus speaks our leader al-Ghazali." When he heard this, al-Ghazali was filled with two conflicting emotions: on the one hand, pride, and on the other hand, disgust with his great intellectual reputation, which, deep inside, he knew had turned into a stumbling block to real understanding, because it inflated his ego. He immediately resolved to leave that town and go where no one had ever heard of al-Ghazali. Inwardly he was being summoned to undertake the mystical journey away from his ego persona and toward his spiritual heart.

Al-Ghazali's period of seclusion lasted eleven years, a time during which he fervently meditated upon Divine Reality and studied all of the mystical schools of thought until he succeeded in

---

98 Quoted from an article on Imam al-Ghazali by G. F. Haddad.

breaking through the limits of his former ceiling of understanding. This condition had been imposed by his scholastic approach to Reality, in which his own nafs had been more before his eyes than Allah. In his autobiography, al-Ghazali states that he had learned all he could by reading; the remainder could not be acquired by study or talk. He further related: "I arrived at Truth, not by systematic reasoning and accumulation of proofs, but by a flash of light which Allah sent into my soul."[99]

Now he was able to champion the mystic insights of Junayd and Muhasibi, presenting their perspective in acceptable orthodox language, and even cogently defending the idea of passionate love for Allah against the arguments of the rationalist *ulama*, whom he says mistakenly deny themselves the possibility of the very divine intimacy which God desires. In his *Mishkat al-Anwar* (The Niche of Lights), al-Ghazali even excuses Hallaj, Bistami and Abu'l-Khayr (already popularized as mystic saints by his time) for their controversial *shatahat*, "I am the Truth," "Praise be to Me! How great is My glory!" and "Beneath this robe is none but Allah," saying they were simply dazed and lost in God's oneness so that their reason temporarily collapsed. However, al-Ghazali adds, "when their drunkenness abates and their reason is restored . . . they know that this was not actual identity, but resembled identity as when the lovers say at the height of their passion: 'I am he whom I desire, and he whom I desire is I; we are two souls inhabiting one body.'"[100]

Here, he is giving these ecstatics credit for realizing Junayd's teaching that the mystic who is given an experience of unity may at first mistakenly assume that he has become the Supreme Being, pure and simple. This is called the "first isolation" (an intermediate station on the path where Allah tests the soul by purposely allowing it to become isolated and inflated in its own higher level, so that the mystic believes he has become the One by his own efforts and thus boldly claims divinity). But ultimately, Allah, in His lordship, will overwhelm the soul with His victorious attribute of *Qahhar*. The soul will humbly realize a further level of longing, dependence and

---

99 Glasse, *The Concise Encyclopedia of Islam*, 138.
100 Zaehner, *Hindu and Muslim Mysticism*, 164.

love for Allah as the impulse behind his every action—the Divine Sun which is always greater than the individual sunbeam (or soul) which emerges from It and ultimately returns to It. Despite the fact that al-Ghazali has much in common with Junayd, he is also enamored with some of the less orthodox ecstatics and does not hesitate to echo Abu'l Khayr, when he states that "All is He and apart from Him there is nothing at all."[101]

In his *Kitab Jawahir al-Qur'an,*[102] al-Ghazali offers another image, that of cleansing the rust from the mirror of the soul so that the light of the Divine Essence may be revealed. He says:

Nothing, then, is incumbent upon you except to cleanse turbidness from the eye of the soul and to strengthen its pupil [to be able to receive more light]. In that case God will be in the soul as the picture is in the mirror, so that when He suddenly reveals Himself in the mirror of the soul, you hasten to say that He is inside the soul and that the human nature *(nasut)* has put on the divine nature *(lahut),* until God strengthens you with the firm word (Qur'an 14:27) so that you realize that the picture is not [really] inside the mirror, but only reflected in it. If the picture were to rest inside the mirror it would be inconceivable that it could be reflected in many mirrors at one time; rather [the case would be that] at that time when it rested inside one mirror, it moved from another. Such, however, is not the fact in the least, for God reveals Himself to many of the gnostics at the same time.

In modern times, the example of a television would likewise serve to show a similar analogy: a particular image which appears on TV is indeed one with the broadcast signal that is appearing on all television sets which are tuned in to that signal. Also, the image itself seems to be contained in the television; yet, strictly speaking, the totality of that broadcast signal is not contained in one single TV. Rather, what is seen on a particular television screen simply represents one of many expressions of one-and-

---

101 Ibid, 150-53, 167.
102 M.Quasem, *Jewels of the Qur'an,* 27.

the-same the image, projected into various television sets from a source transcending the TV, which unites them. Similarly, every soul is an expression of the One Being, yet one particular soul, with its distinctive qualities and goals, is not functionally identical with all other souls. Nevertheless, when the soul of the mystic merges in divine unity, all sense of separation disappears, and the soul experiences an eternal mystery which cannot be explained in words.

In his famous opus, *Ihya Ulum ad-Din* (Revival of the Religious Sciences)—also abridged as *The Alchemy of Happiness*—al-Ghazali says:

> Those who deny the reality of the ecstasies and other spiritual experiences of the Sufis merely betray their own narrow-mindedness and shallow insight . . . A wise man, though he himself may have no experience of those states, will not therefore deny their reality, for what folly can be greater than his who denies the reality of a thing merely because he himself has not experienced it! Of such people it is written in the Qur'an, "Those who do not have guidance will say, "This is manifest imposture."[103]

AL-GHAZALI ON MUSIC IN ISLAM

IN THE SAME WORK, al-Ghazali defends the use of music and sacred dance among the Sufis, saying that music brings out whatever is already in one's heart. Hence, the one who has love for Allah finds their love increased by hearing poetry and sacred music. Thus, it is lawful *(halal)* and laudable for that one to take part in Sufi ceremonies which promote divine love. However, the one whose heart is full of sensual desires, finds only sensuality stimulated by music and poetry, making its use unlawful *(haram)* for them. For the one who simply listens for amusement, the music is neutral—

---

103 Al-Ghazali, *Alchemy of Happiness*, 78.

thus, neither lawful nor unlawful for them.

He mentions clear cases in which music is considered lawful within Islam: when the pilgrims sing during *hajj*, the music-making of the prophet David *(Da'ud)*, joyous music at wedding celebrations, music going into battle, and so forth. Al-Ghazali also mentions several precedents in the life of the holy Prophet, two where he allowed music and one case where he stopped some singing-girls from improvising songs in his honor. In one case, the Prophet held 'A'isha up so that she could see and hear some black musicians performing music in a mosque on a festival day, while on another occasion two girls had come to their home to play and sing for 'A'isha. Shortly thereafter, the Prophet came in and did not object, but lay down on the couch, turning his face away. When 'A'isha's father, Abu Bakr happened by and entered, he exclaimed, "What! the pipe of Shaitan in the Prophet's house?" But the Prophet turned and answered, "Let them alone, Abu Bakr, for this is a festival-day."[104]

As for the use of music and dance among the Sufis of al-Ghazali's time, the imam freely admits that these matters are comparative novelties *(bid'a)*[105] in Islam. Yes, Imam al-Ghazali concedes, some of these practices were not received in exactly this form from the first followers of the Prophet; however, "we must remember that not all novelties are forbidden in Islam, but only those which directly contravene the Sacred Law *(shariat)*. For instance, the *tarawih* [the extra night prayers during Ramadan] was introduced by Caliph 'Umar. The Prophet said, 'Live with each man according to his habits and dispositions,' therefore it is right to fall in with usages that please people, when non-conformity would vex them."[106]

It is interesting to see how this discussion, based on the

---

104 Ibid, 75-76.
105 Innovation, or *bid'a*—changing the customs of the Prophet or deviating from what is taught in the Qur'an—is generally *verboten* in Islam. The injunction against innovation in Islam is designed as a protection so that people who are not on a prophetic level will not be tempted to casually change the religion according to the subjective propensities of their own nafs. If such alterations were allowed unchecked, the authentic understanding and practice of Islam would gradually become corrupted and diluted, until eventually, there would be little left of the original teaching to be passed on to future generations.
106 Ibid, 84-85.

misconception that the Prophet unconditionally forbade all music in Islam, continues to persist up to our time. When various Sufi groups presented their music-filled Islamic ceremonies of Divine remembrance to the American and European public in the late

1970's and early 1980's, the question of whether music was *haram* in Islam occasionally surfaced, usually posed by skeptical Muslims or students of religion from the universities. When this question arose during a question and answer period after a musical recitation and public dhikr at Cooper Union in New York City (April 2, 1980), Muzaffer Efendi offered this explanation:

There are two types of music: *shaitani* music and *rahmani* music. When anyone remembers and calls upon Allah with the use of music, that music is *rahmani*. Conversely, music that is insinuating and stimulates one's fleshly desires is *shaitani.* It is not only music which can be distinguished into two such categories; there are many acts in life which seem similar, yet are not the same, such as adultery and married love. Both acts are physically the same, but one is a sin and the other a blessing. [At Harvard University, on March 30, 1980, he again spoke about music, saying:] Music is very much connected with our path. When the Rasulullah entered Medina, the whole city came out with drums like we use in our dhikr, and chanted hymns to receive him.[107]

In the *'alam-i arwah* (universe of souls), when our Creator asked, *"Alastu bi-Rabbikum?"* (Am I not your Lord?") all souls answered, "Yes." That is why, in our essence, we all share this sweet taste which our souls have experienced beyond time. The music, then, evokes a memory, a faint echo reminiscent of the voice of Allah pronouncing those words which all souls heard and to which they responded. So when a musician sings, chants or plays an instrument, his soul is inspired by nostalgia for the beauty of that celestial sentence which Allah uttered in the soul's eternal realm.

On the other hand, when the flesh takes the place of the essence, that sound becomes worldly; but when it reaches up to that pure level from whence it has come, it reflects the voice of divinity. When one reaches to the third level—to the human soul—then one will have a taste of the sound of Allah and it will affect their art, whether it is music or some other form of artistic expression. Otherwise, the person on the first two levels—vegetable and animal—will simply produce what is compatible with vegetable and animal life.

In the universe of the souls, every soul melted with the beauty of Allah. Allah's beauty is such that whoever has eyes to see, disappears with love and the taste of divine beauty. [Allah's] flute cannot be seen in this world; one can only perceive it with the eyes of the heart, when divine beauty is reflected there. Though it is impossible to directly see the

---

107 The words and melody of the famous *segâh ilahi, Tala'al Badru Aleyna,* have been preserved since that time over 1400 years ago. It remains a popular Muslim and Sufi hymn to this day.

beauty of Allah's Essential Being, one can see the reflections in His attributes. Hazrat 'Ali said, "I wouldn't pray to a God I hadn't seen." The way he saw Allah was through seeing the divine attributes reflected and distributed in the realm of earthly life.

Sometimes, extremely shariatic Muslims, when they hear the music of our Sufi ceremonies, will ask if what we are doing is not *haram*. I tell them: Islam is built on five pillars, one of them being to fast during the month of Ramadan. In the morning, drummers wake the Muslims up before sunrise in order that they may eat a snack before prayers. Why isn't that *haram*? In battles, Muslims are also permitted to beat drums. Our path is the greatest battle against our own nafs. Does one realize the sincerity of the situation? In Islam, we take beauty wherever we see it. Some Islamic leaders may be against playing drums and chanting, but as for us, we will go on beating our drums, chanting and calling out to Allah.

From the words of both of these respected mystics—both of them highly esteemed imams in their times—we see the importance of sacred music in stimulating the soul to divine realms of ecstasy, while neither in the Qur'an nor the ahadith of the beloved Prophet do we find any wholesale prohibition of music, much less sacred music. In fact, the Qur'an, like other ancient scriptures, such as the original Hebrew Psalms *(Zabur)* of David, is almost always chanted with a musical cadence, and the recitation of the *adhan* (the Islamic call to prayer) is certainly a musical expression, one which is chanted or sung in various musical modes *(makamat)* by knowledgeable muezzins. Music and poetry was popular in sixth century Arabia as it was in the 'Abbasid courts. Thus, it was gradually incorporated into the ceremonies of the Sufi Orders, along with the chanting of Qur'an, some of the ninety-nine divine names *(esma)* of Allah, the mystic odes (which express the realization of the adepts), as well as the sacred rhythmic movements of the dhikr. These dhikr movements can only loosely be designated as "dance."

It is only degenerate music and poetry, as well as lewdly sensual dancing, which is actively discouraged by Islam, and the authentic Sufi Orders never included these in their ceremonies of Divine remembrance. Some poets of al-Ghazali's time, such as Omar Khayyam (of whom al-Ghazali was not enamored), did write allegorical poetry that may have seemed to extol wine-drinking and an earthly beloved rather than Allah. Yet, those who know the mystic symbolism of Persian poetry will see what is behind the metaphors; and even if they do not, the love poetry can still be appreciated as a secular realization of the truth that human love is a step on the way to divine love.

As Abu Hamid al-Ghazali would say, whether one makes use of music and poetry or avoids it, what is important is to penetrate into the depth of whatever form of worship one practices. He is scornful of those who regularly utter pious phrases which they don't actually take to heart, such as *"Na'udhib'illah!"* (I take refuge in God). In his *Ihya*, al-Ghazali says, "Shaitan laughs at such pious ejaculations. Those who utter them are like a man who should meet a lion in a desert, while there is a fort at no great distance, and, when he sees the evil beast, stands there exclaiming, 'I take refuge in that fortress,' without moving a step towards it. What will such an ejaculation profit him? In the same way the mere exclamation, 'I take refuge in Allah,' will not protect you from the terrors of His judgments unless you really take refuge in Him."[108]

It is the same with any practice or spiritual concentration, whether it be *salat*, fasting or reciting dhikr; one has to really enter into the spirit of the practice beyond the surface level to experience its optimum benefits. It is said that Rasulullah once offered to give his own mantle to any of his companions who could focus complete concentration during two *raka'at* of *salat*, without any stray thoughts whatsoever occurring to them. One of the companions who tried came very close, but in the end admitted that he had failed. "You looked very concentrated. What happened?" they inquired. He answered, addressing the holy Prophet, "I maintained

---

108 Ghazali, *Alchemy of Happiness*, 11.

perfect concentration until almost the end of the prayers, but when I realized I was about to be successful, the thought came to me, 'The Prophet has two cloaks. I wonder which one he will give me?'" They all laughed with him.

On the other hand, Hazrat 'Ali's absorption in *salat* was so complete that he felt no pain or outward sensations during his prayers. This fact came out when he was injured in battle. His thigh was pierced by an arrow which broke off and was going to be painful to remove. Hazrat 'Ali asked the others to wait until he was engaged in his *salat* and then remove it. They did so, and were able to remove the arrow, without 'Ali being aware of any pain. When he finished his prayer, 'Ali asked if they had removed it yet.

There are two further stories on this subject, on the lighter side, related by Muzaffer Efendi, about some not fully-concentrated imams of Ottoman times. One imam, a professional prayer leader, was leading the faithful in congregational *salat*, and just as he raised his hands to his ears to utter the traditional phrase, "*Allahu Akbar*," a *madzub* in the congregation—a man overwhelmed with divine intoxication—*mooed* loudly like a cow. Everyone continued to complete their prayers, but afterwards some of them asked him why he had *mooed* like that during the prayers. He told them, "I was inspired to *moo* the way a cow does when it wants food because the imam was leading the prayers, not for the sake of Allah, but for the wages he receives. My *moo* was just an imitation of him."

Another imam was leading Jum'a prayers one Friday, when his mind began to wander off from its concentration on the words of the *salat*. In his mind, he was planning ahead to later in the day when he would ride his donkey to his vineyard, but he realized he didn't have a stake with which to tether the animal. Suddenly, from the back, a *madzub* yelled out, "You need to lie down on your back and tie the animal just below your waist!" After this outburst, some of the congregation was ready to beat up the *madzub* over this impropriety, but the imam said, "Don't touch him; he was right. I was thinking about where to tie my donkey in my vineyard after the prayers, and he offered a suggestion."

Such stories illustrate, in passing, another point about the approach of Sufism, as compared to the purely scholastic, legal approach to the religious life: a teacher does not have to be dry or deadly serious to teach people how to live a spiritual life, especially one that includes joy. Certainly we could say of al-Ghazali that the light of mystical understanding, of deep insight into inner teachings of Islam, if not humor, made the difference between his remaining a half-forgotten Islamic jurist of the medieval period and the great reputation which he still enjoys today, even in the West. He is known as one who facilitated a measure of reconciliation between Islamic mysticism *(tasawwuf)* and the more legalistic, shariatic Islamic viewpoint.

The reader should note that we avoid saying, as many Orientalists do, that al-Ghazali reconciled mysticism with "orthodoxy." The schools of legal jurisprudence and *kalam* which arose simultaneously with the development of the mystical wing of Islam in the ninth century do not in themselves represent the one true orthodox view of Islam; nor can *tasawwuf* be accurately understood as some peripheral, even heretical addition to the faith, which could only later be grafted onto the main body of Islamic theology by some authority like al-Ghazali. Rather, the *shariat* and the *tarikat* are both intrinsic facets of Islamic orthopraxis, two wings of the faith which have coexisted from the time of the Prophet and are part of the primordial religion. Despite orientalist comparisons, the development of Islamic jurisprudence was never strictly analogous to the historical Church councils who legislated Christian orthodoxy with its precise creeds from whom no believer might legitimately deviate to the slightest degree. Ideally in Islam, there is much legitimate room for latitude within certain basic parameters of the faith; whenever Muslims have denied this, their stern intolerance has only signified a distortion of the faith. The sacred law without the mystical depths would be like a corpse without life-breath and heart, just as a mysticism devoid of a shariatic body of practices for the individual and community would suffer from lack of foundational structure like a will-o'-the-wisp without bodily container.

Some authors have doubted whether al-Ghazali can rightly be credited with any decisive reconciliation of these two poles or wings of the religion, especially when we note that one of his brother's dervishes, Ayn al-Qudat Hamadani, was executed for publicly teaching what was alleged to be Shi'ite-inspired *hululi* doctrines not long after Abu Hamid's death. Though he studied with Sheikh Yusuf an-Nassaj in Tus, Imam Abu Hamid Muhammad al-Ghazali never, himself, became a true *sheikh at-tarikat*, nor does he seriously figure into any of the major Sufi *silsilas*. Nevertheless, he stands as an important theologian in his time with mystical leanings, one who helped usher in the second major period of Islam, and was known as the "Reviver of the faith," and the "Proof of Islam *(Hujjat al-Islam)."* After his eleven years in meditation and self-imposed retirement, Abu-Hamid al-Ghazali was persuaded by the ruling sultan to teach once again in Baghdad. Toward the end of his life, he returned to Tus, where he associated with his followers at a Sufi convent until he died in 1111 CE.

SHEIKH AHMAD AL-GHAZALI

WHILE ABU-HAMID was generally possessed of a sober, scholarly disposition, his younger brother, Ahmad al-Ghazali (d.1126 CE), was a true ecstatic, a *sheikh at-tarikat* who found his affinities within the "drunken" school of Sufism. It was he, in fact, who played a significant role in his brother's decision to leave his post at the *Nizamiyya* and break his bonds with the world. One day when Abu-Hamid was preaching, his brother, Sheikh Ahmad, entered and recited:

> *You stretched out your hand to those who lagged behind, and now they have gone ahead of you.*
> *You chose the role of guide, but will not be guided;*
> *You preach, but do not listen.*

O whetstone, how long will you whet iron,
but will not let yourself be whetted?[109]

Like his brother, Sheikh Ahmad al-Ghazali was a writer. One of his most interesting texts is a treatise on the *sama*[110] entitled *Bawariq al-ilma*, in which he describes the kinds of mystical secrets, states of union, subtle lights and unveilings which can arise in the heart of the gnostic *(arif)* who attends the sama and is genuinely lifted up by the aid of sacred music and poetry. Citing supporting traditions, he insists that all of these things—including sacred music and reverent bodily movements (or "dance")—are fully in line with the *sunna* of the Prophet. He even asserts that jurists who are against these things are themselves, in reality, opposing the sunna. Sheikh Ahmad assumes an especially important role during this period, serving as sheikh for a number of prominent Sufis, the most renowned of them being Pir Diya'addin 'Abdul-Qahir Abu Najib as-Suhrawardi, the founding pir of the Suhrawardi tarikat as well as an esteemed pir in the Halveti-Jerrahi lineage.

PIR ABU-NAJIB AS-SUHRAWARDI

ABU-NAJIB WAS BORN in Suhraward in 1097. He was descended from the first caliph, Abu Bakr Siddiq, into a family with its own initiatic line *(nisbat al-khirqa)*. In his youth, Abu-Najib made his living as a water server. While still a young man, he left for Baghdad where he studied *usul al-fiqh* (jurisprudence) and much later in life accepted a teaching post at the same *Nizamiyya* college where both Ghazali brothers had taught.

After completing his studies, Abu Najib left the academic world for a time, receiving *bayat* from the hand of Sheikh Ahmad al-Ghazali, the mystic guide colorfully described in the old accounts

---

109 Murtada az-Zabidi, *Ithaf as-Sada*, 8.
110 *Sama* (lit. "the listening") indicates a recitation including music and poetry, often accompanied by whirling, as in the Mevlevi ceremonies.

Artist's copy of a Rembrandt sketch showing four great founding
pirs: (left to right;) 'Abdul Qadir Gaylani, Abu-Najib Suhrawardi,
Moinuddin Chisti and presumably the Naqshibandi Pir al-Hamadani.

as having "wafted the breath of felicity" *(nasim as-sa'adat)* upon
Abu Najib. Though Sheikh Ahmad was Abu Najib's primary guide
on the Sufi way, Abu Najib also received training from two others.
The first was his own uncle, Vejihiddin al-Qadi, the sheikh who
precedes him in the Halveti-Jerrahi silsila. The second was the
famous Sheikh Hammad ad-Dabbas (d.1131 CE), the master who
first summoned Sayyid 'Abdul Qadir Gaylani to the mystic path.

For a time, Abu Najib cut himself off from ordinary society and lived a secluded life, punctuated by lengthy retreats *(khalwa* or *khilvat)*. Gradually disciples came and received his guidance as the fame of his *baraka* began to spread. He built a *ribat* on a ruined site on the banks of the Tigris, and the lodge became a place of refuge. He gathered a number of distinguished disciples, two of whom subsequently served as khalifas of Najmaddin Kubra, the pir of the Kubrawiyya Order. Abu Najib's nephew, Shahabuddin Abu Hafs 'Umar as-Suhrawardi also studied at this ribat and helped found the Suhrawardi line. Inasmuch as Sheikh Abu Najib eventually emerged from his seclusion and returned to Baghdad to accept a teaching post, he conforms to a prevalent tendency among the great mystics of his era toward balancing academic scholarship with periods of seclusion and renunciation. This pattern culminates in an integrated re-emergence into the world during the sage's mature years, for the sake of serving humanity.

Abu Najib Suhrawardi is most famous for his manual on the rules of *adab* for the Sufi novices, *al-Kitab adab al-muridin. Adab* is an Arabic word referring to the courteous manners or etiquette on the path. Some common examples of *adab* would be: serving others before oneself, not raising one's voice in heated argument with one's brother or sister over some matter of faith or practice, not backbiting, gossiping, nor ever denying that another professed believer is a Muslim (since Allah alone best knows what is in one's heart). In matters of faith, a Muslim would never attribute sinful acts to the prophets (even what might outwardly resemble an error would come under Allah's guidance working toward some greater good); nor does a Muslim attribute the evil actions and intentions of humans to Allah's guidance, even though, essentially, everything comes from one Divine Source.

Other matters of *adab* more specifically within the sphere of the tarikat would include respect and deference to one's seniors on the path, especially one's sheikh; not chatting idly with someone else in the presence of the sheikh, nor leaving without paying one's respects to him. As the early twentieth century Halveti-Jerrahi grand-sheikh, Fahruddin Efendi, advised, the dervish should never leave the presence of the sheikh. Clearly this attitude of always being psychologically in the sheikh's presence extends to the experience of dwelling continually in the Divine Presence, as Hazrat Junayd's dervish did when he could not find any place "where no one could see him."

Abu Najib's text, for the most part, addresses novices *(muridin)* on the mystic way who were able to live together in community. He teaches them to "choose only pure food, drink and clothes," to "render service to one's brethren," to "associate with people of his kind and those from whom he can benefit," and not to "separate from his sheikh before the eye of his heart opens."[111] Another *adab* which he also endorses is the concept of *rukhsa* ("dispensation" or "indulgence"), which relaxes the obligation to fulfill some of the more severe ascetic practices. This was originally intended to make it easier for the lay community, but was later adopted by the whole brotherhood. (Later, the Suhrawardi Order would regain a reputation for strictness). The beloved Prophet, upon him be peace, said that "gracious manners *(husn al-adab)* are an important basis of the faith." In his manual, Abu Najib quotes this hadith and goes on to observe that "the whole of Sufism is *adab*; each moment *(waqt)*, each state *(hal)* and each spiritual station *(makam)* has its own *adab*."[112] Let us look at an example of adab in action.

One day Hazrat 'Ali was detained in starting out to the mosque for prayers; he had heard the *adhan* and was trying to walk there quickly but mindfully, hoping to arrive before the congregation, led by the Prophet, finished their first *ruku* (ritual bow). (At a certain point early in the salat, it becomes too late to join in and follow the sequence of the congregation, in which case one has to make an individual prayer.) Meanwhile outside the mosque, 'Ali came up behind an old woman who was walking very slowly ahead of him, and though he greatly desired to hurry into the mosque, out of *adab* (owing to respect for her age), he refused to scurry around her or rudely cut in front of the old woman, and instead patiently and slowly followed behind her until she finally passed by.

---

111 Abu-Najib Suhrawardi, *Adab al-muridin,* 26, 31, 34.
112 Milson, *A Sufi Rule for Novices,* 17.

Meanwhile inside, the Prophet, having begun the prayers on time, realized that 'Ali was running late and said a very long *sura,* deliberately prolonging the first part of the prayer. Finally, when he had finished the *sura* and felt he should not delay any longer, he uttered the customary, *"Allahu Akbar,"* and everyone bowed forward into the first *ruku.* Just then, Hazrat 'Ali entered and, seeing that he was still not too late, joined one of the rows of prayer and quickly caught up with the others. When the Prophet finally spoke the next words of the prayer, *"Sami Allahu liman hamida"* ("Allah has heard the one who glorifies Him."), 'Ali arose from the *ruku* along with the rest of the congregation and uttered an exuberant exclamation of thanks to Allah: *"Rabbana lakal-hamd!"* ("Our Lord, all praise is for You.") According to tradition, the Prophet was inspired to incorporate this beautifully spontaneous cry at that point in the prayer as a permanent responsory supplication in the salat. Born from a small, but significant, observance of *adab*, the resultant words of praise have remained as part of the salat ever since, for fourteen centuries.

Abu Najib Suhrawardi's *Manual of Adab* represents the first full-fledged set of guidelines for a mystic organization. In it, he details the basics of Islamic belief and theology, stressing the divine unity, then continues, outlining the adab and rituals of the Sufi path (poverty, love of Allah, the sama ritual, etc.). He mentions three grades of Sufis, each characterized by the adab proper to their level: the novice *(murid)*, the initiate *(mutawassit)* and gnostic *(arif)*. He also takes into account the *muhib*, or non-initiated friend or lover of the dervishes and their sheikh. Next, Suhrawardi gives an account of the stations *(makamat)* and states *(ahwal)* on the Sufi path, finishing with an account of how the Sufi faces certain tests in life, including illness and death. He stresses that, for those who realize it, illness is capable of purifying one—a fever can burn away sins or impurities—or, if there is little that needs to be purified, it is possible for illness to raise one's station to a higher *makam*. However, for the one who doesn't know its purpose, sickness is merely perceived as a valueless annoyance.

The Prophet Muhammad mentioned that those who die young or are innocent victims of war, starvation or disease, die as martyrs and easily attain paradise. Once a messenger came running to Rasulullah and informed him that the child of a certain woman in the community had just died. The Prophet asked the messenger to console her with the news that paradise is freely granted to those who trust in Allah and remain steadfast in their faith when faced with unavoidable suffering.

Having alluded to this potent secret, it may give added perspective to recount a story[113] from the nineteenth century, about the blessings that can come to the believer as the result of an illnesses such as cancer. At the same time, the story warns us that asking for patience to bear with an illness is not always the most appropriate response.

During the time of the sixteenth Halveti-Jerrahi grand-sheikh, Yahya Galib Efendi (the grandfather of Fahruddin Efendi), there was a sheikh who became very ill, with foul-smelling boils breaking out all over his body. The family built a shed behind their residence where he could lay, and the wife of the sheikh sought out Galib Efendi. She asked him to pray for her husband, either that he would recover or die soon and be out of his misery.

Galib Efendi came to see the sheikh and found him laying there in a terrible condition, repeating over and over to his Lord, "I patiently accept whatever You give me, and am satisfied with it." When Galib Efendi saw the sheikh's wretched situation and heard his prayer, he reached down and gave the man a hard slap on the body and said, "What are you doing? Do you think you're some sort of great martyr or *waliyullah* like Imam Husayn or Hazrat Yunus (Job)? Stop trying to be so patient and accepting of your afflictions, and repent!" The sick sheikh was surprised by this advice, but, seeing the wisdom of it, repented with tears and asked forgiveness of his Lord. His sores soon cleared up and he was well again.

This shows that illnesses are often brought on by internal conflicts which, once brought to light by the cells of the body and understood by the patient as a physical manifestation of toxic imbalances or constrictions in the psyche, can be released, having

---

113 As recounted by Safer Dal.

served their function. The illness is not a punishment by which the ailing one earns redemption through suffering, but a way in which the body reflects some inner situation that calls for purification. The wisdom of the body thus has something to teach the soul; illness can provide an opportunity to physically burn or clear away psychic toxicities through fever, coughing, boils, etc. An injury accident or near-death experience can serve to wake up the soul, while the bed-rest that accompanies a serious illness can provide much needed respite from over-activity and stress. Hence, we can see that the idea of turning to Allah, as that sheikh did, and asking for patience in order to continue suffering, rests on a misunderstanding of the place of saintly forbearance.

Returning to Suhrawardi's *Adab al-muridin*, we note that, while explicating the subject of *adab*, he includes a section on the various levels and states which the mystic experiences on the path. He uses a tripartite division, listing *makamat* (spiritual stations; plural of *makam), ahwal* (spiritual states; plural of *hal)* and a third division which includes such indescribable things as *fawatih* (revealed signs), *lawa'ih* (appearances of light), and *mana'ih* (graces). The first category, the *makam*, is the station or spiritual level of understanding upon which a soul is established for a certain period of time, while a *hal* is a passing spiritual state or peak experience, usually reaching higher than one's *makam* and at the same time providing a glimpse of states beyond one's present level which may eventually be part of one's station of realization.

Some of the *makamat* listed by Suhrawardi include: *inibah* (awakening out of carelessness), *tawba* (repentance), *intiba* (returning), *muhasabat an-nafs* (examination of the soul, or conscience), *faqr* (poverty), *sidq* (truthfulness), *tasabbur* (forbearance—the final station of the novice), *rida* (or *riza*— satisfaction), and last, *tawakkul* (absolute trust in God). One's spiritual level can be depicted through such *makamat*, representing, to some extent, the fruit of one's efforts to purify oneself and to arrive at some deep understanding of Reality. However, from the perspective of Sufism, one's level is ultimately granted to one by Allah, beyond one's own efforts or volition.

The *ahwal* (mystic states) are of a somewhat different nature from one's *makam* (station), coming to the individual through divine grace, but on a temporary basis. Abu Najib quotes Junayd, who defined the *ahwal* as forms of "inspiration which come down to the heart but do not stay in it permanently." (In one of his lists, Abu Najib even includes *fana* and *baqa* as *ahwal*, though these are usually included as stations *(makamat)* by other writers, such as Hujwiri and Abu'l Khayr. Other *ahwal* listed by Suhrawardi include: *qurb* (nearness), *mahabba* (love), *khawf* (fear or awe), *uns* (intimacy), *tuma'ina* (serenity), *yaqin* (certainty), and *mushahada* (experience of vision).[114]

In conclusion, we would note one other categorization by Abu Najib. He divides *tasawwuf* into three stages: first, the acquisition of knowledge; secondly, the assimilation of that knowledge by putting it into practice; and from there he says, one finally reaches to the stage of Allah's religion. The first stage lifts the curtain, giving one a sense of the goal; the second—putting it into practice—stimulates one's longing, while the deep truths of the religion of Allah, approached with profound self-knowledge, lead one to the ultimate goal.

OTHER NOTABLE SUFIS OF THE PERIOD

Shahabuddin 'Abu Hafs Umar Suhrawardi

THE SUCCESSOR OF Pir Abu Najib Suhrawardi in the Halveti-Jerrahi line was Sheikh Qutbuddin Abhari (d.1221 CE) and from him the chain of transmission proceeds within a few generations to the first two of five great masters who stand at the beginning of the Khalwati (Halveti) line, Pir Ibrahim Zahid Gaylani and Pir

---

114 Suhrawardi, *Adab al-muridin*, 20-21.

Muhammad ibn Nur al-Halveti. Before moving on to these masters of the tarikat and of the *khalwa* or *khilvat* (spiritual retreat), there are other important sheikhs of Abu Najib's time who deserve special mention, namely: Abu Najib's nephew, Shahabuddin Abu Hafs 'Umar Muhammad as-Suhrawardi, *Sayyid* 'Abdul Qadir Gaylani, *Sayyid* Ahmad Rifa'i, *Sayyid* Ahmad Badawi and Ibrahim Dusuki. all heads of important Sufi orders which began during this era.

Abu Najib also had several sons ('Abdul Rahim, 'Abdul Latif, and Sheikh Ziauddin) who helped develop the Suhrawardi tarikat, and may have been involved in the spread of the order to India and modern-day Pakistan. Another of his famous disciples was Sheikh 'Abdullah ibn Masood Rumi. But by far the most celebrated developer of the Suhrawardi Order was the son of Abu Najib's brother, Sheikh Shahabuddin 'Umar Suhrawardi (1145-1234 CE), who is sometimes credited with the actual founding of the *Suhrawardiyya*. Certainly, his widely-read and comprehensive treatise on the way of Sufi mysticism, *Awarif ul-Ma'arif*, became a classic in its field, expanding upon the more specific subject matter of his uncle's manual of adab to produce a full-fledged manual of Sufi discipline, with chapters on every facet of the Sufi path.

Shahabuddin himself related that when he was a young student at the Islamic university, he was very interested in philosophy and *'Ilm ul-Kalam*, memorizing several books on these subjects. His uncle, Abu Najib, tried to dissuade him from such pursuits and warned him of the possible harm arising from such studies, yet all his efforts were to little avail. Finally, one day, he took Shahabuddin with him to visit the sheikh whom everyone in Baghdad and beyond acknowledged as the greatest living saint and *qutb* of his age, Sayyid Sultan 'Abdul Qadir Gaylani. Pir 'Abdul Qadir looked at the young man and asked him what books he had studied. Shahabuddin proudly listed all the books on *kalam* and philosophy which he knew by heart; then the elder saint of Gaylan put his hand on Shahabuddin's heart for minute. As Shahabuddin relates it, suddenly he felt as if every word of all the books he had read faded from his memory, as if he had never read them. All interest in those speculative intellectual pursuits vanished and his heart was flooded in the ocean of Allah's love and mystic knowledge *(ma'arifat-i-Ilahi)*. 'Abdul Qadir then predicted, "You will be the most famed and respected man in Baghdad after me."[115] And indeed, he was to become the greatest sheikh and statesman of the generation following that of 'Abdul Qadir (to whom we will return shortly).

After this, Shahabuddin intensified his Sufi training and undertook a number of forty day spiritual retreats *(khalwat)* at his uncle's *ribat* and wrote his definitive manual of retreat and Sufi practice based on the inner and outer knowledge he received during this training. He was not to live out the life of a recluse. In accordance with his uncle's *rukhsas* which permitted the dervishes to work in society and even associate with heads of state, Shahabuddin entered into the service of the caliph, an-Nasir. The ruler appointed him *sheikh ash-shuyukh* (sheikh of sheikhs), the official Sufi master and *sheikh al-Islam* of the Baghdad capital. He also served as the caliph's ambassador to the Ayyubid rulers of Syria and Egypt and to the Turkish Seljuk capital of Konya, where the family of Mevlana Jalaluddin Rumi would settle a few decades later.

During this period, the long-reigning Caliph an-Nasir (1180-1225 CE) was engaged in a process of revitalizing the 'Abbasid dynasty and institutionalizing the *futuwwah* codes of chivalry. His aim was to reunite all the Islamic countries in a vast Sufi-inspired fraternal order whose noble ideals would bring the Muslims together to answer the threat of Mongol invasions, as well as attacks from Western Crusaders. The *sheikh ash-shuyukh*, Shahabuddin 'Umar Suhrawardi was an integral part of this design, functioning as Nasir's spiritual director and chief architect in a plan which was not only shrewd and effective politically, but also served to diffuse the sheikh's spiritual teaching throughout the *Dar al-Islam*. It is interesting to note that the sheikh, a former enthusiast of philosophy, participated whole-heartedly in Nasir's ideological attack against Greek philosophy, waged during this time. The *futuwwah* featured a number of customs, such as the investiture of "*futuwwah* trousers" and the girding of the novice with a special

---

115 Aziz Urfi, *Ghous ul Azam Dastgir,* 143-44.

belt and headgear, which represented clear parallels to the rites of the Sufis, with their conferring of the *khirqa* (dervish cloak) and *rakiye* (dervish cap). Besides initiatic rites, the *futuwwah* orders also emphasized a code of ethics which celebrated honor, bravery, and noble generosity—in a word, "spiritual chivalry"— and ritualized the practice of hunting and martial arts within its military ranks.

Throughout this period, the sheikh had a great influence on the people and was widely sought out for his counsels. He also traveled and taught a great deal, lodging in *khanaqas* in places such as Damascus and Aleppo. Caliph an-Nasir presided over the final moment of 'Abbasid glory before its inevitable decline. However, the *Suhrawardiyya,* as one of the first organized international Sufi orders—having come into high profile as a result of Sheikh Shahabuddin's fame—flourished steadily, spreading to India and throughout the Middle-East. It split off into many branches and survived as a family *ta'ifa* (organization), continued by Shahabuddin's sons and their heirs. One of the distinctive hallmarks of the order became its emphasis upon the continuous repetition of *La ilaha illallah*, until the remembrance of the tongue has become the remembrance of the heart.

Suhrawardi on the Khalwa (Spiritual Retreat)

Next we turn to a consideration of Shahabuddin Suhrawardi's classic treatise, *Awarif ul-Ma'arif,* focusing in particular upon his chapter on *khalwa (khilvat,* or in Turkish, *halvet).* His descriptions of the Sufi retreat are important in laying the groundwork for the formation of the Khalwati Order in the following century.

Sheikh Suhrawardi begins by noting that *khalwa*, in the way of the Sufis, is an innovation insofar as, during the twenty-three years of active prophethood, the *sunnat* of Muhammad consisted only of spiritual unfoldment within society (*suhbat*). Yet, the tradition of the forty day retreat or *khalwa* in seclusion, accompanied by some degree of fasting, actually dates from the time of the earlier prophets, such as Moses and Jesus, and from Muhammad's retirement to the caves of Mt. Hira before he announced his prophecy. After the time of the companions of the Prophet Muhammad, society became overwhelmed so that *khalwa*, a period of spiritual renewal and repose away from the crowd, become not only attractive, but *wajib* (necessary) for mystics on the path of spiritual attainment.

For the one who undertakes the forty day *khalwa*, under the guidance of an experienced master, "every morning, a veil should lift and a nearness (to Allah) appear, so that in forty mornings, the forty-fold veil should lift," revealing divine wisdom *(hikmat)* and eternal knowledge to the heart of the retreatant.[116] Retreat conduct includes: very little eating and sleeping, silence, shunning society, repeating *dhikr*, negating conventional thoughts in favor of contemplation, and practicing *riyadat* (ascetic spiritual practice, the austerity of abandoning desire). The daily rhythm of five obligatory periods of *salat* is also retained throughout the retreat. Suhrawardi recommends an annual retreat, but says that the *khalwa* does not have to last a full forty days. However, experience has shown that the manifestation (of Allah's bounty) begins to appear after the completion of the fortieth day of retreat. The sole object is to attain to a state of divine nearness. As the desires concerning this world and the next are put away, and the activity of the *nafs* begins to fade, the heart becomes cleansed and peaceful, allowing true thoughts and unattainable knowledge to arise from the depth of the spiritual heart.

Next, Suhrawardi expounds upon the dreams and grades of revelation that may come to the one on *khalwa*. The dream or *waqi'ah* can have elements of *ruh*—revealing the soul's truth—as well as *nafs*—coloring the dream with the ego's false distortions; so some dreams can be true, others false, still others confused and uninterpretable. However what is called *mukashafah*, represents revelation coming from a state of union in the soul, devoid of earthly

---

116 Suhrawardi, *Awarif ul-Ma'arif,* 72.

thoughts, and is never false. An example of this is given from the life of the Caliph 'Umar. Once, while delivering the *khutba* (sermon) to the people of Medina, he saw in a flash of *mukashafah*, his officer Sariyah, whom he had sent out with an army to Nihazar not long before, about to be ambushed. 'Umar stopped his sermon and cried out, "O Sariyah! (go) to the mountain!" Sariyah heard, went to the mountain and gained the victory.

Dervishes in retreat.

If in sleep one dreams of something that one didn't previously know, such as the location of a treasure, and upon waking finds that it is true, this is called *kashf-i-mujarrad*, pure revelation or insight. On the other hand, imaginary or fancied revelations are called *kashf-i-mukhayyal*; whether they occur in waking or sleeping-dream, these are revelations in which the soul's true understanding, by the power of the imagination, puts on a suitable fanciful garment, thereby rendering it in some sense false, but not totally false, since it is not void of the soul's understanding. A third possibility is that one dreams self-aggrandizing dreams which a true sheikh will recognize as being purely the result of vain desire or compensation. In these, the truth never appears because, in it, the *nafs* is devoid of the partnership of the *ruh* (soul or spirit).[117] Such are a few of the explanations of khalwat and dreams provided by Sheikh Suhrawardi in his *Awarif ul-Ma'arif*.

---

117 Ibid, 84-92.

Yahya Suhrawardi, the Martyr

We should mention, in passing, one further famous mystic from Suhraward, Yahya Shahabuddin Suhrawardi (1154-1191 CE), the martyr, who became the victim of shifting court sympathies and was executed at the age of 38 in Syria. He represents a tendency, also being mirrored in Islamic Spain at the same time, of incorporating Neo-Platonic and Hermetic wisdom into the body of Islamic mystical teachings.

This young Persian master of "the theosophy of illumination" *(ishraq)* was also boldly bringing elements of gnostic Zoroastrian metaphysics into *tasawwuf*. These involved a hierarchy of angelic presences whose light is part of the *Nur* of Allah, the Supreme deity, idealized as the Light of Lights, the Radiant Source Who illuminates the soul with divine light as it progresses on the spiritual path. In the equivalent language of Qur'an, he is describing *"Nurun 'ala nur,"* (Light upon light: the divine light of the Original Source illuminating the soul, whose inner light is derived from and returns to "the orient of light.")

Suhrawardi, a favored friend of the Syrian governor, al-Malik al-Zahir al-Ghazi (the son of Saladin), became known as *al-Maqtul* (the slain), after he fell foul of the religious authorities and was executed on orders of Saladin. Suhrawardi penned a number of treatises on Sufism before his death, several of which have been translated into English by Henri Corbin.

Pir 'Abdul Qadir Gaylani

We now turn to one of the greatest masters of the tarikat, known as *Ghous ul-Azam* (the Greatest Helper) and *Pir-i Piran* (Saint of Saints), the noble founding pir of the *Qadiriyya* order, Sayyid

Sultan Muhyiddin 'Abdul Qadir Gaylani (1078-1166 CE). His greatness was acknowledged by all of the saints and sheikhs of his time, including Pir Abu Najib Suhrawardi and his khalifa, Sheikh Shahabuddin 'Umar, who said of 'Abdul Qadir: "He is unique among the saints, and has no match in the spiritual world. Why should I not respect him, since he has been granted superiority over all the saints by Almighty Allah?" Still another highly-venerated Sufi master of that time, a relative of 'Abdul Qadir and founder of the *Rifa'iyya* Order, Pir Ahmad Rifa'i, testified concerning him: "No other saint has been so honored by Allah with powers as the Saint of Gaylan. He deserves the high station he occupies, and is the only saint who has been elevated to such an exalted position."[118]

Shrine of 'Abdul Qadir Gaylani in Baghdad

Just two years after the launch of the first crusade, 'Abdul Qadir was born in Bushteer, in the Persian province of Guilan or Gaylan.[119] 'Abdul Qadir was a *sayyid*, a descendent of the Prophet on both sides of his family, through Imam Hasan on his father's

118 Urfi, 157.

119 Note: the name of this province has been transliterated into English with a variety of different spellings, including: Geylan, Gilan, arabicized to al-Jil or al-Jilan; this also carries over to his name, 'Abdul Qadir [Kadr, Kadir] al-Jilani, etc. In the Kadiri orders of Turkey and Egypt Gaylani is pronounced with a hard "G".

side and from Imam Husayn on his mother's side. When the illustrious order bearing 'Abdul Qadir's name came into being, its *silsila* read very much like the silsila of the Halveti-Jerrahi lineage, from Hazrat 'Ali and Hasan Basri down to Pir Junayd. From Junayd, the Qadiri Order passes to Sheikh Abu Bakr Shibli, to Sheikh 'Abdul Wahid Tamini, to Sheikh 'Abdul Farah Tartoosi, to Sheikh Abu'l Hasan Qarashi, to Sheikh Abu Sayyid al-Mubarak ibn 'Ali Muharrami, and finally to the founding pir of the *Qadiriyya* order, Sheikh 'Abdul Qadir Gaylani.[120]

Sayyid Abdul Qadir Gaylani and
Sayyid Ahmad Rifa'i

Tradition has it that as a newborn baby, 'Abdul Qadir refused his mother's milk every day during Ramadan until sunset, thus keeping the fast and amazing those who witnessed this remarkable sign. He became a hafiz, having memorized the entire Qur'an before his eighteenth birthday, at which time he set out for Baghdad in search of knowledge. His mother sowed forty dinars in the lining of his coat and in parting, made him promise to always tell the truth in every situation. During the journey to Baghdad, his caravan was attacked by highwaymen who robbed everyone, but couldn't find 'Abdul Qadir's hidden money. When they asked him, as they were leaving, whether he had any money, he astounded them by truthfully answering, "yes" and even volunteering where it was hidden. Upon confirming the truth of these statements and

---

120 Another version of the Qadiri *silsila* passes from Imam 'Ali, to Imam Hasan and Imam Husayn, on down through several of the other twelve Imams, including Imam Jafar as-Sadiq, before reaching Junayd.

hearing 'Abdul Qadir explain that he had acted according to his mother's advice, since his journey to find true knowledge could not begin on a foundation of deceit, the robber chief's heart was touched. He decided to return everyone's money in the caravan and renew his allegiance to Islam, as did all sixty of the other bandits who followed him.

'Abdul Qadir made his way to Baghdad at a time when the Iraqi capital was still a great center of learning, though it had become somewhat secularized and factionalized due to the pull of various rival political and religious groups: Seljuks, Fatimids, Batinis, Hanbalites, Shi'is, Isma'ilis, and 'Abbasids. A climate of political instability and chaos was in the air; the Assassins had become a terror among the Muslims, murdering a number of caliphs and high-ranking members of the 'Abbasid government. Furthermore, the Crusaders had recently captured the *Bayt-ul Muqaddas*, the Temple Mosque in Jerusalem, killing 70,000 Islamic scholars, an event which had left a great shortage of knowledgeable teachers for the Muslims, and whose effect could be felt even in Baghdad, where Imam Ghazali had recently passed away.

When 'Abdul Qadir arrived there, he secured admission into the renowned *Jamia*, or university, the *Bab al-Azj*, where Qadi Abu Sayyid al-Mubarak ibn 'Ali al-Muharrami served as head teacher and college administrator. There, 'Abdul Qadir studied Hanbalite *fiqh* (Islamic jurisprudence), specializing in hadith and graduating with honors, a favorite pupil of Abu Sayyid Muharrami. Another tradition relates that Hazrat Khidr met 'Abdul Qadir at the gates of Baghdad when he first arrived from Gaylan and communicated to him Allah's order that he was forbidden to enter the city for seven years. Then Khidr led him to a desert ruin where he spent years praying, fasting and struggling to perfect himself. He would pray all night and go for days without food or water, exposed to the heat and cold of the wilderness. On more than one occasion he refused food although he was quite starved; the reason being that, as a *sayyid*, there remained doubt as to whether it was permissible for him to consume this food.

At the end of this period of isolation and soul purification, 'Abdul Qadir was at last directed to go to Baghdad, serve the people, and associate with Abu Sayyid Muharrami. Both traditions which we have mentioned agree that Abu Sayyid bestowed his own *khirqa* (cloak) upon him and gave him *Khilafat* (deputyship), predicting that people would flock to 'Abdul Qadir, who would infuse new life in the waning *Din-i-Muhammad* (Islamic faith). He further predicted that 'Abdul Qadir would become "a highly revered saint," saying: "at his call, all the saints will acknowledge his superiority."[121]

Later, 'Abdul Qadir would settle in Baghdad and accept a professorship at Abu Sayyid's *Jamia*, but first he embarked on a course of travel, as far as Ceylon. His goal was to bring Islamic knowledge to the illiterate peasants beyond the capital cities, given his sense that there had been a great deterioration of the most basic knowledge of the religion in the outlying regions. During his travels, 'Abdul Qadir witnessed first hand not only the refugee problems which the Crusades had caused throughout Iraq, but was dismayed to find that in many towns, no one possessed even such rudimentary knowledge of Islam as how to properly perform salat, including the local imams and scholars. Pondering on how best to redress this situation, he received divine guidance inspiring him to return to Baghdad and begin training people who could be sent out all over the Muslim world.

At age forty, 'Abdul Qadir returned to Baghdad and rejoined his teacher at the *Bab al-Azj*. He began to live a simple life, trying to avoid the degenerate spirit which prevailed in Baghdad's high society with its corrupt political regime. Finally he became so uncomfortable living in Baghdad that he decided to abandon the capital once and for all. He made it as far as the outskirts of the city before a divine voice stopped him and ordered him to return. He spent that night in Baghdad in a state of prayer and supplication for divine guidance. He was in for a surprise the following day.

While walking through a neighborhood called Muzaffariyya, an old sheikh called out to him from a door-way, saying "O 'Abdul Qadir, where were you going yesterday and what did you pray for last night?" 'Abdul Qadir turned in amazement just in time to catch

---

121 Ibid, 30.

a glimpse of a white-bearded man before the door closed, raising dust everywhere. Uncertain as to whether he should approach that door, 'Abdul Qadir walked on, trying to remember what he had prayed for. When he remembered, he stopped and tried to return but couldn't find the house again. By now, 'Abdul Qadir was thoroughly intrigued by the sheikh's words; he realized that the sage was very close to Allah, and felt a great longing to meet him again.

A few days later, he encountered the sheikh in the market and was invited to his house, where he would soon receive *bayat* from him. He was Sheikh Hammad ad-Dabbas, well-known in Baghdad Sufi circles as a great master of the tarikat, with as many as 1,200 dervishes. His profound mastery of the heart was in marked contrast to the intellectual knowledge of *fiqh* which 'Abdul Qadir had received from others, such as Abu Sayyid Muharrami. The scholars and jurists in those days were quite isolated from the people of *tasawwuf*, so it took a great deal of courage for 'Abdul Qadir to attend his sheikh's *sohbets* at the local *tekke*, where some of the other dervishes would tease him about being out of his scholarly element. 'Abdul Qadir continued to study with other scholars but always returned to Sheikh Dabbas when the others could not answer his questions. He stayed with him until the sheikh passed away in 1130 CE. His other principal teacher, Abu Sayyid, died in 1119, after turning over the leadership of his *Jamia* to 'Abdul Qadir.

During this period, 'Abdul Qadir married four wives, with whom he was to produce forty-nine children. He spent time educating both his daughters and his sons. One of his daughters, Seyyidah Zahra, became a scholar of hadith and taught women students, while a number of his sons were prominent in the tarikat. Though 'Abdul Qadir was a Hanbalite jurist, he was made a guardian of the tomb of Imam Abu Hanifa for several years.

Around that time, a new caliph came to power. He was more spiritually inclined than his more secular predecessors and began to work toward the revival of the shariat. Meanwhile, the *Jamia* grew in size and stature with 'Abdul Qadir at its head, but because he was an *Ajami*, a Persian whose command of Arabic was not perfect, he held back for many years from preaching in public. In his fiftieth year, he received a vision in which he was directed by the Prophet Muhammad to preach to the people, despite any insecurities about his fluency in Arabic.

After this, he began to speak publicly, and did so with great confidence, soon becoming a famous orator as well as a teacher. People of all persuasions and even other religions began to crowd into the mosque where he spoke, until a succession of larger gathering-places had to be found. Ultimately, he had to speak to the crowds outdoors when the audience swelled to as many as 70,000 people. At such times, vast lines would form to accept Islam directly from the hand of the saint. 'Abdul Qadir became an advocate of justice for the people and was fearless in speaking out against government corruption and oppression. He warned the caliph by name on a number of occasions, resulting in immediate corrective policy changes. The caliph, Muqtafi al-Amar Allah was in awe of 'Abdul Qadir and actually became his devotee; he would attend the lectures and humbly kiss the sheikh's hand with the rest of the crowd, seeking his blessing.

'Abdul Qadir had great compassion for the people and helped establish free places of lodging for travelers and the destitute, as he advocated giving "both to the deserving and undeserving, just as Allah gives to all without differentiation between the worthy and the unworthy."[122] The people began to turn to him and called him *Pir Dastgir*, meaning in Persian "the great succorer—the one who clasps the hand of those who are falling and saves them." Though he was gentle and loving by nature, he could also be severe in standing up to injustice. Once, when he issued a warning to the caliph, the caliph sent his minister to see if he could get 'Abdul Qadir to tone down his threats and public criticism of the caliph's affairs; but when the minister joined the vast crowd who had gathered to listen to the saint, he heard 'Abdul Qadir say, "Indeed, I would behead him too!" Sensing that this referred to himself as well as the caliph, the vezir was terrified and hurried back to tell the caliph what he had heard. The caliph wept and said, "Truly, the

---

122 *Bahjatul Asrar,* 305-06. (quoted in Urfi, *Ghous ul Azam Dastgir).*

Sheikh is great."[123]

On another occasion a young woman in Ceylon, who was a follower of 'Abdul Qadir, had gone out to a lonely place and found herself about to be attacked by a strange man. She cried out to 'Abdul Qadir to save her, and at that moment the sheikh, who was making his ablutions in a public place, stopped and angrily threw his wooden shoe up into the air so that it disappeared from sight, descending upon, and killing the attacker in Ceylon.[124]

As the sheikh grew older and closer to Allah, his *karamat* (miracles) increased, and all his prayers seemed to be answered. Finally, his superiority over the other saints was brought out in a sermon at his *ribat* in which he was inspired to say: "My foot is on the neck of all saints," a metaphor, meaning that the path he trod—his tarikat—was unequaled in his day. All of the scholars and sheikhs who heard this, and those outside Baghdad as well, attested to the truth of this. Among those who confirmed this were such notables as Pir Abu Najib Suhrawardi, 'Abdul Qadir's nephew, Sayyid Ahmad Rifa'i, as well as another young maternal nephew in Ajmer, Khwaja Moinuddin Chisti, who came to visit his uncle for several months after this announcement and himself became the great founding pir of Sufism in India, the head of the noble *Chistiyya* tarikat.

Though the development of Sufism in the Indian subcontinent lies outside the immediate scope of this book, we would note in passing that Islam was introduced and accepted in that part of the world, not by means of a legalistic, militant, Islamic approach, but primarily by Sufis who were tolerant of the indigenous Hindu traditions. They emphasized the commonality of truth within the various mystic traditions wherever they found them. Hazrat Inayat Khan, the first Sufi master to bring *tasawwuf* to the West,[125] received his training in the Chisti Order,

---

123 Al-Jilani/Tosun Bayrak, *The Secret of Secrets*, xxiv-xxv.
124 Ibid, xxvi.
125 Hazrat Inayat Khan (1882-1926), born into a Muslim family of musicians in Baroda, India, brought Sufism to Europe and America, beginning in 1910, spreading the message in a very universal form which emphasized respect for all the world's major religious traditions.

and also studied the other three prominent *turuq* of India: the Suhrawardiyya, the Naqshbandiyya, and the Qadiriyya (which spread to India in the centuries following 'Abdul Qadir's passing).

When 'Abdul Qadir Gaylani preached, the people of Baghdad used to sit spellbound in silence, but by the climax of his sermon hundreds of them would be weeping in repentance. The sheikh himself recounted that on one occasion, as many as one-hundred thousand people of ill-repute repented before him, and received hand at the end of his sermon. One day, one of 'Abdul Qadir's sons, Sheikh Sayfuddin Sayyid 'Abdul Wahhab, a prominent scholar in the community, asked his father if he, 'Abdul Wahhab, could address the people who had gathered to hear his father speak. Having obtained 'Abdul Qadir's smiling permission, 'Abdul Wahhab addressed the congregation in his finest oratorical style, including as many fine points of learning as he could, but try as he might, he felt unsatisfied with his talk and realized that he was simply not capturing the interest of the audience.

After he finished, his father went to the *minbar* just to add a few words. He said: "Umme Yahya [his wife] fried a few eggs and put them away in a bowl for her husband's meal. The bowl was kept in a hanger suspended from the roof. Meanwhile, a cat jumped at the hanger, the fried eggs dropped down and were eaten by the cat ..." No sooner had he finished with this simple story, than the people became overwhelmed with emotion, deeply satisfied just to hear a few words from the saint. Later, 'Abdul Wahhab asked his father why the people were so uninterested during his initial sermon, which he gave to the best of his ability, while they were deeply moved when 'Abdul Qadir stood up and spoke a few words of no great significance. The sheikh smiled and answered: "Son, when you spoke, you relied on your acquired knowledge, but when I delivered the sermon, I relied on Allah. I speak with absolute faith that whatever comes out of my mouth is from Him."[126]

On another occasion, the people gathered to hear 'Abdul Qadir speak, but he sat there quietly not saying a word. Then the congregation felt a strange ecstasy and quietness of mind that

---

126 Urfi, 81-82.

made them wonder what the sheikh was experiencing. Sensing their question, he finally spoke, saying, "Just now a man was transported from Mecca to Baghdad in an instant, repented in my presence, and flew back." Then the thought arose amongst them: "Why should a man who could fly in an instant from Mecca to Baghdad need to repent?" 'Abdul Qadir answered: "To fly in the air is one thing, but to feel love is something else. I taught him how to love."[127]

A Turkish mystic hymn, often sung in dervish dhikr circles, extols this great Sultan of the saints in the following words (as freely rendered in English by Sheikh Nur al-Jerrahi):

> *None can equal him, Prophets by his side;*
> *Light of the whole earth, Exalted by Allah;*
> *Souls amazed, angels amazed by his sanctity,*
> *Sayyid Sultan 'Abdul Qadir Gaylani.*
>
> *Qutb of the Wise, Axis of the Saints;*
> *The Throne and the Pen shine within his heart.*
> *Souls amazed, angels amazed by his mastery,*
> *Sayyid Sultan 'Abdul Qadir Gaylani.*
>
> *Roads from Baghdad flow with his sweet presence;*
> *I am his dervish beyond both the worlds.*
> *Renounce division, Truth is one pure identity,*
> *Sayyid Sultan 'Abdul Qadir Gaylani.*

Several collections of writings have come down to us from Sheikh Muhyiddin 'Abdul Qadir Gaylani; two are collections of sermons from his *ribat*, entitled, *Al-Fath ar-Rabbani* (The Conquest of the Divine) and *Ghunyat at-Talibin* (Wealth for Seekers). Two others, which deal more directly with the mystical principles of Sufism, are: *Futuh al-Ghayb* (Revelations of the Unseen) and *Sirr al-Asrar* (The Secret of Secrets). In the last mentioned work, the sheikh delves into the mysteries of the spiritual heart. He mentions the Qur'anic injunction, "Guard the prayers, especially the middle

---

127 Jilani/Bayrak, xxxi.

one,"[128] which is often taken to mean something like: "Be sure to do all the obligatory *(farz)* prayers, and don't become so busy that you forget to do the third prayer *('asr)* in the middle of the afternoon." Rather, says 'Abdul Qadir, the first phrase refers to the participation of the material body and self in the movements of the prayers, while "the middle prayer" refers to the prayer of the heart, because the heart is in the middle of the body, the central point of balance for the entire being.[129] Sayyid 'Abdul Qadir goes on to explain:

> True worship is the worship of the heart. If one's heart is heedless of true worship, the ritual prayer of the material self is in disorder. When this happens, the peace of the material self that one hopes to obtain from ritual prayer is most realized. That is why the Prophet (peace and blessings be upon him) says, "Ritual worship is only possible with a quiet heart."[130]

'Abdul Qadir says that during prayer, servant and Lord are able to meet in the heart, but only if the heart is open and not closed down. It was to this end that the Prophet said: "There is a piece of flesh in the body; when it is in a good state, it strengthens the whole being, but when it is in a bad state, it weakens the whole being. Take heed: it is the heart." The sheikh continues, noting that the outer ritual prayer is performed with standing, bowing, and prostrating five times a day, facing Mecca, optimally with a congregation and imam in a mosque. Then he describes the prayer of the heart, saying:

> The time for inner worship is timeless and endless, for the whole life here and in the hereafter. The mosque for this prayer is the heart. The congregation is the inner faculties, which remember and recite the Names of the unity of Allah

---

128 Qur'an 2:38.
129 The spiritual heart or heart chakra resides in the center of the breast; its wisdom and divine inspiration goes far deeper than the emotions of the conventional heart or any ego-centric feelings.
130 Jilani/Bayrak 74.

in the language of the inner world. The leader of this prayer is the irresistible wish. The direction of prayer is toward the oneness of Allah—which is everywhere—and His eternal nature and beauty. The true heart is the one which can perform such a prayer . . . When the ritual worship of the material being and the inner worship of the heart unite, the prayer is complete. It is perfect worship, and its rewards are great. It brings spirituality to the realms of the proximity of Allah, and physically to the highest level of one's possibility.[131]

'Abdul Qadir's Teaching on the Spiritual Heart

In *The Secret of Secrets*, 'Abdul Qadir goes on to describe the inner layers of the heart and the souls which reside therein. He describes four levels of the heart, corresponding to the four spiritual realms: shariat *(sadr,* the outer heart), tarikat *(qalb,* the inner, spiritual heart), hakikat *(fu'ad,* the heart of hearts), and marifat *(lubb,* the transcendent kernel of the heart).

The outermost chamber of the heart, the breast *(sadr* in Arabic), houses the human soul, and is connected with the senses and the surface of the mind, forming a bridge between the inner and outer worlds. The breast is the place of struggle between the potential negative propensities of the *nafs* and the positive influence of righteous decision and action. It reflects the light of shariat, which is in turn supported by the light of faith, which illuminates the next, more inward level of the heart *(qalb).*

The heart is the home of the *moving soul* or *angelic soul,* and its concern is with the inner world and following the spiritual path—the level of tarikat. With the angelic realm constantly within its view, this level forms still another bridge, connecting the human and the divine qualities of the heart. The *qalb,* the spiritual heart, exists

---

131 Ibid, 74-75.

as Allah's treasure-house, the seat of pure luminous wisdom and guidance, which is untouched by any tarnishing effect that might result from the human *nafs*. The clouds of darkness, confusion and unbelief can only veil, but not extinguish nor penetrate the brilliant divine light radiating from the spiritual heart.

The further depths of the center of the heart *(fu'ad)*, or heart of hearts, is the locale where the sultan soul is found, the soul corresponding to the level of *Firdaws*, or heavenly paradise in the hereafter. The station of this inner heart corresponds to the hakikat, the heart which sees the inner truth of things. 'Abdul Qadir contrasts the vision of the outward part of the heart with that of the inward heart's perception, saying: "The outer knowledge of appearances is like rainwater, which comes and goes, while the inner knowledge is like a fountain whose source never runs dry." One simply has to purify the heart and dig deep enough to tap into that luminous fountain of wisdom, which everyone has within them. That is why the Prophet said, "If anyone spends forty days in sincerity and purity, the source of wisdom will gush from his heart to his tongue."

The innermost level of the heart, which corresponds to the station of marifat and the secret of secrets soul, is called the *lubb*, the very kernel of the heart. Around this divine heart, which has descended from on high, the *fu'ad* forms a buffer which shields it from creation, a very fine and special nonphysical container, a temple in the heart which houses Allah on His holy throne. 'Abdul Qadir says that one spark from this divine heart could cause the material world to burst into flames, destroying all of creation. Its vision is secret; its light is the light of unity. As 'Abdul Qadir says, "The station where the Holy Spirit reigns is the secret place that Allah made for Himself in the center of the heart, where He deposited His secret *(sirr)* for safekeeping." This mystery was alluded to by the holy Prophet when he spoke on behalf of Allah Most High, saying: "Humanity is My secret and I am the secret of humanity."[132] The divine mystery of the innermost heart was also mentioned in another *hadith qudsi* in which Allah says: "My heavens and my earths are not vast enough to contain Me; and yet,

---

132 Ibid, 23-24.

the heart of my sincere, loving servant does contain Me."

When the layers of the heart have been purified, the eye of the heart is able to open and see heavenly inspirations reflected in the mirror of the heart. Then the Truth becomes evident without distortion; this is possible because, as the Rasulullah expressed it, "The faithful sees by the light of Allah."

In his tarikat, 'Abdul Qadir systematized the noble seven steps, the original number of divine names given on the mystic path. These first seven names, or *esma-i saba*, are given by the sheikh to the dervish in sequence, but only as he or she is ready for them. They are: *La ilaha illallah, Allah, Hu, Haqq, Hayy, Qayyum, and Qahhar.* In *The Secret of Secrets*,[133] 'Abdul Qadir goes on to mention twelve *esmas* or divine names, extending by five names the basic seven *esmas*. Later on, these twelve names would be used by the Khalwati (Halveti) order to signify the number of stations through which the dervish passed before becoming a sheikh. Eventually, other mystic orders would use fourteen, then twenty-one names; and finally, in the time of Hazrati Pir Nureddin Jerrahi, by divine inspiration, the number would be increased to twenty-eight divine names.

'Abdul Qadir lived to the age of 91 and actively continued his work until his final breath on the eleventh of Rabi II, 561 A.H. (1166 CE). Two of 'Abdul Qadir's sons, 'Abdul Razzaq and 'Abdul Aziz, carried on their father's teachings and helped establish the order on the scale of a true movement, which would eventually become one of the largest and most important *turuq* in the world. Eshrefoghlu 'Abdullah Rumi (d.1469) and Ismail Rumi (d.1631), who both trained with the Khalwatis, helped establish the Qadiriyya respectively in Anatolia, then in Istanbul. Besides Turkey, the order has also become popular in North Africa, Iraq and throughout the Balkans. Thus, the green and white turban of the Qadiri (Kadiri) order would come to be worn by thousands of sheikhs over the centuries. The *türbe* or tomb of 'Abdul Qadir remains one of the holiest sites in Baghdad to this day. Even in the Gulf war of 1991, and again in 2003, the Western powers

---

133 Ibid, 77.

were careful not to bomb the final resting place of this powerful protecting saint during their repeated missile attacks on Baghdad.

Besides the respected title, *Ghous ul-Azam*, some of the many spiritual sobriquets bestowed upon Sayyid 'Abdul Qadir Gaylani included: *Muhyiddin* (Reviver of the Faith), *Baz al-ashhab* (Grey Falcon or Hawk), *Sultan al-awliya* (Sovereign of Saints), *Taj al-muhaqqiqin* (Crown of the People of Truth), *Burhan Allah* (Proof of God), *Sayf Allah* (Sword of God), and *Sultan al-arifin* (King of the Gnostic Initiates). His given Arabic name, 'Abdul Qadir, means the Servant of Divine Power.

As we have mentioned, the period during and following 'Abdul Qadir's lifetime was a very rich era in terms of the formation of Sufi fraternities; a number of great founding pirs lived and interacted with each other during the twelfth and thirteenth centuries CE. 'Abdul Qadir Gaylani was the first of four major *qutbs* of that time, known as the *Aktab-i-arwah*, the Masters of the souls. Though a number of other Sufi pirs and saints lived during this period, these four pirs are endowed with a special significance, akin to the four khalifas of Rasulullah, peace and blessings be upon him.

Each of them also was known by a special tarikat title. Sayyid Ahmad Rifa'i (d.1182 CE), is called *Abu'l-Alamayn*, the Father of the Two Worlds; after him, Sayyid Ahmad Badawi (d.1276 CE) became known as *Abu'l-Aynayn*, the Father of Two Noble Lines (the tarikat transmission through the lines of both Hazrat 'Ali and Hazrat Abu Bakr Siddiq); and finally, Ibrahim Dusuki (d.1288 CE) was dubbed *Abu'l-Uyun*, the Father of the Eyes (i.e., mystic insight), as well as *al-Sheikh al-Arab* (the teacher of the Arabs). Somewhat later in time, the noble Halveti-Jerrahi pir of Istanbul, Muhammad Nureddin Jerrahi (d.1721), would be the direct recipient of the gift of the exalted spiritual influence of these four qutbs, and would be acknowledged by the rank and spiritual title of *Hatem-al Mujtahidin*, the Seal of the Pirs; he is also called *Abu Füyuzat* (the Father of Spiritual Emanations, or Knowledge).

Among the dervishes, there is an adage, which succinctly describes the spiritual *meshreb* (attunement) of each of these *qutbs* and their *khalifas*: If you walk with a Qadiri sheikh, you will experience time speeding up or stopping, or have the sensation of flying. If you walk with a Rifa'i sheikh, you will feel emanations of great power, or perhaps be protected from some passing danger. If you walk with a Badawi sheikh, you will experience great beauty, and people will begin to notice you. If you walk with a Dusuki sheikh, you will experience *nazar*, the power to attract with spiritual love. And finally, if you walk with a Jerrahi sheikh, you will feel dead hearts coming alive with divine love *(ashk or ishq)*.

Pir Ahmad Rifa'i

Sayyid Ahmad ibn 'Ali ar-Rifa'i (1106/1118-1182 CE) was born into an Arab family in the Bata'ih section of southern Iraq, near Basra, in the village of Umm 'Ubayda, where he spent most of his life. Not much is known about his history, although a number of his sayings and writings have been preserved, including his two most well-known works: *al-Burhan al-Muayyad* (The Confirmed Proof) and *al-Hikam* (The Wisdom).

Orphaned at the tender age of seven, Ahmad was raised by his maternal uncle, Mansur (Rabbani) al-Bata'ihi (d.1145 CE), who bequeathed to him a family *silsila*, which he developed into a highly popular order. Ahmad did not choose the life of an university professor in *fiqh* like 'Abdul Qadir in the Baghdad capital; however, he did become a hafiz at the early age of eight and became well-versed in Islamic law through his studies in the Shafi'ite school. Rather than a scholar, he best fits the prototype of the naturally ecstatic holy man, a compassionate man, known for kind acts of generosity, such as gathering firewood for poor widows and orphans.

Before Ahmad's birth, his uncle, Sheikh Mansur, had a vision of the Prophet, who informed him that Mansur's sister would give birth to a male child who would become famous and be known by the name "Rifa'i" (meaning "exalted"). He was further instructed that, upon reaching the proper age, the child was to be educated by Sheikh 'Ali Abu'l-Fazl al-Qari al-Wasiti. The auspiciousness of this birth was further enhanced by the fact that the child would be a *sayyid*, a direct descendant of the Prophet from both his father's side (through Imam Husayn) and his mother's side (through Imam Hasan). In accordance with his uncle's vision, Ahmad received his training and first *khirka* from Sheikh Wasiti (Vasiti). Ahmad would receive his second dervish cloak of investiture and throne of spiritual direction *(sajjadat al-irshad)* from Sheikh Mansur shortly before the latter's death.[134] During this period, Ahmad gathered a large and enthusiastic following of *fuqara* ("poor ones" or dervishes) and developed a Sufi fraternity that seems to have initially spread much more quickly than the more gradual growth of the Qadiriyya.

Detail of a 19th century Rifa'i dhikr painted by F. Zonaro

---

134 Öztürk, *The Eye of the Heart,* 110.

As Sheikh Mansur was a wealthy individual, he was able to leave a substantial inheritance to his nephew. Rather than keeping this great wealth, Ahmad chose to distribute it all to the needy. Out of his great love for his fellow human beings, he kept nothing for himself, saying, "*Ashk* (love) is enough for me." Just as he spread his money out to everyone impartially, Ahmad emanated his compassionate energy toward everyone he encountered. He took the path of burning love, of love's fire—accepting every person as they were, even taking in their negativity, transforming it, and giving it out as positive energy. In this way, he rose to a high, exalted station of love.

The Rifa'i line passes through Hazrat 'Ali to Hazrat Junayd, like the Qadiris and the Halveti-Jerrahis, then to Abu Bakr Shibli and 'Ali Ajami down to Ahmad's sheikh, Abu Fazl ibn Qari. Rifa'iyya sources connect Sayyid Ahmad Rifa'i closely with Sayyid 'Abdul Qadir Gaylani, to whom he is said to have been related, perhaps as a nephew. According to the traditions, Ahmad Rifa'i once went into an ecstatic state, plunging his feet and legs into a basin of burning coals, and was immediately cured by the healing breath and saliva of 'Abdul Qadir. This divine healing power was thereby transmitted to Ahmad Rifa'i, who was subsequently able to bequeath it to all of the sheikhs who would succeed him, down to the present day.

Since that time, the Rifa'i order has maintained a focus upon the powerful *jalal* forms of worship, chanting their dhikr ceremonies with great strength, often punctuated with multiple drums and cymbals, evoking a strong ecstatic setting (called *halat*), a powerful state in which the dervishes are carried beyond themselves and are capable of performing extraordinary acts of mastery with little or no pain. These include walking on burning coals and eating them, stabbing themselves with knives without causing serious injury, handling snakes, rolling in fire, licking red-hot brands, cutting the tongue off and replacing it so that it is no longer severed, and so on.

After the completion of such feats during the course of the ceremony, the sheikh visits each of them in turn and breathes upon them, licking his finger and rubbing the wounds with his healing saliva, offering prayers for their speedy recovery (if they were injured at all), so that, traditionally, within twenty-four hours, no trace of such a wound can be found.

During the eighteenth and nineteenth centuries, Western observers who witnessed the Rifaʻi ceremonies, with their loudly accented and eccentric style of chanting, dubbed them "the Howling Dervishes," in contrast to the more refined musical lyricism of the Mevlevi "Whirling Dervishes."

Ecstatic Rifa'i dervishes   Dervish with a skewer

Although some, like Jami, have claimed that such "aberrations" as fire-eating and snake-handling were not introduced by the founder of the Rifaʻiyya, the likelihood is that Pir Ahmad Rifaʻi initiated some of these practices, however much they may have been elaborated (or degenerated) since his time. One of the more common and relatively mild varieties of such Rifaʻi activity, which the author has witnessed firsthand, is the practice in which, in the midst of the clamorous standing dhikr ceremony, the sheikh—in a collected state—inserts a special shish (a long, thin knife or skewer with a handle ornamented with Arabic calligraphy) through the two cheeks of selected dervishes. Throughout the dhikr, these dervishes show no signs of pain and evidence negligible bleeding when the sheikh later removes the shish, with a smile and touch of saliva upon the nearly invisible wounds.

The sheikh himself may also tear open his shirt, then hurl his own body about while pressing a razor-sharp lance into his neck or stomach, all without apparent injury or pain. A brightly-colored painting of Hazrat 'Ali on the wall of the tekke serves to remind one of his imperviousness to pain from an arrow wound, while deeply concentrated in salat. Finally, the sheikh closes the ceremony with a series of ecstatic prayers and *salawats* to the Prophet, after which everyone relaxes and cordially partakes of after-dhikr hot tea and refreshments.

The importance of the wounding and healing in the Rifa'i ritual actually lies more in the act of healing itself, the wounding being only a necessary prelude to the healing that follows it. Sayyid Ahmad Rifa'i was credited with great powers of healing; for instance, curing a lame, hunchback girl from the village of Haddahiya, whose mother was a Rifa'i disciple. The Rifa'is, in turn, attribute their Pir's miraculous healings to his link with his noble ancestor, the Prophet Muhammad, may peace and blessing be upon him.

The Prophet's Mosque in Medina (photo by the author.)

Around the year 1162 CE, a miraculous occasion of healing is said to have taken place at the tomb of the Prophet during the month of Hajj, when Sayyid Ahmad Rifa'i made a pilgrimage to Mecca and Medina in the company of a number of noted scholars and sheikhs of his time. When the Pir approached the Prophet's

Mosque in Medina, the guard would not let him into the special interior section where the sayyids enjoy intimate access to the Prophet's tomb.

Facing Muhammad's tomb inside the Prophet's Mosque in Medina.

The guard refused admittance to Ahmad because he was not attired in the traditional garb of a sayyid, but instead, wore simple clothes which seemed to belie his claim of Muhammadan descendency. When he saw that he would not be permitted to approach the tomb, Sayyid Ahmad Rifa'i became sad and began petitioning loudly in the direction of the Prophet's tomb, crying, *"As-salaamu 'aleikum, ya jeddi!"* (Peace be upon you, O my ancestor!) and imploring that, if he could not approach the Prophet's tomb, that he might at least have the honor of kissing the Prophet's hand. To the amazement of all the witnesses, whose spiritual eyes and ears were dramatically opened, a voice was heard from the tomb answering Sayyid Ahmad Rifa'i, *"W'aleikum as-salaam, ya waladi!"* (And may peace also be with you, my son.) To their further amazement, they saw the Prophet's hand extend from the tomb and his tearful descendent kissing it.

The Prophet's tomb in Medina (peace and blesssings be upon him)

Overwhelmed with emotion, Ahmad's companions began flailing about and stabbing themselves with their swords and knives in a state of *wajd* (spiritual ecstasy). When Ahmad finally turned around, he saw that his companions had all fallen to the floor, covered with blood which flowed from the wounds they had inflicted on their bodies. Collecting himself, the Pir went around compassionately licking his finger and healing each wound he touched with his saliva, until each one of them had stopped bleeding and was fully recovered. From this time forward, Pir Ahmad Rifa'i was able to use this gift of divine grace to quickly heal any wound he encountered.

The real essence of Ahmad Rifa'i's dynamic being is revealed in a story which tangentially involves his uncle, Sayyid 'Abdul Qadir Gaylani. When a seeker came to Baghdad and asked 'Abdul Qadir about love, the man was advised to go to Sayyid Ahmad Rifa'i and ask him for the answer. The man traveled to see Ahmad Rifa'i, and after conveying 'Abdul Qadir's salaams, inquired about the nature of love. Upon hearing the question, the Pir stood up and passionately responded, "Love is fire! Love is fire!" And so saying, he began to whirl until he disappeared completely from the man's sight. The man was bewildered and was wondering what to do, when suddenly he perceived the spiritual presence of 'Abdul Qadir before him, urging him to pour rose water on the exact spot where he had last seen Ahmad Rifa 'i. When the man did so, Sayyid Ahmad Rifa 'i reappeared still whirling in the same place.

When the seeker returned to Baghdad, 'Abdul Qadir asked him, "Did you see what love is? My brother Sayyid Rifa 'i has attained stations that have not been reached by many of Allah's intimate friends." This love and respect was mutual. After 'Abdul Qadir's death, Ahmad Rifa 'i would tell his students that whoever visited Baghdad and failed to pay respects at the tomb of 'Abdul Qadir would be received neither by his spiritual community nor Allah.

Though Pir Ahmad Rifa 'i was childless, the Rifa 'i tarikat continued in his family beginning with his sister's son, 'Ali Ibn 'Uthman. It soon spread into Egypt and Syria, then to Anatolia and the Balkans, spawning various suborders and becoming one of the largest and most popular of all Sufi orders. After the fifteenth century, the Rifa 'iyya declined somewhat and was even banned for a time by the Ottoman Empire, owing to the notoriety of its rituals. However, it remains a vital order in modern times; indeed, it is possibly the most wide-spread tarikat in the world at present. For years, until the breakup of Yugoslavia with its subsequent wars and devastation, Bosnia was a strong center of Rifa 'iyya activity.

The noble *taj* or turban of the Rifa 'iyya is black— representing a dynamic mystic blackness—in the spirit of Rasulullah, who often wore a black or dark green turban.

Pir Ahmad Badawi

Sayyid Ahmad al-Badawi (1199-1276 CE), the third of the four *aktab-i-arwah,* was born in Fez, Morocco, during the period of the third and fourth Crusades, a time of great political upheaval. In Iraq and much of the Near East, the Turkish Seljuk government would soon be swept away by Mongol invaders, headed first by Ghengis Khan (d.1227 CE), then by his grandson, Hulagu. By 1250 CE, Egypt and Syria would be controlled by the Mamluk Dynasty (1250-1517 CE); and in Fez, where Ahmad Badawi's Arabian ancestors had migrated, the Moroccan government was overthrown during Ahmad's boyhood by a religious reformer from the Atlas Mountains. Ahmad's family (who were *sayyids* descended from Husayn) fled, making a pilgrimage to Mecca, where they settled after dwelling for a time in Egypt. In Mecca, Ahmad memorized the Qur'an and studied Shafi'ite canon law; but besides religious studies, he also earned a reputation as a powerful horseman and duelist. Tall and broad in stature with classic Arabian features, he adopted the Moroccan Bedouin custom of veiling his face, thus earning the epithet *al-Badawi*.

After his father's death, Ahmad dreamed that both Pir Ahmad Rifa'i and Pir 'Abdul Qadir Gaylani invited him on the mystic path and pledged him their help. There was already a link between Ahmad Badawi and Ahmad Rifa'i in that one of Pir Rifa'i's Sufi teachers, Abu Maydan, was the great-grandfather of Ahmad Badawi. Inspired by his dreams, Ahmad and his brother, Hasan, set out on a journey to the Sufi heartland of Iraq, where they visited the shrines of many famous saints, finally arriving at the Rifa'iyya headquarters in Umm Ubayda. There, Ahmad trained to become a Rifa'i sheikh. Ahmad's keen sense of his own destiny is revealed in the words he uttered there: "It is as if a king of the Arabs has settled at this place, pitched his tent, and unfurled his banners."[135]

In 1238 CE, he returned to Mecca—his brother having preceded him—and meditated in the caves at Hira as the Prophet himself had done. In his fortieth year, Ahmad received word—either from an inner voice or perhaps Rifa'i orders—that sent him to Tanta in Egypt to replace a deceased sheikh and serve as spiritual director there. There, a sheikh by the name of Rukain received him with honor after Ahmad the Bedouin's unannounced coming was foreseen by another holy man. Like Joseph, the prophet of old, Ahmad Badawi used his mystic knowledge to help his benefactor

---

135 Reeves, *Hidden Government*, 46.

The Formation of the Great Sufi Orders

and the people of Tanta by advising Sheikh Rukain to store up grain in order to offset a severe coming drought.

There, in rural Tanta, Ahmad's reputation and following grew very swiftly. By divine permission, the Arabian sheikh founded his own Badawi (or *Ahmadiyya*) Order, featuring red turbans and banners. One distinctive practice of Sayyid Ahmad Badawi was to stay on the roof of Sheikh Rukain's house for forty days, performing *khalwa*, fasting and meditating. In his ecstasy, his hair became long and matted and his clothing ragged as he stared directly into the sun, his eyes beaming like burning coals. (In modern times as well, certain ascetics are known to be able to gaze for hours at the sun without damaging their retina.) Even in this, the pir attracted a large following of dervishes, who became known as the *Sutuhiyya*, "the People of the Roof." One of these was Ahmad's *khalifa*, 'Abd al-Al, his primary successor, who himself developed a great spiritual reputation, constructed the saint's shrine, and greatly expanded the order after his master's passing.

People used to bestow great gifts upon Sayyid al-Badawi, which he would accept and, in turn, donate to others. However, the well-to-do religious leaders jealously withheld their charity from the saint, coveting their own share of the wealth. In some cases, it is difficult to separate fact from legend. For instance, some of the festivities of the order reflect pre-Islamic Nile flood and fertility customs, according to the solar Coptic calendar, while the founding pir of the Badawiyya is famous for his power to cure barrenness in women. Another modern custom of the order involves the donning of iron collars and chains, which is said to be in commemoration of Ahmad Badawi's participation in the war against the Christian Crusaders, in which he miraculously freed captive Muslims of their chains. It is also told that when Sheikh Ahmad Badawi visited Cairo, the secular Mamluk leaders, including Zahir Baybars and his army, came out of the city to greet him. It does seem to be a matter of clear historical record that in 1462 and 1463, the wife of the Mamluk Sultan Khushqadam and her retinue made two pilgrimages to the shrine of Sayyid Ahmad al-Badawi, and when she died in 1466, her royal tomb was covered with the red dervish

— *231* —

cloak and banners of the Badawi order.[136]

In time, the Badawiyya produced several suborders and spread to parts of Turkey, the Hijaz, Syria and Tunisia. The order remains popular in Egypt up to the present day, along with the *Shadhiliyya* and *Burhaniyya (Dusukiyya)* turuq. Though the Badawi order is considered to have emerged from the Qadiri and Rifa'i line, its *silsila* does not duplicate those two orders but passes from Hasan Basri and Habib al-Ajami to Mahmud at-Tabrizi through 'Abdul Razzaq al-Andulusi, finally to Ahmad's own sheikh, 'Abdul Jelib.

Like several other Egyptian turuq, including the *Dusukiyya*, the teaching of the *Badawiyya* stressed the soul's *nur* (light, or luminous intelligence) which was created from the original Muhammadan Light, or *Nuri Muhammad*. In the *hizb* of Ahmad Badawi, which is recited by the Badawi dervishes, Muhammad is described as "tree of the luminous origin, the brilliance of the handful of the Merciful, . . . mine of the divine secrets . . . owner of the original handful [of light from which the *Nuri Muhammadin* was created]."[137]

One of the distinctive portions of the Badawi dhikr ceremony, which was later bequeathed to Pir Nureddin Jerrahi as a spiritual gift to be used in the Jerrahi dhikr, is what is known as the *Bedevi (Badawi) topu*. In this section of the dhikr ceremony, the dervishes stop circling around the sheikh and, upon his signal, crowd in toward him in the center of the *meydan*, their bodies collectively pulsing up and down while loudly and ecstatically chanting the name of the Everliving Source of Life, *Ya Hayy! Ya Hayy! Ya Hayy!*

One of the Halveti-Jerrahi hymns fervently extols the saint,[138] exclaiming:

> *Ah! Ahmad Badawi, Axis of the Sufi way,*
> *We will enter your ecstasy!*
> *Ah! Ya Saki! You offer drink from Kawthar;*
> *Ya Hu, Ya Badawi! Help us, O Badawi!*

---

136 Ibid, 50-51.
137 Hoffman, *Sufism, Mystics, and Saints in Modern Egypt*, 59-60.
138 English rendition by Sheikh Nur al-Jerrahi.

Ya Saki! Paradise is right here. Ya Hu, Ya Badawi!
O beloved friend, I only long to drink your wine
And plunge into the essence of your love!...
Ya Hu, Ya Badawi!

Pir Ibrahim Dusuki

Ibrahim ibn Abu'l Majid ad-Dusuki (1246-1288 CE) was an Egyptian contemporary of Ahmad Badawi who was born in the small village of Dusuk on the banks of the Nile. Ibrahim's father was a sheikh, Abu Madha, and his uncle was the great Egyptian pir from Morocco, Abu'l Hasan ash-Shadhili (1196-1258 CE), the founder of the *Shadhiliyya* Order, one of the largest and most important of the Egyptian Sufi brotherhoods. Imam ash-Shadhili for a time studied with Ibrahim Dusuki's maternal grandfather, Sheikh Abu'l-Fath al-Wasiti, the khalifa of Ahmad Rifa'i who brought the Rifa'iyya to Egypt in 1253.

Although a book of Ibrahim Dusuki's instruction to his mureeds has survived, entitled *Jawahir*, not too much is actually known about the life of this saint. One story which survives from his childhood is similar to one also told about 'Abdul Qadir Gaylani. Ibrahim Dusuki (Dasuqi) was born one day before the beginning of the month of Ramadan. The next day, there was some doubt among the people as to whether the new moon had appeared—the sign that the fasting should begin. Some of the people went to a wise local sheikh named Muhammad ibn Harun. Through mystic insight, he knew that a blessed child had recently been born in their village to the daughter of the famous Sufi sheikh, Abu'l-Fath al-Wasiti; so Sheikh Muhammad asked the people go and inquire of the child's mother as to whether her new-born son was nursing. Ibrahim's mother reported that the baby had not nursed all day since the *fajr* prayer at dawn. From this, the sheikh concluded that Ramadan had indeed begun and sent word back to the worried mother assuring her that the child would resume nursing after the sunset prayers in the evening. The child did so and continued to fast from sunrise to sundown for the entire month of Ramadan. Indeed, Allah was to grant young Ibrahim a number of cosmic visions and mystic revelations before the age of fifteen.

Ibrahim would later receive *bayat* in the Suhrawardi, Rifa'i and Badawi orders, after which he would receive permission to found his own independent Dusuki (or *Ibrahimiyya*) tarikat, thus combining the lineages of several of these prominent *turuq*. The Dusuki line, like the Halveti-Jerrahi line, passes through Junayd down to Abu Ishaq (or Najib) Suhrawardi. From there, it passes to Sheikh Shahabuddin 'Umar Suhrawardi to Sheikh Nejubiddin ash-Shirazi to Sheikh Nureddin 'Abdul-Samad Natnazi, and finally to Sheikh Nejmeddin Tasulsi, the teacher of Ibrahim Dusuki.

A few of Pir Ibrahim's noble sayings follow. He urged his disciples not to be satisfied with any station on the path but to always continue in one's efforts to progress to a higher station, saying: "Every *makam* in which you stop veils you from your Lord." Like many Sufis, Pir Ibrahim held those in the tarikat and higher levels to a stricter standard of behavior than the average Muslim, saying:

> Just as the people of the *shari'a* void prayer when it is done in a corrupt form, the people of the *haqiqa* void prayer accompanied by corrupt morals. If a person harbors hatred, envy, a bad opinion about a Muslim, or some other such defects, his prayer is void in their opinion. All of these are signs of love of this world, and whoever loves this world is veiled from the presence of God and expelled from entering it.

While worldly love detains one, divine love is the key to entering Allah's exalted presence. In a noble verse the pir says:

> *I have placed you as an intimate friend in my heart,*
> *And have granted my body to whoever wants to sit with me.*

For my body has assemblies for the Beloved,
And the Beloved of my heart is sitting with me in my heart.[139]

One day, toward the very end of his life, Ibrahim Dusuki asked one of his closest dervishes to go to his brother, Musa Dusuki, who was teaching at the Azhar mosque, and to convey Ibrahim's salaams along with this message: "Cleanse the inside, the heart, before cleansing the outside. Protect yourself from all character defects such as pride, arrogance, jealousy, and vengefulness. May the peace and blessings of Allah be with you." The student delivered the message immediately to Musa. Though engaged in the middle of a lecture, Musa instantly sensed what was behind the message and, excusing himself from the class, rushed to his brother's house. There he found Pir Ibrahim in *sajda* (prostration) upon his prayer carpet. In this noble position, forehead to the earth, the pir had breathed his last, attaining the mercy of Allah.

In modern times, the order founded by Ibrahim Dusuki is commonly known as the *Burhaniyya*. Numbering at least three million adherents, this popular revitalized Egyptian-Sudanese tarikat is a branch of the original Dusuki order, founded in the nineteen-thirties by Sheikh Muhammad 'Uthman al-Burhani of Sudan (1894-1983) and further propagated by Sheikh Gamal as-Sanhuri. Some of the order's specialties include the mystic symbolism of the letters in the Qur'an and the healing of diseases. The tarikat combines the teaching of Sheikh Burhan with the mystic teachings of Pir Ibrahim Dusuki and Pir Abu'l Hasan Shadhili in an order known, in its full title, as the *Burhaniyya Dusukiyya Shadhiliyya* Order.[140]

Before leaving our consideration of Pir Ibrahim Dusuki, it is incumbent upon us to mention a remarkable passage in a book by his son-in-law. The daughter of Pir Ibrahim was married to Imam Ahmad ibn 'Uthman Sharnubi (d.1586 CE), who was a khalifa of the pir. Hazrat Sharnubi wrote a book entitled *Kashf al-Ghuyubi* or *Tabaqat ul-Awliya* (Ranks of the Saints) which discusses the miracles of four *qutbs* (*al-Aktab al-Arbaa*)—'Abdul Qadir

---

139 Hoffman, 157, 146, 189.
140 Ibid, 300-1.

Gaylani, Ahmad Rifaʻi, Ahmad Badawi and Ibrahim Dusuki—in the form of answers which Imam Sharnubi gave to the questions of his pupil, Muhammad al-Bulkini.

Of particular interest is a section in which he discusses the lives of future *awliya* (saints) who would live between the years of 1592-1864. Amazingly, one of the noble *awliya* whose life and death was foretold—three hundred years before his birth— was the Halveti-Jerrahi pir, Nureddin al-Jerrahi. Several copies and printings of this manuscript have been closely checked for agreement on this point. One copy, which can be found in the Fatih Library of Istanbul (#3286), was signed next to the passage by Hazrati Pir Nureddin himself, confirming his acceptance of it. The passage is quoted in full below, as given in a copy obtained from the *Bibliotheque Nationale de Paris*, manuscript 648, January, 1873, Leaflet 22, side 2:

And among these saints is Sayyid Nureddin Jerrahi who will reside in Istanbul and will appear in the year 1115 A.H. He will live for forty-four years. One of his miracles will be that he will be able to see his station in heaven while still living in this world, and will enter paradise directly upon his passing. The prayers and supplications of those who visit him and pray in his presence will be accepted by Allah.

Indeed, all of this came to pass as foretold by Hazrat Shanubi: Nureddin Jerrahi lived in Istanbul. He was born in 1086 A.H. (May 4, 1678 CE), became active as a sheikh and inaugurated the Jerrahi dergah in the Karagümrük section of Istanbul in 1115 A.H. (Dec. 6, 1704 CE), was active eighteen years and passed away during his forty-forth year in the year 1133 A.H. (July 28, 1721 CE) While Sheikh ʻAli Köstendili was Pir Nureddin's sheikh in the outer, physical world, it was Pir Ibrahim Dusuki who was to function as Pir Nureddin's hidden teacher in the spiritual world.

Although there are many noteworthy saints and pirs who lived during the twelfth and thirteenth centuries, two of them stand out from the others, not only in terms of enduring fame and universality of spirit, but in respect to their momentous contributions to the body of Sufi literature: one a vast ocean of the knowledge of Reality and the other an immense ocean of spiritual love. Known as the two wings of the mystic path, they are: Sheikh Muhyiddin Ibn al-'Arabi (1165-1240 CE) and Mevlana Jelaluddin Rumi (1207-1273 CE). Once we have examined these two important mystics, beginning with Ibn 'Arabi, we will at last be ready to focus on the Khalwati Order itself and its pregnant spiritual offspring, the Jerrahi Order, and the whole milieu of Turkish Sufism, in which Rumi stands as a pioneer.

Ibn al-'Arabi

Muhyiddin Abu Bakr Muhammad ibn-'Ali ibn al-'Arabi was born in Murcia in the Andalusian province of Spain on the Night of Power (27th of Ramadan), 1165 CE. He was a descendant of the famous Arab of the Prophet's time, Hatim at-Ta'i, whose Yemenite clan of Banu Tayy had emigrated to Spain during the initial years of the Arab conquest, three or four hundred years prior to Ibn 'Arabi's time. Abu Madyan (1126-1198 CE), a great Sufi saint and student of 'Abdul Qadir Gaylani, was born in Seville and eventually settled in Algeria. He was, at the time, one of the great Sufi influences in Spain, as well as upon Ibn 'Arabi.

Muhyiddin's father, 'Ali ibn Muhammad ibn 'Arabi, was a high-ranking dignitary in the service of the Islamic Almohad sultan who ruled there, and was himself a Sufi of great spiritual gifts. Long without progeny, he traveled to Baghdad before the conception of his only son, to ask Sayyid 'Abdul Qadir Gaylani's blessing that he might have a son. (He would later have two daughters.) When the saint informed him of what he saw inwardly—that Allah had not decreed any son for him—'Ali pleaded with 'Abdul Qadir to

THE GARDEN OF MYSTIC LOVE

try and intercede for him. After retiring for a short period of contemplation, 'Abdul Qadir, who had many children of his own, returned and offered the elder Ibn 'Arabi one of his own future-destined sons, who was to be named Muhyiddin, after the saint. Gladly accepting the offer, 'Ali ibn Muhammad ibn 'Arabi stood back to back with the saint of Gaylan and felt a warm transfusion of energy enter his spine, which soon bore fruit in the birth of a child whom, as agreed, he named Muhyiddin, a divinely-graced son who would one day become known as *ash-Sheikh al-Akkbar* (the Greatest Master), *Qutb-al Aqtab* (Pole of all Poles), *al-Murshid ul-Mutlaq* (the Absolute Guide) and *Khatem al-Awliya al-Muhammadi* (Seal of the Muhammadan Saints). 'Abdul Qadir died the year Ibn 'Arabi was born.

As a child, Muhyiddin was taught by two elderly women saints, Yasmin of Marchena (also known as Shams Umm al-Fuqara) and Fatima bint al-Waliyya (ibn al-Muthanna) of Cordova, the latter mystic being ninety years old at the time and known for "having the sight of God in everything in the world." She told Ibn 'Arabi, "I am your spiritual mother and the light of your carnal mother."[141]

When Muhyiddin was eight year old, his father moved the family to Seville, where he arranged for his son to attend theological seminary and become a teacher there. Around the age of nineteen, Muhyidden embarked on his first major spiritual retreat *(khalwa),* after which he met his father's friend, the famous philosopher Averroes (Ibn Rushd) of Cordova, who, like a number of others, had already begun to take special notice of young Muhyiddin.

Later, as Ibn 'Arabi intensified his spiritual practice, including renunciation, fasting and retreat, he was rewarded with a vision of Jesus, Moses and Muhammad. He soon thereafter began to receive guidance from Hazrat Khidr and Jesus as well as an earthly teacher, Sheikh Abu'l 'Abbas al-Uryabi, who himself had a strong connection to the station of Jesus, upon him be peace. Around the year 1190 CE, at Cordova, Ibn 'Arabi received one of his greatest visions, in which he was invited to join a vast assembly of prophets from Adam to Muhammad, along with the spirits of

---

141 Claude Addas, Quest for the Red Sulphur, 87.

all the believers who would exist to the end of time. They were there ostensibly to commemorate the passing of a certain sheikh, but from the prophet Hud, Ibn 'Arabi learned the secret that every saint is an heir *(warith)* to one of the prophets, and that Ibn 'Arabi himself was the *Seal of the Saints*.

Later, Ibn 'Arabi would elaborate these ideas in his writings: just as the period of legislative prophecy had ended with Muhammad, the Seal of Prophets *(Khatem an-Nabiyyin)*, the present period of spiritual unfoldment featured Muhammadan saints of various ranks, each in the station or attunement of a particular prophet. Ibn 'Arabi was the one who would seal the Muhammadan sainthood *(walaya Muhammadiyya)*, while it was revealed to him that the prophet Jesus is the seal of saints in general who will close the era of universal sainthood when he returns at the end of time. Though Ibn 'Arabi was usually cryptic about claiming such a title, sometimes speaking ambiguously, as though the Seal of Saints might be another person, in his *Diwan* he states clearly:

> *I am the Seal of Saints, just as it is attested*
> *That the Seal of the Prophets is Muhammad:*
> *The seal in a specific sense,*
> *   not the Seal of Sainthood in general,*
> *For that is Jesus the Assisted.*[142]

Toward the end of the twelfth century, Ibn 'Arabi began to travel extensively, while rumblings of war plagued his native Andalusia. (King Alfonso VIII fought the Muslim Almohads and was defeated in 1195 CE) The year 1198 found Ibn 'Arabi in Fez, Morocco, where he was granted an important spiritual revelation. There, he experienced an extraordinary inner journey of the soul, a *mi'raj* through the seven heavens, in which he met most of the prophets and divine messengers who had appeared to Muhammad in the Prophet's own heavenly ascension; and from this he received many unveilings. Whereas in the vision of Cordova, Ibn 'Arabi did

---

142 See also chapter 43 of Ibn 'Arabi's *Futuhat,* which reads, "I am, without any doubt, the Seal of Sainthood." Chodkiewicz, *Seal of the Saints,* 129.

not speak directly to any of the prophets save Hud, in this instance he enjoyed more intimate encounters with the great prophets.

In the first level of heaven, he met the prophet Adam, the primordial father of humanity, who revealed to him that all humans are on the right of Allah—meaning that every soul, without exception, is destined for bliss. Afterwards, Ibn 'Arabi wrote that, as Allah's mercy was predominant, neither the divine wrath nor punishment was eternal, but would end at the Great Judgment. The duration of the resurrection will be limited—lasting approximately 50,000 years—as will be the period during which any penalties are imposed, after which time the fire experienced by those in hell will become bliss and the atmosphere there will become "freshness and peace."[143]

Ibn 'Arabi received an authentic collection of some of the most secret mystical ahadith of the Prophet. These sayings, for example, speak in merciful terms regarding the punishment of hell, stressing the divine generosity, even to the worst sinners who possess so much as a grain of faith. However, the Prophet warned that he did not want such sayings too widely advertised, lest people should become spiritually complacent and abandon their efforts in the cause of righteousness, or erode their faith through doubting that Allah could be so merciful, even to incorrigible sinners. Predictably, such tidings of divine grace from Ibn 'Arabi did not go over well with many of the mainstream theologians, who rejected the material as false and heretical.

During his *mi'raj* vision, Ibn 'Arabi met Yahya (John the Baptist) and Jesus in the higher realms of heaven, and from them learned various mysteries concerning the raising of the dead. He also met Aaron, who explained that any teachings which categorically deny the world represent an imperfect understanding of the theophanies on the part of those who so teach, since everything is from Allah; only when worldliness begins to seriously eclipse one's awareness of the Source of Being is it undesirable.

After meeting Joseph and Idris, Ibn 'Arabi came upon Moses, who explained the nature of his own prophetic vision of Allah on

143 Addas, 134-35.

the holy mountain. Finally, in bodiless form, Ibn 'Arabi arrived in the seventh heaven, at the site of the Celestial Ka'ba and the Lote Tree of the Far Boundary. He became pure light and discovered himself as the Muhammadan heir. He became aware that all the divine names refer to one single Divine Essence, which was indeed his own essence (and one with the essence of all humanity).

Ibn 'Arabi reported that he was able to realize all of this because of approaching Ultimate Reality in a condition of pure servanthood (*'abd*), without the slightest trace of sovereignty *(rububiyya)*. He says that whoever has a trace of sovereignty in approaching the Divine hastens to return to the sense-world as soon as possible for fear of losing his sovereignty.[144] He also describes the way of descent after the spiritual ascension, saying there are those called *waqifun* who are meant to stay in the contemplation of the One; then there are *raji'un*, those who return to the earthly life for their own self-perfecting and also those who are sent back for the benefit of giving divine guidance to other beings. Ibn 'Arabi was of the last category: at the summit of his ascent into *hakikat*, he was not offered a new prophetic law or religious dispensation—since that station had been sealed by Muhammad—but he was given the mission, as Seal of the Muhammadan Saints, to distribute the wealth of inner knowledge of the tradition to the souls who thirsted for the Truth. With time, Ibn 'Arabi would more than once be tempted to withdraw from teaching disciples and dealing with disapproving critics to simply concentrate on himself, only to be directly reproved by a divine voice, which said: "Counsel My servants!"

By 1201 CE, at the age of thirty-six, Ibn 'Arabi was writing and traveling extensively, wandering throughout Asia Minor and North Africa and frequently making the *hajj* to Mecca. In Baghdad, he met Sheikh Shahabuddin 'Umar Suhrawardi, a brief meeting which apparently consisted of both parties bowing their heads to one another in silence, before parting without conversing. Suhrawardi later said of Ibn 'Arabi that he was "an ocean of essential truths," while Ibn 'Arabi said of him, "He is

---

144 Ibid, 156, 195.

impregnated with the sunna from tip to toe."[145] Years later in
Damascus (where Ibn 'Arabi would eventually settle), he would
meet the young Jalaluddin Rumi, who was tagging along behind
his scholarly father, Baha'uddin (several years prior to the family's
move to Anatolia). Ibn 'Arabi briefly talked to Jalaluddin and was
favorably impressed. He later remarked: "Amazing that an ocean
is following a small lake!"

One of Ibn 'Arabi's acquaintances, Hafiz ibn Najjar said: "Ibn
'Arabi was a *qutb* (spiritual pole) and knew other *qutbs [aqtab]* of
his time. Furthermore, he knew the *qutbs* of the past and future.
Mostly he kept company with the Sufis and spent his time at the
Ka'ba. That seemed to be his only pleasure."[146]

A fateful encounter took place during the first of Ibn 'Arabi's
pilgrimages to Mecca. There, while making *tawafs* around the
Ka'ba, he met a maiden named Nizam, whose father, Sheikh Abu
Shuja al-Isfahani, was the imam of the Maqam Ibrahim. Nizam's
aunt, Fakhr an-Nisa, was also a sheikha. Nizam's beauty and
wisdom were an inspiration for Ibn 'Arabi and years later became
the inspiration for his mystical work on passionate divine desire,
entitled *Tarjuman al-ashwaq*. He would later issue a mystical
commentary on this *diwan* in order to demonstrate that it was not
simply a poetic celebration of erotic love. One of the most famous
and universal sets of verses in the *Tarjuman*[147] reads:

> *My heart has become capable of every form:*
> *a meadow for gazelles, a monastery for monks,*
> *a temple for idols and the ka'ba of the pilgrims,*
> *the Torah tablets, the Qur'an.*
> *I profess the creed of Love,*
> *And whatever direction its mount takes,*
> *Love remains my religion and my faith.*

There were a number of other beloved women in Ibn 'Arabi's
life; though information is sketchy, he seems to have had at least

145 Addas, 240.
146 Ibn 'Arabi, trans. by Tosun Bayrak, *What the Seeker Needs*, xviii, .xvi.
147 Ibn 'Arabi, *Tarjuman*, XI.vv.13-16, 43-44.

two wives as well as two sons, and was very close to his two sisters (his only siblings). Ibn 'Arabi believed in the spiritual sanctity of women, as well as men, and freely proclaimed that "men and women have their share in every level, including the function of *qutb* (the spiritual pole of the age)."[148] He also brought out the feminine form of the name of Divine Essence *(Hiya)* as well as the traditional masculine form *(Hu* or *Huwa)*.

Several mystic visions were bestowed upon Ibn 'Arabi during his stay in Mecca, several in the vicinity of the Ka'ba. One of these experiences occurred shortly after Ibn 'Arabi refused *zam-zam* water at the Ka'ba, exalting in his mind the divine station of humanity above his reverence for the House of Allah. One stormy night, while circling the *Bayt Allah*, he found himself terrorized by a vision of the Ka'ba raising itself up and angrily threatening to crush him over his failure to pay it due respect. Realizing it was a lesson from Allah, he appeased the anger of the Ka'ba by uttering sweet verses which paid homage to the sanctity of the holy shrine.

On another occasion, behind the wall of the Hanbalites, he was allowed to join a spiritual convocation of the highest ranking saints of his age, the seven *'abdal* (substitutes). He made prayers with them and spoke with them, marveling at their absorption in Allah. Another time, he noticed a noble personage circumambulating the Ka'ba, whose body passed through two men who were holding on to each other. Ibn 'Arabi followed him right through the two linked men and finally, after completing the seven *tawafs* around the Ka'ba, was able to greet him. He learned that the man was the late as-Sabti ibn Harun ar-Rashid, the son of the famous ninth century 'Abbasid caliph, and that Sabti was circling the Ka'ba in his spiritual body. Ibn 'Arabi asked him a number of questions and found out that Sabti had been the *qutb* of his time; but Sabti added, "There's nothing in that to cause pride!"

On still another occasion, Ibn 'Arabi dreamed that he was circling the Ka'ba and met someone who was one of his remotely distant ancestors. When Ibn 'Arabi asked how long ago the person had lived, he was told forty thousand years. Amazed, Ibn 'Arabi

---

148 Addas, 87.

pointed out that Adam, the first man, had only lived around six thousand years ago. "Which Adam?" was the reply. "The one closest to you, or another before that? Know that he is but the last of one hundred thousand Adams, who came and passed away before him." Then Ibn 'Arabi remembered the hadith of the Prophet which indeed stated that Allah had created one hundred thousand Adams.[149] Another hadith of this type states: "Allah has created 18,000 universes and this, your world, is just one universe from among them."[150]

In his *Fusus al-Hikam*, Ibn 'Arabi elaborates, saying "I have spoken to the soul of Adam, upon him be peace, and he has said, 'I am the last of the six generations (eras of time).'" The amazing tradition which he transmits goes on to spell out the six major races, or types of being (as they are not exactly like modern homo sapiens), who existed before the race of our present Adam, each race lasting approximately one million years. The earth itself, then, is not merely thousands of years old (nor does the Qur'an itself actually allege such a scientifically untenable date of earthly genesis); rather—according to Ibn 'Arabi's report—it is some 3,313,000,000 years old. This tradition also has its corollary in the Torah, where, in the *Sepher Bereshith* or Book of Genesis it states that there were giants *(nefelim)* or "sons of God"[151] inhabiting the earth in the days before the *Elohim* brought forth Adam, and Cain went forth among them. Some of the *nefilim* are said to have "taken wives among the daughters of men," producing a new mixed race on earth.

Ibn 'Arabi names the generation before humankind as the race of *Jann (jinn),* who were created from fire, rather than earth and water, as humans are. Iblis (Satan) is said to be the only creature left of this type from before Adam's time—a race that was hermaphrodite, with one leg male and the other leg female. A million years prior to this existed the race of *Ten*, a human-like species created from water. Before that was the race called *Ben*, created only from moisture or water vapor. Before this was the race

149 Ibid, 215-16.
150 Ibn 'Arabi/translated by Bursevi, *Kernel of the Kernel*, 9.
151 Genesis 6:1-2.

called *Sen*, created from the wind, and so forth. The idea that there were others before our present human race is implied in the holy Qur'an, when the angels ask Allah prior to the creation of Adam:

"O Lord, are you going to create a being who will tyrannize the earth and shed blood?" Why should they have thought to ask that, queries Ibn 'Arabi? He answers: it was because their knowledge was based on prior generations who did precisely these things.

Returning to the life of Ibn 'Arabi, we find that, after years of traveling and writing, visiting Jerusalem, Hebron (the site of Abraham's tomb), Cairo, Anatolia, and many other places including the *Maghrib*,[152] he was finally directed in a vision to settle in the East. In 1223 CE, he moved to Damascus, where he lived the remainder of his days, left this world, and was buried in 1240.

Toward the end of his life he produced two works within an astonishing forty day period. One was his vast *summa mystica*, the *Futuhat al-Makkiyya* (The Meccan Openings [Illuminations])—a 2800 page work which he placed on top of the Ka'ba and, in spite of inclement weather, retrieved undamaged one year later. The other was his shorter, more controversial work on the stations of the prophets and their inheritors, *Fusus al-Hikam* (Bezels of Wisdom). The latter book was given to him spiritually by the Prophet Muhammad in 1229 CE, with an injunction to pass it on to humanity; what Ibn 'Arabi wrote, he insisted, was pure dictation by divine decree, notated precisely as he received it. All told, the prolific *Sheikh al-Akbar*, Ibn 'Arabi, wrote approximately 700 works, some 300 of which have not survived.

Among Sufis in general, he is regarded as the greatest master of the knowledge of spiritual realities, one of the most respected expounders of Sufi or Islamic metaphysics. However, Ibn 'Arabi was always controversial, even in his lifetime (having supposedly fled Egypt after a condemning *fatwa* was issued against him), but

---

152 Maghrib (Arabic: "the West") traditionally refers to Western North Africa as well as Islamic Spain and Andalusia.

even more so posthumously. A half century after his death, Ibn Taymiyya joined the chorus of hostile critics and classified Ibn 'Arabi, along with Al-Hallaj and other traditionally cited heretics, in a register of those holding "reprehensible propositions." He rejected the possibility that *al-Fusus al-Hikam* was divinely inspired, and even went so far as to allege that the work was shaitanically inspired, since he felt it promoted laxity with its descriptions of ultimate divine mercy upon those in hell and its supposed pantheistic doctrine of unity. In seventeenth century India, the religious reformer Sirhindi again attacked Ibn 'Arabi, this time for allegedly not giving enough weight to the aspect of servanthood as the highest possible *makam*, but rather insisting that there are no beings separate from God. Presently, we will quote Ibn 'Arabi himself on some of these major points in his wide-ranging teachings, but will only point out here that, during his lifetime, Ibn 'Arabi was known by many to be a *qutb*, and certainly a respected teacher whose example was blameless in terms of teaching and observing the shariat.

To add world perspective to the latter part of Ibn 'Arabi's life, we may note a few events that transpired during that time. Around 1200 CE, a number of natural disasters plagued the Middle East: severe famine in Egypt, earthquakes in Syria, flooding of the Guadalquivir. In 1204, the Crusaders took Constantinople and the noted Jewish philosopher, Maimonides passed away. In 1207, Genghis Khan was proclaimed Emperor by the Turks and Mongols, his army taking Persia in 1220. In 1223, Frederick II deported the Muslims from Sicily and was ceded Jerusalem in 1229; 1226-7 saw the death first of St. Francis of Assisi, then Genghis Khan. The noted Sufi poet and master, Fariduddin Attar (who wrote *The Conference of the Birds*) was martyred by Mongol invaders in 1229, triggering a great wave of resistance by his people, who had formerly remained passive. Damascus was successfully sieged by Kamil in the same year, and in 1236, Cordova was captured by the Christians. In 1245, five years after the passing of Ibn 'Arabi, Baghdad fell to the Mongols.

The legend of Ibn 'Arabi's passing is an interesting one. Ibn 'Arabi's principal modern biographer, Claude Addas, thinks the

Sheikh al-Akbar probably died undramatically in his old age; but in Damascus, as well as in Istanbul, the following story of his martyrdom is recounted. During his life, Ibn 'Arabi was often showered with gifts, sometimes from persons in high positions. However, he had no interest in the accumulation of money or worldly possessions, and would distribute these gifts to others. Once he was given a palace and immediately gave it away to a beggar who approached him. On the other hand, many of the religious authorities of Damascus were professionals who worked primarily for the pay they received rather than for sake of Allah, and held highly restricted notions about the teachings of Islam. As such, they resented Ibn 'Arabi's high-flown Qur'anic exegeses as well as the abundance of gifts that seemed to flow to him from his admirers.

It is told that one day Ibn 'Arabi went up the mountain in Damascus to a place where he often preached and, walking over to a certain spot, said to a group of jurists congregated there, "The lord whom you worship is under my feet." Upon hearing this, they became furious and beat him to death. Afterwards, the jurists themselves were severely punished and it was decided to bury Sheikh Muhyiddin right where he was martyred. Another version has it that Ibn 'Arabi was jailed after his audacious announcement but was later released when another sheikh, Abu-Hassan, mitigated his words by explaining that his words were *shath*—words from beyond him, uttered in a state of spiritual intoxication—and that he should not be punished for them. Finally, there are still other accounts of his death and funeral that make no mention of such a colorful episode. However, his tomb seems to have been later destroyed by some antagonistic party.

A footnote to this story underscores the regard that the Turkish people have always felt for the *Sheikh al-Akbar*. When the ninth Ottoman sultan, Selim II, conquered Damascus in 1516, he learned of Ibn 'Arabi's enigmatic statement: "When *S* (the Arabic letter *sin*) enters into *SH* (*shin*), the tomb of Muhyiddin will be discovered." Zembilli 'Ali Efendi, a scholar of the time, interpreted the saying as a prophecy which meant: "When Selim (with a *S*) enters the city of Sham (with a *SH*, using the Arabic name for Damascus), he will discover Muhyiddin Ibn al-'Arabi's tomb." From local scholars, they learned where he had been buried and excavated the area. There, they indeed found his tomb; but even more surprising, they found a treasure chest full of gold coins adjacent to the spot. Thus they came to understand the significance of the master's cryptic saying to the assembly of money-hungry professional jurists, "The lord you worship is beneath my feet." Using the recovered treasure, Sultan Selim built a magnificent shrine in honor of Ibn 'Arabi, which still exists today on the mountain Qasiyun near Damascus.[153]

Having examined a few of the salient events in the spiritual life of the *Sheikh al-Akbar*, we can now briefly examine of some of the major themes which characterize his prodigious literary output. Because there is such a volume and rich abundance of ideas, we can only scratch the surface and would refer the interested reader to further investigate the many recent English classics in the field of Ibn 'Arabi study. These include: *The Sufi Path of Knowledge* by William Chittick, *Seal of the Saints* by Michel Chodkiewicz, *What the Seeker Needs*, translated by Sheikh Tosun Bayrak al-Jerrahi and Rabi'a Harris, as well as Claude Addas' excellent biography of Ibn 'Arabi, *Quest for the Red Sulphur*.

Insights from the Teachings of Ibn 'Arabi

Highly characteristic of Ibn 'Arabi's broad understanding of the nature of Reality and the universal character of religious belief is his statement about the authentic gnostic, or knower of Truth, in his *Futuhat al-Makkiyya*: "If a gnostic *('arif)* is really a gnostic he cannot stay tied to one form of belief." That is, he recognizes and penetrates to the inner kernel of truth in a wide variety of beliefs,

153 Ibn 'Arabi, translated by Sheikh Tosun Bayrak, *Journey to the Lord of Power*, quoted from the introduction by Sheikh Muzaffer Ozak, 10-11.

without narrowing his belief system to the point of inwardly imposing upon the Divine Truth one form of external clothing with which he has become familiar.

Without tying himself to any figurative belief, the true *'arif* recognizes and loves the Essential Truth, regardless of what apparel it dons. Two ahadith are cited in support of this teaching: in one *hadith qudsi*, Allah Most High states: "I appear to My servants as they expect Me to appear." In another it is related that some of the people who attain to paradise will behold the revelation of their Lord for which they had longed for so many years; but they will be astonished at the form of the revelation and deny it saying, "Never could you be our Lord!" Three times the revelation will change and they will be upset and reject each one, until finally the Lord will appear to each one according to the degree of their understanding and the expectation of their belief. Then they will each love and accept what they see and praise the Lord as the greatest Reality and become lost in the ecstasy of beholding Allah's Beauty. On the other hand, says Ibn 'Arabi, the gnostic who knows himself or herself and truly sees Reality in this world will easily recognize and embrace the first revelation of the Divine that they are shown in paradise; but as it is said in the Qur'an, "whoever is (inwardly) blind in this world will be blind also in the next world"—except as Allah has mercy upon them. Therefore, seekers of Truth should strive to free their minds from narrow and limiting beliefs in this world, for it is here that one plants the seeds in preparation for the next world.[154]

Never shirking controversy in the pursuit of Truth, Ibn 'Arabi goes on to point out that, as Allah is the source of all that exists, when Muslims reject idols as being non-God, they err in an important sense. He is in complete agreement with the Messenger of Unity, the Prophet Muhammad, that Allah cannot be contained in any idol, but emphatically rejects the more limited assumption—adopted by so many later followers of the Prophet—that there can be anything separate from God, whether an idol, Shaitan or one's nafs. He points out the Qur'anic injunction: "Your Lord has

---

154 Ibn 'Arabi/Bursevi, *Kernel of the Kernel*, 1-2.

decreed (commanded) that you worship none but Him." This is not a divine request which we may or may not choose to obey, says Ibn 'Arabi; rather, it is the statement of an already existing condition, since nothing exists except He—this One Indivisible Divine Reality.

The sheikh goes on to say:

> In every form none but God is worshiped, for there is no non-God in existence. The low one imagines God, that is, a limited deity, in the form of the worshiped ... The sublime one does not so imagine, but says: "This is a divine manifestation and its respect is necessary." ... Whatever you comprehend is God. God is the essence of the possibles ... There is nothing in existence except God.[155]

Ibn 'Arabi further quotes the hadith which was a favorite of Hazrat Junayd: "Allah is and there is nothing with Him." He explains that the second word—*kana* in Arabic—is often used as if it denoted time, so that the saying has been interpreted by some to mean, "[There was a remote time when] Allah *was* and nothing existed with Him." However, Ibn 'Arabi says this distorts the intended meaning of the verse; *kana*, in its true significance, simply denotes *existence* (beyond time) and is not a verb with a tense, precisely as in the Qur'anic saying, "Allah is *(kana)* most gracious and pardoning . . . ." Nor was it accurate when scholars of the past, wrongly understanding *kana* to imply the past tense, further extrapolated from this saying that "Allah is as He was [before time]." The simple, unencumbered meaning of this Prophetic hadith is that "Allah alone exists and . . . there is nothing with Him."[156]

Unlike al-Hallaj, who advocated *hululu'l-lahuti fi'n-nasut*, or the indwelling of the divine in the mundane, Ibn 'Arabi totally rejects the possibility of *hulul*—that there could possibly be some separate divine entity that could indwell something that is non-

155 Husaini, *The Pantheistic Monism of Ibn al-'Arabi*, 175-77.
156 Ibid, 178-79.

God.[157] Though Orientalists have sometimes tried to label Ibn 'Arabi as a pantheist, that idea carries associations with it that are incompatible with his belief—such as the idea that God is (only) the material world of nature, or that God indwells all things. What Ibn 'Arabi actually says is this:

> Do not fall into the blasphemous error of the sect called *Hululiyyah*, who believe that another soul, even another being, can be infused into them and that they may have God materially existing in them. Know that He is never in anything, nor is anything in Him.[158] He is neither inside nor outside of anything . . . None can know Him; only He can know Himself . . .That which hides Him is His oneness . . . The veil that hides Him is His own being . . . Neither a prophet whom He has sent to humanity, nor a saint, a perfect man, nor an angel close to Him can see Him, for they are not apart from Him. His prophets, His messengers, [His perfected ones,] are none other than He, for He has sent Himself, from Himself, for Himself, without any other cause or means besides Himself . . . That is why our Master, the Light of the Universe, the Prophet Muhammad (may Allah's peace and blessings be upon him) said: "I know my Lord by my Lord." He also said: "He who knows himself knows his Lord." By this it is meant that surely you are not you, and you—without being you—are He . . . for you never existed, nor do you exist, nor will ever exist. You have not entered into Him, nor He into you. Without being, your essence is with Him and in Him... If you know yourself as nothing, then you truly know your Lord. Otherwise, you know Him not.[159]

Ibn 'Arabi goes on to point out the common fallacy, claimed by many a spiritual teacher, that you need to make yourself nothing in order to know your Lord. You are not something that can efface

---

157 Ibid, 181.
158 Nor is God a He or She, but an Allness; the limitations of the English language make it difficult to cogently avoid using a gender-specific pronoun in the translation of such passages.
159 Ibn 'Arabi/Bayrak, *What the Seeker Needs,* 30-31.

itself and finally become nothing. Ibn 'Arabi says if you think you exist, and thus need to annihilate yourself in God, this is already the sin of *shirk*, setting up partners beside Allah—because you are claiming that Allah exists and you exist separately. The holy Prophet did not say: "He who eliminates himself knows his Lord," but "He who knows himself, knows his Lord." *(Man arafa nafsahu faqad arafa Rabbahu.)* By "knowing oneself," the Prophet did not mean the limited ego-self, but rather knowing one's truth, one's reality. Likewise, the Prophet also said, "Actually, you do not exist, as you did not exist before you were created."[160]

This is pure seventh level teaching, which is rarely presented in the context of any Western religious training. This is partially because those who are practicing their faith and forming their conception of Reality in terms of a second or third level understanding—where God and the *nafs* (or the world) are still conceptualized as being fairly separate—have great difficulty in receiving such high truths or making any practical use of them. Yet, if we really deeply consider it, we can begin to see that this is not merely some rarified teaching for the most advanced adepts, but is the fundamental truth of our existence as expressions of the One Reality. This teaching—that all existence is one, and that there are no partners beside Allah—is certainly the core significance of *La ilaha illallah*. The Prophet once said of this blessed declaration of unity: "The best statement we have made—both I and the all prophets who preceded me—is *La ilaha illallah*."

Ibn 'Arabi's philosophy has come to be known by the term *wahdat al-wujud*, which may be roughly translated as "the unity of existence" or "unity of being". Although Ibn 'Arabi never actually used this phrase in his writings, it is a useful term inasmuch as it points toward that aspect of Qur'anic hermeneutics and Sufi metaphysics which, in the sheikh's scholarly hands, finally became clearly and coherently articulated as never before. Various Westerns scholars have attempted to apply other labels to Ibn 'Arabi's philosophy, such as *monism*, *pantheism*, and even *existential monism*; but none of these terms have proved

---

160 Ibid, 32.

very satisfactory, primarily because they tend to evoke stray associations which don't accurately represent the sheikhs' views.

One of the subtleties of Ibn 'Arabi's system—a significant spiritual nuance which would elude a simplistic or reductionist analysis of *wahdat al-wajud*—is the sheikh's explanation that, though nothing exists which is separate from the Divine Source of Being, the creation nevertheless is not strictly identical with the Divine Essence. This is because Allah does not manifest the world by means of His Essence *(Zat)*, but by means of His Divine Attributes *(Sifaat Allah)*.

First, a note on the etymology of a word which sheds light on the nature of this explanation. The Arabic word for *world*, *'alam* (plural: *'alamin),* comes from the root word *'ilm*, meaning *to know*; thus, in Arabic, the word designating *the world* or *the created realms* literally indicates "that by means of which one knows a thing". The very word, then, implies that the creation is that by which the Creator is known.[161] This essential idea is shown forth in the famous *hadith qudsi* where Allah says: "I was a Hidden Treasure and I desired to be known; therefore I created the worlds."

Ibn 'Arabi explains that the creation, having become apparent *(Zahir)* as the externalization of the hidden *(Batin),* exists, as it were, as a projected reflection of the Essential Source, which is sustained by means of the divine names or qualities. What depends on another for its being, the sheikh points out, does not truly exist. The manifest universe is both He and not-He. Accordingly, Ibn 'Arabi enumerates three categories of existence:

(1) Allah, who alone has *Being* (but Who has no material, finite existence in time or space).

(2) The created universe, which does materially exist (but which has no Being, except through Allah).

(3) That which neither exists nor doesn't exist (referring to intangible things like knowledge and the imagination).

---

161 Maulana Muhammad 'Ali, The Holy Qur'an, 4.

The first category is *wujud*, a word rich in meanings, which is here being used only to refer to Absolute Being. The second category is *mawjud*, that which manifests physically; while the third is *ma'dun*, not physically manifested.[162]

On the one hand, then, Ibn 'Arabi says that only matter—the material creation—physically exists (this includes the more rarified gradations of created life such as mind and spirit), while its Source, Allah Most High, has no physical existence. He refers to *Surat al-An'am* (6:104) to amplify this explanation: "The eyes cannot see Him (Allah), but He sees through all eyes. He is the Subtle, the All-Aware." Ibn 'Arabi points out that the physical eyes, being created, cannot perceive the Eternal, the Spiritual Origin of creation; but ultimately, he says, there really are no separate parts of creation, such as eyes, but only the One. "The one who does not reach this conclusion cannot possibly come to know himself . . . Allah sees Himself by Himself and none other than Himself. His Essence sees His Essence."[163]

Ibn 'Arabi also quotes two other sayings here. The first one is a hadith of the Prophet which says: "Men are asleep and they will awaken when they die." The sheikh interprets this to mean that whatever we see in our worldly life is like a dream for the sleeper—a drama requiring interpretation—as is everything except the Ultimate Reality, Allah.[164]

The other verse, a favorite of Ibn 'Arabi's, is from the Qur'an. It was revealed after the famous Muslim victory at the Battle of Badr and refers to an incident in which the Prophet picked up a handful of gravel and sand, then hurled it at the charging enemy during the height of the battle. The attacking Meccans stopped their onslaught immediately, astonished by the perception of a powerful force repelling them backwards. They turned and fled the field, giving the victory to the outnumbered Muslims of Medina. Soon afterwards, the *ayat* was revealed in which Allah spoke to the Prophet, saying: "You did not throw when you threw, but Allah

---

162 Chittick, *The Sufi Path of Knowledge*, 6-7.
163 Ibn 'Arabi/Bayrak, *What the Seeker Needs*, 45.
164 Husaini, 187.

threw."[165] This amazing verse affirms the individual reality of the Prophet (. . . when *you* threw), then negates it by revealing that it was Allah who was the reality behind the appearance (*You* did not throw . . . but *Allah threw*). Ibn 'Arabi concedes:

> The clear formation of this question is terribly difficult. Verbal expression *(ibara)* falls short of it and conceptualization *(tasawwur)* cannot define it, because it quickly escapes and its properties are contradictory. It is like His words, "You did not throw," so He negated, "when you threw," so He affirmed, "but God threw," so He negated the engendered existence *(kawn)* of Muhammad and affirmed Himself as identical *(`ayn)* with Muhammad, since He appointed for him the name "God."[166]

This is all connected to the mystery of servanthood. As Ibn 'Arabi notes, the Prophet himself is referred to in the Muslim *shahada* as *'abduhu wa rasuluhu* (the servant and messenger), the servanthood *('abd)* taking priority even over being a messenger *(rasul)*. The Qur'an[167] reveals: "No one in the heavens and earth comes to the All-Merciful except as a servant." The divine name Lord *(Rabb)* denotes the relationship that exists between the Divine Essence, which is Independent of the worlds, and created beings, who are all vassal servants entirely dependent on their Lord for Necessary Being, having none of their own.

The name Lord only has meaning as one pole connecting it with servanthood, but the two qualities are forever distinct and, according to Ibn 'Arabi, never merge; the creature never becomes Lord. The perfection of servanthood *('ubudiyyat)*, which is to become nothing in oneself—i.e., completely transparent to and united with the divine command—brings the servant to the highest possible station, a *makam* in which Ibn 'Arabi says "no whiffs of lordship *(rububiyya)* are smelt from" the servant. He says that "the ultimate illusion is for a person to bring Lord and servant together

---

165 Qur'an 8:17.
166 Chittick, 113-14.
167 Qur'an 19:93.

through *wujud* [Being/existence]."[168] He adds that the *malami* on the path of blame is often the most successful in achieving the state of pure servanthood.

The Holy Qur'an reveals that "All who are in the heavens or earth submit (bow) to Allah, knowingly or unknowingly, as do their shadows, from morning to evening."[169] In respect to this *ayat*, Ibn 'Arabi says there are really two degrees of servanthood. The first is *'ubuda*, which refers to the servant inasmuch as the Lord's acts are spontaneously performed through him or her, without the slightest distance between the divine impulse or command and its immediate performance. In this case (as stated in a famous hadith), Allah "draws near to the servant and becomes his hearing, his sight and his hands," yet the acts are totally owned by Allah: the Lord alone is acting without partner. Jesus' raising of the dead would be an example of *'ubuda*; such perfect servanthood being indicative of the seventh level.

The second form, *'ubudiyyat*, includes the perspective of the earlier-quoted Qur'anic verse where all creation, including inanimate objects, along with their shadows, are at all times in natural accord with the divine will. But beyond this, *'ubudiyyat* also includes the level of conscious participation by humans and *jinn* who, as vassals of their Lord, are divinely bequeathed the prerogative of obeying or disobeying His will. The Qur'an again supports this, saying: "It is up to each one of you to take the straight path if each so wishes. But you cannot wish except what Allah, the Lord of the Worlds, wishes."[170] Clearly then, having the conscious awareness to make choices does not take one out of the realm of servanthood, though some might mistakenly imagine that it does. Nor does the Lord ever become the servant: "The Real is far too exalted to dwell within corporal bodies."[171]

Having said all of this, Ibn 'Arabi, still affirms the basic truth of Bistami and Al-Hallaj's realization of being none but Allah or the Divine Truth. However, he qualifies this, saying that they were not

---

168 Chittick, 324.
169 Qur'an 13:15
170 Qur'an 81:28-9.
171 Chittick, 310, 325.

annihilated in Allah, since they were never self-existent to begin with; rather, they were overcome by a state of divine intoxication which made them claim lordship—a claim outwardly resembling Pharaoh's deluded boast—whereas the messengers, prophets and truly mature friends are always careful to speak with *adab* so that they don't audaciously intrude upon the divine station of lordship.[172] He specifically alludes to an instance in which Abu Yazid Bistami said to his Lord, "How should I gain nearness to You?" The Real answered him, "Leave aside your self and come!" Ibn 'Arabi comments:

> Once he abandons himself, he will have abandoned the property of servanthood . . . Hence, in lowliness and poverty Abu Yazid sought nearness through servanthood, while, in abandoning self, he sought nearness through assuming the character of the traits of God. It is through this that there is a coming together . . . At root the servant was created only to belong to God and to be a servant perpetually. He was not created to be a lord. So when God clothes him in the robe of mastership and commands him to appear in it, he appears as a servant in himself and a master in the view of the observer. This is the ornament of his Lord, the robe He has placed upon him . . .
>
> Someone remarked to Abu Maydan that the people were touching him with their hands with the intention of gaining blessing and he let them do that. [The person asked Abu Maydan:] "Do you not find in yourself the effect of that?" He replied, "Does the Black stone [of the Ka'ba] find in itself an effect which would remove it from being a stone, since it is kissed by messengers, the prophets, and the friends, and since it is the right hand of God?" The person replied that it did not. Abu Maydan said, "I am that stone."[173]

---

172 Ibid, 320.
173 Ibid, 319-23. The anecdote probably refers to Sheikh Abu Madyan rather than Sheikh Abu Maydan, the two often being confused.

Concerning this station, Allah informs the Prophet Muhammad (48:10): "Those who swear allegiance to you, in reality swear allegiance to Allah." The Divine Source also reveals to Muhammad that he has a *khuluq 'azim*, a tremendous nature or character. According to Ibn 'Arabi's *tafsir*, this does not merely indicate that the Prophet possessed a morally upright character, but is indicative of the degree to which he had realized the innate potentialities of his being and given expression to the divine attributes with which Allah had created him, such as generosity, kindness and so forth. This is called *at-takhalluq bi akhlaq Allah*, meaning "assuming the divine traits"—manifesting the manner and characteristics of Allah's own exalted qualities within one's being. The word *khuluq* (plural, *akhlaq*), meaning "character traits" as well as "moral traits," has its ontological roots in the word *khalq*, meaning "creation."

We have already mentioned Ibn 'Arabi's explanation that Allah manifests the creation, not by means of His Essence, but by means of His Divine Attributes or Names. Each soul, then, has been created as a garden of beautiful Divine Attributes. The one who actualizes the beautiful traits through which Allah has created them as well as the divine qualities which form the root of their individual soul is said to be assuming the divine manner *(Akhlaq Allah)*. Thus, the Prophet used to urge the people to embody these noble character traits as a way of participation in the divine milieu. He said, "I was sent [as a prophet] to complete the beautiful character traits," and "Among the best of you is the most beautiful in character."[174]

According to the Sufi teaching based on the Qur'an, there are at least ninety-nine beautiful divine names of Allah (*al-esma al-husna*) which resonate in the human soul. Ibn 'Arabi takes up the tradition, explaining how Allah taught Adam all of the names, and did so to an extent which surpassed even the knowledge of the angels.[175] It was thus through the divine names that everything in existence came into being. According to Ibn 'Arabi, this is the sense in which one should understand the hadith: "Allah created Adam upon His own form." From Adam on, each human being

---

174 Ibid, 22.
175 Qur'an 2:31.

has inherited the potentiality of all the divine names in their being; however, certain qualities are primary in each soul while others are secondary. As a result, each person exists as a unique blend of the divine qualities. One person may manifest divine compassion *(Rahman)* and light *(Nur)*, while another may existentiate the qualities of divine majesty *(Majid)* and power *(Qadr)*.

As Ibn 'Arabi notes, the conflict of opposing qualities contained in the individual soul goes right to the highest level of created existence. It was revealed to the Prophet that even the angels in the higher plenum were disputing over various "expiations" *(kaffarat)* which had their roots in the primal opposites—issues such as whether to go to the mosque on foot, how to do ablutions under difficult conditions, etc. As for the extent to which a given divine name manifests in the human form, more is not always better than less. Just as there are names of mercy, there are also names of severity; to have the quality *al-Jabbar*, the Over-Bearing, coming through strongly in a human, without other qualities to balance it (as we see in many dictators), would not be desirable, either to Allah or other creatures around that person.

In their pure state, all the attributes are encompassed by Allah, Who is the First and the Last, the Inner and the Outer, the Giver and the Taker of Life. In Him, at the very Source, all of these qualities are perfectly balanced and at peace. This has its corollary on a smaller scale for humans, inasmuch as the different qualities can balance one's character in a complementary way. We can observe that great beauty or knowledge is best guarded by modesty, lest one suffer from the jealousy of others; power operates best in tandem with wisdom and mercy, and so forth.

The sheikh points out that, unlike all the other specific divine names, the name *Allah* encompasses all the other names, representing an indescribable combination of all the opposites. It is thus the most basic, all-inclusive name for calling upon God, no matter what divine quality one is seeking.[176] In summarizing this subject, Ibn 'Arabi, notes that, though Allah is "Independent of the worlds," without His creation making Him known and actualizing

---

176 Chittick, 66-68.

His names, He would not be Lord; nor is the human being fully human until he or she manifests the perfect attributes latent within their own being.

Ibn 'Arabi's Elucidations on the Spiritual Hierarchy

We have dwelt on Ibn 'Arabi's ideas at some length because he touches upon so many essential ideas which thereafter became important to the tarikat legacy. In concluding our treatment of Sheikh Muhyiddin, we will revisit one set of ideas to which we earlier alluded in passing: the idea of spiritual hierarchy.

In one sense, everything that is created is equal and there exists no hierarchy; it is not as if Allah were separate or remote from His creation and could only be reached through a hierarchy of intermediaries. Far from it; Allah is the All-Aware, the All-Seeing, the All-Hearing, the Omnipotent and Omnipresent, "closer to us than our jugular veins." However, there is another barometer of divine intimacy and trust. Many souls consciously or unconsciously turn their backs upon the Divine Source of their own being. Through their own heedlessness, they lose their innate awareness of existing nearer than near to Allah. This is one of the primary messages of the Qur'an: a warning to humanity to turn back *(tawba)* toward its own True Source, and to heed the prophets, messengers and *awliya* (saints) who, deeply inspired by their own intimate remembrance of Allah, bid humanity to join in the conscious return to Him.

In such a context, the Qur'an speaks of those upright souls who have drawn near to the Divine Presence, such as the Prophet Muhammad, who mystically drew as close as "two bow-lengths" to the formless and spaceless Divine Essence, and Jesus, who is described[177] as being one of the "very nearest" *(muqarrabun)* to

---

177 Qur'an 3:45.

Allah, honored in both worlds. There is also a description in the Qur'an[178] of one who can probably be identified as either a *qutb (qutub)* or a *ghous (ghawth)*. This unnamed man, who is not a prophet or *rasul* (divine messenger), comes running from a remote part of a city which is about to undergo destruction, and, in an effort to save the people, cries out: "O my people, follow the messenger!" This man closely conforms to the image of a *qutb*: an intimate friend of Allah who is the spiritual pole or axis of his nation, or even the entire planet—frequently hidden or unknown—who, through his prayers and devout spiritual influence, helps protect and preserve the people from harm through his intercessions with Allah.

The well-known biblical story of the Prophet Abraham interceding with Allah to forestall the fate of Sodom and Gomorrah, depicts one aspect of what is meant by a *qutb*. Another aspect would be possession of a deep degree of divine intimacy and penetrating knowledge of spiritual realities which qualifies one to serve as a kind of spiritual commander of one's nation and as a chief among the other saints of the time. The *qutb's* service is performed for the sake of the well-being of the planet or of a large population among whom he or she resides. The various hidden saints, *aqtab* (plural of *qutb*), and *'abdal* may or may not recognize each other and may or may not be outwardly important people, or of the same religion, though all are inwardly Muslims in the sense of being submitted to the One God or Ultimate Reality.

A *ghous*, such as 'Abdul Qadir Gaylani was recognized to be (he was also a *qutb*), is one who brings succor to his people and radiates a harmonious atmosphere which helps protect his community from various dangers and natural disasters. *Ghous* is usually considered to be the next rank below *qutb*; either one of these functionaries may be entrusted with some power to affect the weather, where necessary.

More than any mystic before him, Ibn 'Arabi has a great deal to say about the subject of sainthood *(walaya)*, with its various grades. He

---

178 Qur'an 36:20-27.

speaks about the *Aqtab* (qutbs), in his *Futuhat al-Makkiyya,*[179] saying:

> [Though the *Aqtab* represent] the sum of all the states and all the stations, . . . the meaning of the word "Pole" *(qutb)* may be stretched to cover all those who are pivots of a certain spiritual station and who alone are in full possession of it at any given moment. One may also say of a man dwelling in a certain place that he is its Pole. In the same way, the sheikh who presides over an assembly is the Pole of that assembly. But in the technical sense, and in the absence of any other definition, the Pole is a term which properly speaking can only be applied to one person in every epoch. He is also named *ghawth* [ghous], "help." He is one of the "proximate" *(al-muqarrabun*[180]*)*, and is the head of the community for his time. Some of the Poles possess an authority which is manifested and hold the office of caliph in the external sense. This was so in the case of Abu Bakr, 'Umar, 'Uthman and 'Ali, Hasan and Mu'awiya ibn Yazid [the grandson of Mu'awiya I], 'Umar ibn 'Abd al-Aziz and al-Mutawakkil. Others are caliphs only in the inner sense and possess no apparent external authority, such as Ahmad ibn Harun ar-Rashid as-Sabti or Abu Yazid al-Bistami and most of the Poles.

Though other mystics had previously alluded to the existence of a *qutb* and other ranks, their information was sparse and seldom tallied. There are traditions purportedly reaching back to the time of the Prophet which mention *"The Forty"* and *"The Seven."* For instance, Abu Hurayra reported that the Prophet once said to him: "In a moment a man will come toward me through that door; he is one of the seven men by means of whom Allah protects the inhabitants of the earth." A moment later a bald and disfigured Ethiopian entered carrying a pitcher of water. The Prophet indicated that this man, whose job was to wash down and sweep the mosque,

---

179 Chodkiewicz, *Seal of the Saints,* 95.
180 Qur'an 56:11.

was the one to whom he had referred—one of the seven *'abdal* or spiritual substitutes. Of the Forty Spiritual Elders who uphold the world, Shi'i tradition maintains that 'Ali, Salman Farsi, and various other members of the *Ahl as-Suffa* were among them and that the Prophet encountered their glorious spiritual counterparts during his heavenly *mir'aj*.

Another later story reveals how a disciple unobtrusively followed 'Abdul Qadir Gaylani out of the gates of Baghdad one night. Suddenly they were in another place altogether, and there, while the disciple hid behind a pillar, the sheikh met six men, along with a seventh and an eighth, the last of whom was groaning and at the point of death. Saying that he did so by divine command, 'Abdul Qadir performed a ceremony involving the seventh man, who was in good health. The next day when the mystified disciple privately begged 'Abdul Qadir to explain what he had seen, his sheikh revealed that the six men and the dying man were the seven *'abdal*, while the eighth man was a Christian from Constantinople who had come to take the Muslim *shahada* from 'Abdul Qadir and replace the other *badal*, who was dying. He then ordered the disciple not to divulge the story as long his sheikh was alive.[181]

Though anecdotes such as these existed, as well as a growing literature concerning the "Council of the Saints" *(diwan al-awliya)*, the information remained scattered and vague until the Sheikh al-Akbar took up the subject. Through Ibn 'Arabi's writings, we are given a much more systematic account of the relationship between the spiritual officeholders who secretly uphold the world by the mysterious permission of Allah.

According to Ibn 'Arabi, the *Qutb* of the Age is the highest in rank of the four spiritual pillars *(awtad)* of the world. Only the prophets and messengers, whose function was sealed and completed by Muhammad, rank hierarchically above them. No one on earth has authority over them, so they are directly guided by Allah. Furthermore, the four Pillars of any given age are actually earthly representatives *(nuwwab, plural of na'ib)* substituting for the original four who were divinely appointed after the passing

---

181 Chodkiewicz, 90-1. *(Badal* is the singular of *'abdal.)*

of the Prophet Muhammad; these are the four heavenly immortal messengers: Idris (Enoch), the Pole, flanked by two Imams, Jesus and Elijah, and the fourth Pillar, Khidr.

The two Imams have specific functions, regardless of whether we speak of Jesus and Elijah or their earthly substitutes. They are sometimes referred to as *aftad* (solitary ones). One is called "The Imam of the Left;" his secret name is *'Abdur-Rabb* (Servant of the Lord). As "Sword of the Pole" *(sayf al-qutb),* he watches over the equilibrium of the world and usually succeeds the *qutb.* If he dies before succeeding the *qutb,* his other counterpart, "the Imam of the Right," is next in line of succession, as is the fourth Pillar after him. The Imam of the Right is the one who watches over the world of spirits, his titular name being 'Abdul Malik. It is said that this Imam's knowledge is solely of the heavens and not of the things of this earth.[182] The fourth *watad* (singular for Pillar), Khidr, corresponds to the corner of the Ka'ba which houses the mysterious Black Stone.

Later, in the Halveti-Jerrahi Order, we will see a kind of equivalency in the use of four posts, which are dyed sheepskins of various colors upon which the highest-ranking sheikhs sit during the dhikr ceremony. The grand-sheikh, who is the head of the order, kneels on a blue post, with his two highest ranking elder sheikhs flanking him on either side, kneeling on red posts. One of the holders of the red post specializes in dealing with the events of this world, while the other specializes in dream interpretation and other matters which concern the spiritual world. Adjacent to the blue post is the black post, whose holder is a kind of counterweight to the blue post, and who is further in line of succession for the blue post after the two red posts.

Returning to Ibn 'Arabi, it is possible to deduce from his writings that, as the result of various mystic dreams, he believed himself to have held the position of "Imam of the Left" in his own time, a position he inherited from Abu Madyan, one of the greatest sheikhs of the time, but one whom Ibn 'Arabi never had the opportunity to meet in the flesh. He identifies the other Pillars as being a Sufi

---

182 Ibid, 96.

named Rabi ibn Mahmud al-Mardini, along with a Persian and Ethiopian, neither of whom he names. He also mentions meeting one of the *awtad* in Fez, a man named Ibn Ja`dun, who was so transparent to Allah that few people noticed him or made spiritual inquiries of him. Always wide-ranging in his views, Ibn 'Arabi employs still another complementary system of classification of the *Rijal Allah* (Men of God) in some of his other writings. In the *Futuhat*, he associates the four Pillars with four corners or station of the Ka 'ba in Mecca, saying: "To each *watad* (Pillar) belongs one corner of the corners of the House. The Syrian corner belongs to him who is on the heart of Adam; the Iraqi corner to him who is on the heart of Abraham; the Yemenite corner to him who is on the heart of Jesus; and the corner of the Black Stone to him who is on the heart of Muhammad—and this is my corner, *Alhamdulillah*."[183] In his *Kitab Manzil al-Qutb* he goes on to say:

> The most perfect of the Poles is the Muhammadan Pole. The ones below him are divided hierarchically according to the ranks of the Prophets whose heirs they are; for they are heirs of Jesus, of Abraham, of Joseph, of Noah, and so on; and the position of each pole is determined by the position of the prophet whose heir he is, but all of them proceed from the "tabernacle" of Muhammad.[184]

This teaching relates back to Ibn 'Arabi's great vision at Cordova, where it was revealed to him that every saint is "on the foot of a prophet." That is, they enjoy a spiritual station (*makam*) characterized by a special inheritance from one of the prophets; but these prophetic attunements are, subsequent to the coming of the Seal of Prophecy, all derived through the fountain of the prophets, Muhammad Mustafa, may peace and blessing be upon him. Two centuries before, Sahl at-Tustari had stated something similar: "There is no prophet who does not have someone similar to himself in this community, that is to say, a *wali* (saint, friend) who shares in his charisma." To this the Sheikh al-Akbar added

183 Addas, 66-67.
184 Chodkiewicz, 96.

in his *Futuhat*: "If you are a *wali*, you are the heir of a prophet .
. . And if you have inherited knowledge from Moses or Jesus or
from any prophet in between, all you have actually inherited is
Muhammadan knowledge."

Ibn 'Arabi says that he himself started out in the attunement of
Jesus, then Moses, Hud and gradually all of the other prophets,
until culminating in the station of Muhammad, after which it was
revealed that he had become the Seal of the Saints of Muhammad.
A few of the ones throughout history who seemed to have shared
the *Isawi makam*, the station of Jesus, *'aleihi salaam*, include: the
immediate disciples of Jesus, al-Hallaj, Ayn al-Qudat Hamadani,
Abu'l 'Abbas al-Uryabi (one of Ibn 'Arabi's teachers), Niyazi
Misri, and the modern Sufi saint of Algeria, Sheikh Ahmad al-
Alawi (d.1934) whose Christ-like features can still be seen in
photographs.

Ibn 'Arabi mentions a *Musawi* type (the station of Moses)
named Abu Ya'za whose face was extremely bright like Moses
after he descended from his divine encounter on the mountain.
Ahmad Badawi, a powerful figure who wore a veil, seems to also
be a *Musawi* type as was perhaps 'Abdul Qadir Gaylani. It must
be understood that it is possible for the *wali* to go through several
such stations in his life or combine more than one inheritance,
each of which he or she may receive in full or in part.

The Sufi Ibn Hud (d.1297 CE), the brother of the Sultan
of Granada, seems to have been of an *Ibrahimi* (Abrahamic)
disposition, inasmuch as the Jews of Damascus used to gather in
his house to study Maimonides' *Guide for the Perplexed* under
his direction.[185] It is even possible to see in the Naqshbandi tarikat
an Islamic setting of a Buddhist makam. The order practices a
type of silent meditation and dhikr while its members often travel
around, walking with a staff, in a manner reminiscent of Buddhist
mendicants.

At any given time, Ibn 'Arabi informs us, there are bound to
be at least 124,000 *awliya* living on earth, a number which
represents the minimum requirement if there is to exist one saint

---

185 Ibid, 59, 83.

in the station of each of the prophets who have come to guide humanity over the centuries. As for those saints who directly inherit the Muhammadan station, it is as though they receive a double dose; since one inherits from any of the prophets through the intermediation of Muhammad, the Prophet's direct inheritors receive "from Muhammad through Muhammad".

This was the final makam that Ibn 'Arabi claimed and, as we shall see, it was also very much the station of Hazrati Pir Muhammad Nureddin al-Jerrahi. Pir Nureddin's parents had the same names as the Prophet's parents; his wife was named Khadija; he was born on the Prophet's birthday and even in some fashion resembled him, as revealed through dream confirmations.

No other pir or saint has such specific signs of the Muhammadan inheritance, although all of them share in the Prophet's being to some degree. This is part of the secret of Pir Nureddin's spiritual station, in which he was confirmed as the *Khatem al-Mujtahidin*, meaning the last of the saints who give rulings for a new order— the one who confirms and incorporates the fruits of all the founding pirs before him—in effect, the Seal of the Pirs.

With this we take leave of Ibn 'Arabi. He did not found a tarikat as such, although his stepson Sadruddin al-Qunawi (d.1274 CE) emigrated to Konya and there passed on the lineage to Jalaluddin Rumi, linking the two lines of teaching. Beyond this, the Sheikh al-Akbar left behind a great many dedicated disciples and a prodigious output of writings which were to leave an indelible stamp on the thinking of Sufis who followed him. Though not quite as accessible or easy to popularize as Rumi has proven to be, more and more of the Sheikh al-Akbar's works are currently being translated into English and appearing in print.

Continued in Volume II

APPENDIX I

The Mystery of Intercession

LATE ONE NIGHT, toward the end of the Prophet Muhammad's life, he arose from his bed and mysteriously left his apartment. His wife, Hazrat 'A'isha, awoke to find that the Prophet, who had been sleeping beside her in their bed, was missing. She got up and inquired, first of the other wives, and then of Hazrat Fatima and Hazrat 'Ali, if any of them knew where the Prophet had gone. None of them had seen the Prophet leave, but Hazrat 'Ali suggested that they look for him in the cemetery at al-Baqi. There, they found him in prostration, weeping profusely and supplicating his Lord, saying: "If you punish them, they are your servants. If you forgive them, surely you are Mighty and Wise in all Your works."

When he became aware of their presence and raised his head, Fatima expressed their concern that some harm might have befallen him at the hands of his enemies. The Rasulullah assured them that no harm had come to him; rather, he was fervently praying for his community on this blessed Night of Absolution (the 15th of Shaban), in accordance with the Angel Gabriel's wonderful announcement that on this special night, the gates of mercy would open wide and Allah would accept the Prophet's prayers for his community. The Messenger of God then invited the members of his family, intimately gathered there in the darkness of night, to join him in making intercessory prayers for the sake of all the believers. Thus, the whole gathering engaged in prayerful prostrations and heartfelt supplications to the all-Merciful Source of Being until the break of dawn.

The Islamic tradition holds that complete intercession was granted to the Prophet Muhammad, peace and blessings be upon him, and that the doors of divine forgiveness and acceptance have been opened for his entire community—for all those who turn to their own True Source, Allah Most High, and utter the saving sentence of unity, *La ilaha illallah.* Only the most recalcitrant, who refuse to turn from their faults toward divine reconciliation, will cause themselves to be exempt from the magnanimous offer of paradise promised to all who affirm the divine unity and acknowledge the Seal of Prophets, Muhammad, and all the holy messengers of divine unity who preceded him.

The Night of Absolution, *Laylat ul-Bairat,* is not the only event in the life of the Prophet Muhammad associated with deep intercession for the souls of many. There is also the *miraj,* or mystic heavenly ascension of the Prophet. In Mecca, in the early days of his announced prophethood, Islamic tradition relates that the Prophet ascended by night with the Angel Gabriel through the seven heavens, all the way to the mystic throne of Allah. When they arrived at the "lote tree of the far boundary," the absolute limit of creation where no separate self can pass, Gabriel deferred, but the Prophet continued on, drawn by the ecstatic pull of divine union. There, in a mystic unveiling, he experienced the reality of the essential unity of the individual soul with its Divine Source. This complete annihilation *(fana)* of self in the One Being has long been a goal of the mystic way, a process which clearly transcends the limits of language's ability to describe it. However, the greater mystery lies in the transformation of being that follows divine absorption *(baqa),* when the one awakens, beyond the limited self, as an expression of Divine Reality and Love.

Hence, the true culmination of this encounter came as the Prophet re-emerged from absorption in the Divine Oneness, regaining his individuality in order to respond to a great offer of divine generosity. Given divine permission to ask for whatever his heart desired, the beloved Messenger of Allah requested absolution for his entire community, even all humanity, and for the liberation from the fires of hell of every being who had as much as one drop of goodness and mercy, and who may have even once uttered with sincerity the affirmation of divine unity, *La ilaha illallah.*

The Prophet's prayers were accepted and the particulars of the religious path were revealed as well for the benefit of his people.

These included such acts of devotion as the five-times-a-day prayers, which were modeled after the example of the angels in the various heavenly realms. On one level of paradise the Prophet saw angels standing in prayer *(qiyyam);* on another they only bowed in worship *(ruku);* and on still another the angels remained in constant prayerful prostration *(sajda)* before the all-pervading light of the divine splendor. Consequently, these noble postures became the movements of the traditional Islamic prayers. Certainly, various timeless forms of this *salat,* such as prostration, had also been incorporated in the religions which preceded historical Islam, including Judaism and Christianity (although in recent centuries they have tended to emphasize as their most distinctive prayer postures, respectively, standing and kneeling).

Again, through the night-journey and heavenly ascension of the Prophet, whether in a powerful mystic dream vision or, as tradition usually insists, accomplished by the physical body, the Messenger of Allah engaged in powerful intercessory prayers for his *umma.* When the Prophet's illumined daughter, Fatima, was asked by her father what she desired for her wedding dowry, on the occasion of her forthcoming marriage to Hazrat 'Ali, she asked for nothing in this world but to be a humble channel of intercession for the women of the community, just as her father interceded for the entire community. The next day, the Prophet brought her the good news that Gabriel had informed him of Allah's acceptance of Hazrati Fatima as a channel of intercession for those who mention her in their prayers to Allah.

Certainly everyone who prays for the sake of another is a potential channel of intercession, and tradition credits some of the most effective intercessory power to the sincere prayers of mothers for their children. However, the Qur'an makes clear that not every form of intercession is accepted by Allah (particularly prayers to idols, false deities, or to limited created beings whether seen or unseen), saying, "Who could possibly intercede on behalf of others, except those mysteriously permitted by Allah?"[186] Certainly, the Qur'an implicitly acknowledges the intercession

---

186 Qur'an 2:255.

of such exalted souls as Moses *(Musa)*, upon him be peace, the Messiah Jesus *(Masihu Isa)*, upon him be peace, and his holy virgin mother Mary *(Mariam)*, upon her be peace, and freely grants that Jesus was given the power to heal the sick, bring sight to the blind and raise the dead to life, all through the permission of Allah Most High. The mystic tradition, in fact, reveals that the ability to raise the dead is indicative of a saint who is established in the seventh and highest level of the soul.

The ahadith of the Prophet indicate that there are many mystic friends of Allah *(waliyullah)*, some of them hidden saints and others well-known; they are lovers of God whose consciousness has become so intimately merged with the divine will, that whatever they ask of Allah is likely to come to pass. Nothing is outside the realm of possibility for Allah to grant; as the Qur'an says, "Allah simply says, *'Kun!'* (Be!) and it is."[187] Two well-attested al-Bukhari *ahadith qudsi* (on the authority of Abu Hurayra) attest to these illumined words of the Rasulullah:

> If Allah loves one of His servants, he summons the Angel Gabriel and says, "I profoundly love this servant; may you also love this servant." Then Gabriel loves that servant and travels throughout the heavens spreading the news of Allah's love for this servant and encouraging all of the heavenly beings to likewise love this one. Then a great love for this servant begins to be established in the hearts of the people on the earth.

> When my servant draws near to Me through acts of selfless loving kindness, intimate devotions and prayers which go beyond the duties of religion, and does these things for My sake alone, then I love him (or her). And I become the hearing with which he hears, the seeing with which he sees, the hand with which he grasps, and the feet with which he walks. Were this intimate of Mine to ask anything of Me, I would certainly grant it.

---

187 Qur'an 2:117.

Appendix I

Now let us look more deeply into the mysterious process of intercession. In Islam, one never prays to any limited, created being or derivative power, but only to the Ultimate Source, Allah. In addition to one's own direct supplications to Allah, it is permitted to ask someone else, especially of devout character, to also pray on your behalf to Allah. As to whether the soul of a departed saint or *waliyullah* exists beyond death and would thus be capable of spiritual intercession, the Qur'an states: "Do not say of those who have died in the way of Allah, that they are dead. Certainly they are alive, only you do not perceive them."[188]

On the other hand, we should also take note of the important Qur'anic injunction that "no soul can bear the burden of another."[189] Here, Islamic teaching clearly differs from the doctrine of vicarious messianic atonement found in traditional Christian teaching. Perhaps because of this, and reinforced by various ayats of the Qur'an which deny the intercessory power of false deities, many Muslims consider every form of intercessory prayer to be un-Islamic in nature.

Many devout Muslims practice intercessory prayer; but those who oppose it ignore many valuable ahadith from their own tradition, and are satisfied to conclude that such intercessory prayers must be an innovation *(bid'a)* or a carry-over from Christianity or from the dark ages of paganism. Most of the faithful who hold this opinion, however, are not averse to making a simple personal prayer *(dua)* of supplication to Allah for the sake of their loved ones. It may or may not be realized, but this itself is a basic form of intercession which all believers do for each other: one soul is praying on behalf of another to their shared Creative Source of Power, connecting with the well-spring of Divine Essence, which deeply unites all lives.

As every soul is essentially one with every other soul through the divine unity, there need be no boundary of separation in healing. For instance, because of the deep natural physical and spiritual bond between children and their mothers, it is said that a mother's

188 Qur'an 2:154
189 Qur'an 6:164.

prayer for her children is exceptionally propitious (especially if her children also desire that for which she supplicates).

It is important to see that the healing or change in one's being which may be accomplished through divine acceptance of the intercessory prayers of another, is never done "by another," "for one" any more than a mid-wife or doctor assisting a pregnant woman could give birth to the child "in her place." At a deep level, the person receiving spiritual help or intercession must whole-heartedly desire to be healed or the healing probably will not occur. When a person is not whole-heartedly ready to change, repent, or be healed, whether they pray on their own behalf or even a saint prays for them, the supplication does not find a divine resonance in the soul, and it is said, "Allah did not accept the prayer."

This brings in one of the secrets of human destiny *(qadr):* that Allah, the All-Knowing Spiritual Source, while honoring the individual's freedom of choice, ultimately desires that each soul should draw lessons from its experiences in life, clarifying the soul's direction and helping it to consciously realize and draw upon the power of its own exalted spiritual essence. As long as the soul, like the prodigal son of the Gospels, is intent on experiencing and exploring the realms of separation and heedlessness, Allah allows the soul its freedom and never repents for one or heals one against the soul's will.

Essentially, we could say that it is the lack of clarity and self-realization in one's life which accounts for most of the lack of success that one experiences. Thus, even if one who is unclear attempts to pray, the focus and intention *(niyat)* may be weak and indeterminate and therefore ineffectual in its results. Of course, there are other reasons why prayers may be delayed, such as waiting for the right time or place for its fulfillment, or the right person to interact with one in one's destiny. However, mystically speaking, the divine initiative is always compassionately at work to help us awaken to self-knowledge and to love.

The Bukhari hadith quoted previously affirms that Allah first loves a servant and implants that divine love in their heart; then, in return, the heart of the servant burns with love for Allah. It is all really part of one action or movement of divine love which is cumbersome to speak of sequentially in the language of cause and effect, especially when all souls are, in reality, intimate expressions of the One Being. For such reasons, the sages of our tradition advise against too much discussion of the mystery of free-will and destiny, since one cannot hope to adequately comprehend such things with the limited mind.

Ultimately, not only the mystic, but every true Muslim will affirm the fundamental Qur'anic viewpoint that every impulse, without exception, originates from the One Divine Source, whose nature is mercy and compassion. "Not even a leaf falls without divine sanction and awareness,"[190] and in matters of destiny, "no soul is ever wronged by so much as a date stone."

---

190 Qur'an 6:59

APPENDIX II

The Four Worlds

IN THE COURSE OF THIS WORK, we have spoken primarily of two levels: the *shari'a (shariat* in Turkish)—the main road of the sacred law (including the five basic pillars of Islam, observed by all practicing Muslims)—and the *tariqa (tarikat* in Turkish), the mystic path of inner development (associated mainly with schools of Sufism). However, there are actually seven levels which are delineated by the mystics of Islam. As the final three tend to function as extensions of the fourth, we usually speak of four main levels or four worlds of Reality. Three of these are mentioned in a hadith of the Rasulullah: "The *shari'a* are my words *(aqwali),* the *tariqa* are my actions *(a'mali)* and the *haqiqa* my interior states *(ahwali)."*

The *shariat* is the cornerstone of Islam; it forms the foundation of all Islamic belief and is the substratum of all the other levels. The *tariq* is the "path" off the main highway of the *shariat,* the word *tarikat* having become synonymous with the mystic orders of Islam, popularly known under the banner of Sufism. Each *tarikat* or Sufi order functions as an esoteric school within Islam, headed by knowledgeable sheikhs who (along with sheikhas) instruct dervishes and seekers of truth in the education and training of the *nafs* (or "limited self") and the way of divine unity and love.

The *tarikat* does not abrogate the sacred law *(shariat),* but rather compliments it, endowing it with a deeper significance which carries the aspirant beyond the model of the lone, alienated soul seeking divine favor from without. While the common religious understanding focuses the individual on the attainment of paradise in the afterlife (through righteous adherence to the precepts of the faith), the *tarikat* leads the seeker to become the Truth in this lifetime and to realize non-dualistically that we are all expressions of Divine Reality and Love. The realization of one's relative non-existence and essential unity with Truth properly belongs to the spheres of *haqiqa* and *ma'rifa*

The *haqiqa* (or *hakikat* in Turkish) represents the level of Absolute Truth, the Ultimate Reality which is beyond all conventions of religion, beyond time, space and separation; it is pure essence, formless, transcendent oneness, an infinite ocean of divine light. In this regard, the noble Prophet, upon him be peace, spoke of the heights (or depths) of his meditative "interior states," saying: "I have a time when I enter such a state that there is nothing between me and my Lord, neither the angels, nor Michael, nor Gabriel; and no words can describe it."

The fourth and "highest" state is *marifat*. *Ma'rifa* refers to *gnosis* or the level of knowing, of being Reality, the "I amness" and presence of the soul which has realized itself as Truth *(Haqq)*. A few schools of thought—and here we may include the Kabbalistic schema of the four worlds as well as a few Sufi orders—list the transcendent Truth *(hakikat)* as the highest level, above knowledge *(marifat)*. However, most Sufi schools see the *marifat* as the summit of the path for the following reason. On the path to mystic realization *(suluk)*, one first passes away (or becomes *fana*) in God or Ultimate Truth *(Haqq)*, and this stage may be marked by states of great ecstacy. But this is not the end of the path. After *fana* comes the resurrection *(baqa)*—becoming alive in Allah, becoming the awakened servant whose will is one with the greater will, who becomes the eyes through which God sees, who becomes the hands and healing breath of God, and the instrument of divine love and compassion moving about in this world. First one is lost in Truth, then found as Truth; first one awakens from the perspective of the limited self into the realization of divine unity, then Allah awakens within the human form. The former stages (of *fana*) are known as the minor mysteries while the latter stages *(baqa)* represent the major mysteries—how the infinite Lord of the Worlds can fit into the human heart.

Certainly the Prophet embodied the state of *marifat* and alluded to it when he said, "Whoever has seen me has seen *Haqq* (the

Divine Truth or God)." Likewise, the Master Jesus, who also made similar statements, exemplified this station and showed it forth in its aspect of humble servanthood when he washed the feet of his disciples, thereby illumining their minds and hearts with love.

The highest three levels are respectively: *Qutubiyya* (cardinality or the level of *qutb* or mystic pole), *Qurbiyya* (proximity or station of intimate nearness), and *'Ubudiyya* (the supreme station of servanthood: one serves the Truth with one's whole being, the instrument having become of one accord with the Essential Reality behind it). Each of these seven levels has seven sub-stations within them, producing a total of 49 spiritual stations *(makamat)* on the mystic way.

The Seven Levels of the Soul

Over the centuries, many teachers have taught and written, using various systems which are essentially derived from the holy Qur'an. Some speak of four, others of seven levels of *nafs*, or various levels of *ruh*. In general, we can say that the stations up to the human level may be thought of as *nafs*, and above this as *ruh*.

The Arabic word *nafs* can be translated by a number of English words such as: *essence, soul, self,* and *living breath which animates life*. *Ruh* is usually translated in this context simply as *soul* (although it can also mean *spirit*, as in the appellation *Isa Ruh Allah*, or Jesus, the Spirit of God). There is a famous ayat in the Qur'an (17:85) in which an answer comes to the holy Prophet after he has been asked by some of his contemporaries about the very nature of the *ruh* or spirit. Soon, the divine response was revealed to the Prophet: "Say (to them), *Ruhu min `amri Rabbi*—The spirit is from the command of my Lord; and of its knowledge only a little is communicated." Thus the *ruh* is defined in the Qur'an as a mysterious divine action or command *(amr)* of the Lord. All life and all selves, then, can be taken as "actions" animated and sustained by the Divine Source; likewise, the nature of the spirit *(ruh)* is more aptly conceived as a verb in process than as a static noun form, since the latter would wrongly tend to imply some material existence to the *ruh*.

Inasmuch as we can speak of a system of levels of the soul or self, we should realize that this is not a hierarchy of progressively superior levels, in which the "higher" or "deeper" levels are favored over "lower" or "external" ones. Rather, each level has its own vital, essential function in the whole scheme of selfhood, from the "inert" material level, to the animal nature, to human nature, to the infinite level of the Divine. Just as the body is a corpse without the animation of the spirit, the spirit cannot act without the support of the bodily vehicle. Therefore, each level is equally essential for the fulfillment of one's earthly life. Perfection comes in the balanced interaction of all the levels of soul. Having said as much, we can briefly survey the various levels of the self as they have been developed and taught in the *tarikat*.

We can begin with reference to the story in which 'Abdullah ibn al-Mubarak asked the wise child about the difference between the *ruhu haiwani* (animal nature) and the *ruhu insani* (human nature) as they interact within the human psyche. 'Abdullah was given a beautiful, immediate response in which he could practically taste the difference in the tone of his two attitudes which indeed all of us have within. The first voice was self-centered and low in its estimation of others, while the second resonated with a more loving and generous heart-quality. By the term *ruhu haiwani* or "animal nature" there is no intended denigration of animals—they are by nature as Allah created and intended them to be—a collective nature and inheritance which we also share, ranging from the most noble and affectionate domesticated pet to the most archaic, wild, reptilian beast.

Generally speaking, it could be said that such qualities as modesty, self-reflective awareness, higher thinking, and spiritual love are key factors in distinguishing human behavior from animal behavior. Also, according to the perspective of the tarikat, the reason human beings have been placed on earth together with animals is so that the animals may serve as a mirror to show humans what sub-human behavior is like. By sub-human we mean behavior which is appropriate in animals, but out of place in a fully human existence. (Doubtless, this works interactively so that animals also learn something valuable from their contact with humans.)

For instance, it is not difficult to see the resemblance between a person who struts about and a peacock, or a slothful person and a pig. A timid person has a nature akin to a mouse or a chicken, while an extremely stubborn person is exhibiting the traits proper to a donkey, or is being "bull-headed." Interiorly, each one is manifesting qualities which are characteristic of the animal kingdom, though in outward form they may give the appearance of being human. This is why Rumi said: "Be as you appear, or appear as you are." The goal of spiritual transformation is to become *truly human* both inwardly and outwardly—since that is what we are intended to be—a synthesis of mineral, vegetable, animal, *jinn*, angelic and divine spirit called *ruhu insani*. This is not simply an esoteric teaching, but a basic understanding within the shariat that every man and woman of faith *(mumin* or *mumina)* is under the obligation to try to reach the level of *rajil* (a truly actualized human being; or literally, a "man" in the highest sense of the word).

According to the classical teachings of mystical Islam, the purpose of the soul's descent is to experience life on earth and, having accomplished that, to find release from the realm of physical density, returning to the soul's point of origin. Like a ray of the sun of the Divine Essence, every soul comes forth from the First Light of Eternity (called in Islam, the *Nuri Muhammad*) and passes from the level of the divine throne *(arsh)* and footstool *(kursi)*, descending through the seven heavens.

On its journey, the soul accrues a body of light from the angelic spheres, mental acuity and imagination from the world of the *jinn*. Entering into the material realm, the *ruh* passes through the four elements and evolves through the mineral and vegetable levels, finally accruing an animal body which is built up out of the dense physical fabric of the earth.

Ultimately, one reaches the nadir of the soul's circle of descent *(nuzul)*, incarnating as a human being, who is created to be the *khalifa* or representative of the Divine Source on earth. Then this encrusted diamond soul—which has become blackened while passing through the realm of fire, rusted in the watery elements, muddied with a covering of earth, dried out by air, and surrounded with ether—finally begins a process of purification.

In the second portion of the soul's journey, it undertakes a reverse procedure of stripping off, mining, cleansing and polishing the gem from its coating of earthly layers. When the soul has completed its earthly sojourn, it returns to its heavenly origin through an ascending arc of involution called *uruj*. Along the way, it gradually sheds the various bodies which it had donned in the course of its incarnation, ultimately returning to union with its Original Source, purified and enriched by the experience of the journey.

According to the Qur'an, each soul, on its return journey, passes through a realm of fire, which it may experience as the purifying fire of love—the radiant light of paradise *(janna)*—or the remedial purifying fire of remorse—called *jahannam*. Either of these realms may seem long-lasting or eternal; however, they are actually stations of the soul which exist out of time, through which all eventually pass. The Qur'an affirms that in the end, everything will return to its Lord (6:164) and nothing will remain except the Divine Countenance (55:25).

Islamic mysticism views the sojourn of an individual soul into earthly incarnation as a one-time, round-trip journey; each configuration of the soul is unique, so that we can never speak of a true re-incarnation. (However, the inner teaching is that when one person dies, another "similar" being, with their same basic qualities, comes into the world to replace them, to don their hat, so to speak, just as one president or king follows another and assumes his office or crown and scepter.) In reality, every soul represents an emergence of the One and Only Divine Being, Allah, Who is all that exists.

The seven levels of self or soul which together comprise the full range of human potential during its span of life on earth, are as follows:

1. *Ruhu Madeni.* The mineral soul refers to the inheritance, in the physical body, which constitutes the foundation of the skeletal structure, bones and teeth.

2. *Ruhu Nebati.* The vegetable soul refers to the growing and metabolic functions of the body, especially the digestive system and liver, along with the hair and nails which grow out of the human body just as vegetables grow out of the soil of the earth. A person in a coma or a stupor is operating mostly on the vegetable and mineral level with little more than the autonomic nervous system of the body functioning.

3. *Ruhu Haiwani.* The animal soul refers to the more evolved aspects of the body, including the circulatory system which is centered in the heart, self-preservation instincts, the ability to move from place to place and find food, libido, the principle of pursuing pleasure and fleeing from pain—all of the primal instincts associated with the limbic brain. Aggression and sexual differentiation can also be considered distinctive aspects of the animal inheritance.

In terms of brain physiology, the *ruhu haiwani* most closely correlates with the two most primal portions of the tripartite brain: the brain stem—sometimes characterized as the "cold-blooded" reptilian, survival brain—as well as the mesocortex, the "warm-blooded" primitive mammal brain associated with the limbic node of the cerebellum. By contrast, the most evolved outer covering of the brain, the neo-cortex, would find its affinities more in the realm of higher human faculties associated with the *ruhu nafsani* and the *ruhu insani,* described below.

Every animal life form possesses *ruhu haiwani,* an aspect of the soul which ceases to exist at death. The levels of the soul beyond *ruhu haiwani* are proper only to human beings.

4. *Ruhu Nafsani.* The personal soul could also be called the personality soul or the conventional self. At this level, which is associated chiefly with the brain and nervous system, the qualities of higher thinking, rationality and ego-functions are introduced. These are accompanied by the self-correcting and inhibiting faculties associated with the cerebral cortex. Shadow qualities which come into play at this level are hypocrisy, arrogance, manipulation, "getting ahead" by any means necessary, and other self-serving workings of the intellect.

According to Islamic ontology, our mental inheritance is connected with the sphere of mind which exists on the plane of the *jinn*. (*Jinn* are an unseen variety of being, distinct from the angels; the etymology of their name is connected with the English words *genius* and *genie*.) In Islam, the divine adversary, the *shaitan* (satan, called *Iblis* in the Qur'an) is considered to be a *jinn*, created of smokeless fire *(nar)*, rather than one of the angels, whose being is composed of light *(nur)*. Thus, dreams, thoughts, and imagination—as they come through the human mind—are capable of reflecting "*shaitanic*" as well as angelic and prophetic levels of divine inspiration.

There are many positive qualities also associated with the personal soul level; but however worthy they may be, the qualities of mental attention and personality cohesiveness are, at best, fleeting and evanescent in nature. Because of this, the fourth level of the soul, like the others that support it, perishes along with the physical body.

Only the levels above the *ruhu nafsani* truly survive death. This is because the first four soul levels are built up from below and are thus transient parts of our makeup which decay and pass away, returning to the earth. The uncreated spiritual part of us, which is received from "above" and temporarily housed in the human body, is eternal. It has entered into physicality as the breath which Allah breathed into Adam, and upon the death of the physical body, it returns to its own true abode of spirit.

5. *Ruhu Insani.* The human soul, in some Sufi systems, indicates the highest level of our development, including our spiritual inheritance. With its seat located in the inner spiritual heart *(fu'ad),* the human soul brings divine compassion, wisdom, generosity and love to the being and those around them, beyond the confines of narrow self-interest. A human being is not complete in his or her humanity until having fully realized and awakened to the level of *ruhu insani,* the level in which the soul becomes aware of its divine inheritance and reason for existence. The whole of earthly life, and humanity in particular, has been built up as an accommodation to house Allah's exalted Spirit; however, the lower souls—the dense, foundational aspects of the body and personality—are like

windows which can easily become clouded over with pollution and thus require polishing and cleansing in order to allow the divine light to shine through.

6. *Ruhu Sultani.* The sultan (of the) soul or kingly soul is a still higher aspect of the human soul and is also associated with the angelic level of the soul. The sultan soul is always there but is not always active in people's affairs, except at a subtle level. For example, one might sense it when one is guided by a powerful intuition coming from the sultan soul, or when, through intervention, one is aided in an emergency by a "higher force;" or it may break through in an epiphany so that the rest of the self becomes palpably aware of the splendor of its powerful awakening presence. The sultan of the soul is the divinely enlightened inner master, whose will is one with the Absolute, and whose rightful purpose is to rule over the rest of the self and receive cooperative support from the animal soul and ego. Unfortunately, this ideal is rarely the case in human society which, as a collective, rarely rises even to the level of the heart. If the divine aspects of one's being have not been realized, the more instinctual components in one's nature tend to take over while the master of the house remains idle. When the animal passions assume command, the *ruhu sultani* and the *ruhu insani* go to sleep, as it were, and one's situation becomes like that of a horse rebelling against its carriage-driver, galloping without restraint wherever it pleases.

This is the reason for the greater *jihad* in Islam. If the animal soul or ego soul, instead of serving the Lord of one's being, usurps the throne for its own ignoble purposes, it is the duty of the spiritual warrior to struggle to return the scepter of power to the true sovereign of the soul. An image of yet another kind used in this regard is that the male sultan, the *ruh* (representing the divine inheritance), marries the queen, the female *nafs* (the earthly inheritance of the self), and through this spiritual marriage they peacefully work together, hand in hand.

7. *Ruhu Sirr.* The seventh level of the soul is called the secret soul, or soul of mystery. This highest level may also be called the *sirr al-aswar*, the secret-of-secrets soul (in that case, the sixth level would be called *ruhu sirr*). Regardless of which nomenclature is

used, the seventh level is an utterly transcendent plane of Divine Spirit which defies description because it has no place inside or outside of the body or soul, and it is timeless. However, the *ruhu sirr* should not be thought of as separate from the other levels of the soul nor as remaining in some remote heavenly locale while the other souls fill the body. It does "come down" from heaven, so to speak, yet it is placeless. If the light of this soul does not provide some illumination to the lower souls, that person's experience of the soul will be like a dark prison of unbelief and alienation from the Source. If it illumines the soul, it is like being continuously refreshed by fresh air and water.[191]

The fourteenth century pir of Konya, Mevlana Jalaluddin Rumi, penned some beautiful verses on the subject of the inheritance which we receive from all the different levels:

> I died as a mineral and became a plant.
> I died as a plant and took on animal form.
> Having died as an animal,
> I have become a human being.
> Hereafter, I will assume angelic form
> and continue life in the heavenly spheres.
> When have I become less by dying?
> That form too will perish, as does "everything
> except His face."
> Therefore, let me never, in any of these forms,
> regard myself as separate from the Source of Love,
> To Whom everyone and "everything in
> the end will return."[192]

The Seven Levels of the Nafs

There is yet another important system of classifying the seven levels of the self, or *nafs*, which is similar to the seven levels of

---

191 The *Ruhu Sirr* description is based on a *sohbet* by Muzaffer Efendi.
192 Rumi's poem twice quotes from ayats in the Qur'an: 28:88 and 6:60 (3:83, etc.).

ruh and again makes use of Qur'anic terminology. This way of categorizing the levels, however, focuses more on earmarking the stations of spiritual evolution through which the individual passes on the mystic path to human perfection *(insan-i kamil)*.

1. Nafs al-Ammara. In this system, the first level is called *al-nafs al-ammara*, translated variously as the *commanding self*, the *domineering self* or *tyrannizing self*; it could also be called the *carnal soul*, due to its link with the physical body, with all of its inherent animal soul qualities. Although the command *(amara)* of Allah is mentioned frequently in the Qur'an, the human expropriation of this command *(ammara),* as such, is only mentioned once in the entire Qur'an (12:53). There, it is characterized as the self which "goads one toward evil." Every living thing has *nafs al-ammara*, but it is only humankind who has the capacity and spiritual need to struggle against its base influence. Some of the qualities of the "commanding self" include obsessive self-gratification of the cravings of the physical body: for instance, alcohol, drugs, sex and food addictions. Other manifestations of the *nafs al-ammara* include: greed, lust, miserliness, arrogance, insolence, rebelliousness, envy, malice toward others, and a quick temper.

We can give a simple example of how this comes out in a person: a religious scholar studies books and becomes an expert on the verities of the faith, yet if someone disturbs him or even slightly disagrees with his opinion, he suddenly becomes very angry and irritable. This is the *nafs al-ammara* showing itself. We could take another example of say, a prominent married politician or evangelist who, despite his better judgment, engages in clandestine sexual affairs until he eventually brings ruin upon his career. He has fallen under the sway of the *nafs al-ammara*, the soul which commands him to heedlessly satisfy the momentary urges of the body, regardless of the long-term cost. Human beings are naturally endowed with an alarm that goes off throughout the body—especially in the area of the solar plexus—which functions as a warning against involvement in such misguided acts. It is called conscience. However, if one constantly overrides it, the alarm eventually grows so faint that one no longer notices it.

THE GARDEN OF MYSTIC LOVE

Also characteristic of the activity of the *nafs al-ammara* is the control drama, the desire to manipulate and dominate others. This may take many forms, such as physical intimidation, seduction, shaming, guilt-tripping, passive-aggressive behavior, or imposing excessive moral or religious restrictions on another. Even in relationships ostensively based on love, many attempts at subtly controlling another may creep in without one being aware that the nafs is asserting itself.

How does one deal with the *nafs al-ammara?* First one has to dispassionately observe it for what it is, and, when the second level perspective is brought in, there is a natural tendency to curb it. But as this may involve further controlling behavior, one must recognize the degree of inner struggle it will arouse. In many cases the struggle to go against the nafs is appropriate and will stimulate growth in the soul, while in other cases, the path of least resistance and merciful self-acceptance will prove more useful in transforming the nafs. Helpful models in this regard are the judo practitioner who overcomes by sidestepping the force of the opponent and Christ's saying, "Resist not evil with further evil."

Some tendencies which appear negative cannot simply be repressed but must be sublimated and skillfully harnessed into more acceptable outlets. Often this occurs when the divine desire coming through the individual is misunderstood and rejected, thus becoming distorted from its authentic intention; yet the impulse persists, seeking some appropriate expression. Thus the wise look for the true purpose behind every impulse which Allah has decreed. With anger or irritation, for instance, the dervish is advised to remain calm and "swallow one's anger" when faced with the unpleasant manifestations of other egos or unavoidable frustrating circumstances; yet this checking of the impulse must be carefully distinguished from the legitimate kind of anger which moves one to struggle against injustice and oppression (fulfilling the Islamic injunction to "forbid evil" when one encounters it). Many a sheikh has become like a lion in the defense of Truth.

Traditionally, the remedy associated with the *nafs al-ammara* is repentance (*tawba*). What the soul requires is not mere surface words of repentance, but a deep seeing into the nature of the *nafs*

— 288 —

as it really is—as one would see and become alert when confronted by a poisonous snake in one's path. This recognition is followed by the struggle to curb these thorny, unattractive traits in one's nature; also the practice of repeating the name of divine unity *(tawhid), La ilaha illallah,* is given to help lift one's consciousness above the *nafs al-ammara* and up to higher levels.

This is precisely where the concept of *jihad* or sacred struggle comes into play in Islam. The spiritual warrior has to call upon his or her human intelligence and compassion—indeed, affirming one's divine inheritance. In this way, the warrior of the spirit takes pity upon the rest of one's being, and strives to rescue the authentic, essential self from the intrigues of the *nafs*—this puerile usurper of the command of self who has no higher aim than to indulge the ego. The famous Turkish poet and waliyullah, Niyazi Misri says, "Do not call that *nafs* which leads you astray yourself—he's a dragon."

The noble Prophet Muhammad, peace and blessings be upon him, once told his wife, 'A'isha that everyone has not only a guiding angel, but a *shaitan* (a *jinn* spirit with an inclination toward evil). She asked him, "Even you, O Messenger of Allah?" And he replied, "Even me. However, I have been given the gift of knowing my *shaitan*, and, with Allah's help, he has become *muslim* (submitted to the higher aspects of the soul and to the divine command)." When this transformation has taken place for an individual, Allah no longer allows the *nafs* to act in accord with the *shaitan* as a mischief-maker against the good of the greater self; rather, the *nafs al-ammara* becomes a useful friend and servant of the king (one's inner sultan or divine aspect), and the peaceful soul has no further need of inner struggle.

The dream symbols at this level include wild or ferocious animals (scorpions, wolves, tigers, boars, mice, etc.), especially those whose flesh humans would not normally consume. Other symbols include: rodents and insects, thorns, unpleasant situations, falling in the mud or from heights, satisfying lusts, jealousies, revenge, etc. When one begins to see blue landscapes, blue forests and so on, one is beginning to move toward the next level.

2. *Nafs al-lawwama*. The second level of the nafs is called *al-nafs al-lawwama*, the critical self which regrets and blames itself for its mistakes. It is also called the self-accusing *nafs* or the censorious self. On the first level, the self is in denial about the consequences of its negative impulses; the *nafs* is unchecked and unrepentant, gratifying its base, destructive behaviors with impunity. But at the second level, one has "seen the problem" and the conscience is at work trying to awaken from the spell of the *nafs al-ammara*, with all of its heedless, narcissistic desires. One is sincerely trying to face up to one's shortcomings and making an attempt to bring about self-improvement through abstinence *(wara)* from the indulgences of the unchecked nafs.

In Islam, fasting during the month of Ramadan has this intention behind it at its most basic level, as does *zakat* (alms-giving; practicing generosity instead of hoarding, in order to counter the self-serving tendencies of the nafs). In fact, at this level, one can develop a quite decent and spiritual persona and even indulge in feelings of self-righteous sanctimony. Here, even with the best of intentions, one is still very prone to the phenomenon of hypocrisy—covering-up and rationalizing in order to save face. Or, like a reformed alcoholic or zealous religious convert—ever fearful of backsliding—one might become a rigid fundamentalist, forming harsh judgments of others who do not share and reinforce one's own world view.

Guilt and prohibition, following on the heels of relapse, is how the cortex learns when advancing beyond the instinctual level of the brain. There is a pendulum swing in which one must, in effect, divorce oneself from instinct and instead go by reason. But even reason, in and of itself, is not sufficient to truly guide us; and still less is the ego vantage-point. As the Qur'an explains (2:216): "It could well be that you hate something which is good for you or, conversely, love something which is actually bad for you. Allah knows, though you may not know." This is why the Prophet said: "The secret of wisdom is to fear *(khauf)* God." But we should not glibly misconceive this idea—a deep love and amazement underlies this fear or devout respect for Allah, Whose divine unity includes not only *jamal* (all beauty and sweetness) but also *jalal* qualities (powerful, like a mighty storm). Just as one appreciates the domestic benefits of electricity or fire, the mature person certainly knows better than to play with them in a reckless manner. The true lover constantly regards the good pleasure of the Beloved, hoping never to even inadvertently fall out of divine favor through some unfortunate chain-reaction originating in a heedless moment of self-indulgent behavior. We especially see this quality of divine awe highlighted in the lives of the early Sufi ascetics. When the seeker's faith is primarily motivated by hope of reward and fear of punishment—which is still based on self-interest rather than selfless love—this is indicative of a second level religious understanding.

For the one who repents and backslides again and again, the sign that their repentance has been divinely accepted is that the forbidden lure of their compulsive negative pattern of behavior (or sin) disappears and one finds oneself completely free of the desire to ever do it again. One is, in effect, finished with that behavior. But until then, while operating on the second level, one simply tries to keep it in check, prays to be spared the intrigues and disasters of the ego, and awaits the signs of divine forgiveness and grace which serve one as an invitation to the next *makam*, or spiritual station. The divine *esma* (name) given to the spiritual seeker at this level is the name of majesty, *Allah*, which is meant to penetrate and soften the heart. The human heart is rightfully the divine throne, but first it must be cleared of the idols of self which have assumed a place there.

The critical faculties are intrinsic to the nature of the *nafs al-lawwama*. At the second level, one analyzes and critiques not only oneself, but other people and their behavior. While positive criticism is very useful, it can easily devolve into a negative tendency of criticizing people and situations, giving one a complaining, pessimistic outlook which is spiritually destructive to oneself and to others. As Sheikh al-Jabri of Tunisia wisely observed: "You cannot respect yourself unless you respect others. This is a great secret." A healthy amount of doubt, scepticism and refusal to accept injustice can be helpful in achieving positive social and religious reform; when applied to oneself, it can keep one honest and relatively free of self-deception. The optimism and inspiration that is needed to balance and positively direct the critical self comes from the third level.

Second level dreams tend to feature less wrathful, more domesticated animals (cows, horses, fish, tamed birds, honeybees, pets, etc.), especially *halal*, edible ones, as well as fruit trees, food, places of commerce, boats, fishing, or lawfully earning one's daily bread, shaving, cleaning up, donning (proper) clothing, seeing religious people or sacred spaces, hugging or reconciling with a friend or family member, etc. The second level is associated with the color red.

The reader should note that our aim here is simply to give general types of dream symbols in order to convey a clear feel for the stations. The reader is advised against trying to extrapolate too much from these brief indications, since there are so many other factors involved in accurate dream interpretation, including the necessity of receiving permission to interpret dreams within the tarikat. The dream symbols depend largely upon their context in the dream and the level of the one who is dreaming it. The symbology of the snake is a perfect example, as it may take on such varied meanings as: ego, deceptiveness, kundalini energy, rebirth (shedding its skin), and wisdom. Another example would be the horse, whom we mentioned in association with the second level; however, it could symbolize anything from the first level (if it is a wild, fierce and rebellious horse), to the fourth level, as interpreted by Muzaffer Efendi, who noted that the horse and the palm were, respectively, two of the highest animal and plant dream symbols.

3. *Nafs al-mulhima.* The third level of the self, *al-nafs al-mulhima*, is known as the *inspiring nafs* and is perhaps the highest level which a person might be expected to reach naturally without undergoing spiritual training or being an exceptionally gifted soul. It is the level at which love and ecstasy begin to move one's being—a fire of love that burns away impurities. The Arabic word *mulhima* (or *mulhama)* refers to the root word *ilham*, meaning inspiration, even divine revelation. At this level, one begins to disidentify with the limited self, dying to old habits and shedding the tight

clothes of ego identification to become free of unresolved fears and outmoded defensive patterns. A sense of spiritual freedom and independence blossoms with the recognition that neither material possessions, fame, the pursuit of pleasure, nor slavish conformity to the expectations of others are intrinsic to inner fulfillment. As this renunciation *(zuhd)* of the conventional world takes root in the self, the nafs undergoes a purification which allows other more subtle and inspired creative energies to come through. The practice given for this level is the name of Divine Essence, *Hu*.

As one matures to the third level, one gradually becomes more thoughtful, peaceful, humble, thankful, generous, knowledgeable, content and patient in the face of adversity. Instead of taking offence at others, one becomes charitable in one's opinion of others, seeing the best in them while overlooking their faults. In essence, this level represents the culmination of human fulfilment, as far as the world would recognize it; it is where conventional psychology ends and the process of spiritual enlightenment begins.

Many people in the fine arts, with their emphasis on enriching and beautifying the culture, attain to the third level. Similarly, there are many thoughtful, educated persons in various fields who, having achieved success and recognition in their careers and perhaps having raised families as well, reach this level only to discover that they are being called to a still deeper form of self-discovery and fulfillment. They begin to recognize an inner thirst for the next level of human evolution, which is the beginning of the soul's mystic return to its original heavenly state. Not every soul penetrates to this level during the span of their earthly life. However, if one who has already "found success in the world," turns to the spiritual path and is fortunate enough to find a true guide, then that individual is often better prepared for inner renunciation of the world than the spiritual aspirant who has yet to succeed in the world and may thus have unfinished business there.

The first three levels involve the human journey towards God and learning about Reality. This is followed by the journey within God and finally, at the very highest levels, the journey of God within humanity. Whenever a soul assumes a physical body, it naturally inherits these seven levels of nafs, each of which consists of some 10,000 veils which obscure the soul's realization of its own True Source.

Traits such as arrogance, jealousy, animosity, love of wealth and rank all have to be overcome and purified in this university of life so that the soul may traverse the seven levels and 70,000 veils where it finally arrives at the consciousness of perfect unity. This being the case, one can see that the lifting of the veils which leads to spiritual enlightenment isn't likely to come all at once in some single great *satori* experience resulting in a permanent awakening. Rather, one has various spiritual peak experiences *(ahwal)* and unveilings *(tejelli)* which give one insights into the reality of one's own nature and the world. One is granted glimpses beyond one's present station *(makam),* and gradually, one becomes established at the next level and can truly live at that level of realization. The veils are thus lifted gradually as we are ready to face ourselves, take responsibility for our faults, and also have the courage to humbly accept more and more the truly exalted Reality of which we are a manifestation.

Referring to the most sublime level of formless Divine Essence and the lowest level of the soul in the earthly body of flesh, the Qur'an says (96:4-5): "We have created humankind in the very most sublime of molds *(ahsani taqwim)* and then We bring humankind to the very lowest of states *('asfala safilin)."* Then comes the divine command (which represents the goal of the tarikat): "Return to your Lord." (85:28) That is, return the state of your soul back to its heavenly consciousness, even before the death of the physical body.

The third level is a very expansive stage. Where the first level represented a rather libidinous expansion without boundaries or safeguards, the second features a more restricted, self-contracted state. The third is again expansive and optimistic, like a wave which carries the dervish with the ecstacy of love, dhikr and beautiful mystic hymns. The fourth level again recapitulates the contracted state as the whole being moves toward a state of integration. And this alternation of expansion and contraction continues on into the higher, more subtle levels of the soul's development.

The dreams become more varied. Where there were animal dreams in the lower levels, these tend to be replaced by animal trainers, honey sellers, grocers, gardeners—various symbols that are more human (a hunter or butcher might indicate that the dreamer is lacking in compassion). At the higher levels, dreaming of an animal may simply indicate a momentary weakness or rebellion. Other symbols include doing good deeds, religious or academic activities, holy scriptures—(especially Qur'an, mosques, sheikhs, sheikhas), and dreams that show whether one (who is now more consciously aware) is inviting negative or positive things into the heart. At this state, the traveler on the path is not yet fully able to distinguish what is good for self and others from what is harmful; however he or she might be tempted to imagine that they "have arrived" at the culmination of the path, since they are now receiving some inspiration from the higher (angelic) levels. The color associated with the third level is green, which might manifest symbolically as green vegetation, etc.

4. *Nafs al-mutma'inna.* The fourth level, *al-nafs al-mutma'inna*, is known as the secure nafs or tranquil self. The word *mutma'inna*, as used in the Qur'an to describe the soul (89:27), means to be content, quiet, serene, safe and secure, as well as acquiescent in nature. The soul at this level is becoming an expression of Truth *(Haqq)* as the divine attributes *(sifaat)* begin to unfold and manifest in one's being. One is sincere and genuinely living from what one has learned, what one has assimilated, and what one knows to be true for oneself. It is traditionally the *makam* or station of the *fakir* (the poor, or "poor in spirit"), who has become almost entirely free of the intrigues of the *nafs al-ammara* and the wants and desires associated with the love of this world. One is contented with little, and like Ibrahim Adham or Rabi'a al-'Adawiyya, has learned not to complain if misfortune or sickness comes. The one who truly lives on the fourth level is very clear that everything, whether seemingly good or bad, comes from Allah, Whose divine wisdom knows best when and if the fulfillment of one's prayers is truly propitious. In other words, one in the station of the *nafs al-mutma'inna* is secure in Allah and, as the saying goes, knows better than to presume to

"teach Allah how to be Allah" by instructing one's Creator on what is best for oneself in life.

One who is established in this station no longer inwardly grumbles, "Why I am I not getting my fair share of all these desirable things and opportunities that I see everyone else getting? Why doesn't Allah see this unjust state of affairs as clearly as I do and answer my prayers and complaints?" Verily, the wise know that even an "unanswered" prayer can be an appropriate divine response, if one could only see beyond the limited and self-encapsulated perspective of one's own nafs.

The one who is stationed on the fourth level is still not immune to slipping back into lower level behavior; for instance, depression, or pride over one's spiritual experiences would be reverting to second level behavior. Barring such regressions, the fourth level represents a level of true sincerity of heart, honesty, generosity, love, joy and serene trust in Allah. It is the real commencement of the process of *fana fi'llah*, losing oneself in the Divine Source, and may be accompanied by dreams and various other manifestations of nearness to the mystic saints and prophets of Allah. In many turuq, including the Halveti-Jerrahi, a special ribbed hat, called a *dalli arakiye*, is given to the dervish who reaches this station. The sheikh verifies whether or not a dervish has attained this station of Truth from the content of their dreams and other indications known to them.

The fourth level is the beginning of two stages of sainthood, the first being the level of the common saint *(avam evliya)*. Though Allah has made things easier for the saint at this stage, he or she must still occasionally struggle to keep the nafs under control. The saint may think lowly of the self because of its imperfections, though not everyone else can see these. Whereas the third level represents the pinnacle of human fulfilment, it is at the fourth makam that the human nature and divine nature begin to merge.

Sayyid 'Abdul Qadir Gaylani offers some interesting advice for the one entering this station. He says that the seeker on the mystic path should not get waylaid by miracles and psychic phenomena at the fourth level, nor venture off into speculative philosophy (delving into ideas such as *wahdat al-wajud*, the unity of being, etc.). Rather, at this critical stage, one should push on, aided by the power of *jesbih* (divine attraction) and *dhikrullah*. 'Abdul Qadir states that the station of *nafs al-mutma'inna*, which must be reached with the help of a *murshid* (sheikh or spiritual guide), can actually be considered the end of the formal path *(suluk)*.

The further stages could perhaps be characterized as "post-graduate" work which may be realized primarily on one's own, once one has been set on the proper course by a guide who truly knows the way to the final destination. The mystic way, as a school or system for the *salik*, says 'Abdul Qadir, really boils down to three levels. The pure *nafs al-ammara* is really sub-human and pre-path, and thus does not actually comprise a makam on the mystic way. What is counted is the second, third and fourth stages. After this, one is no longer dealing with strictly human qualities but is awakening within further gradations of the divine life.

Interestingly enough, certain dream symbols that might at first glance seem violent and indicative of the *nafs al-ammara* (cannons, swords, arrows and flags), can reappear at the fourth level, indicating that they are fighting on one's side (for the sake of truth) and bringing one victory in the greater jihad. Also at the fourth level one may dream of sultans, saints, khalifas, divine messengers, martyrs, tombs of saints, and the color white, which signifies the level of *nafs al-mutma'inna*. The *esma al-Haqq* (Truth) is associated with the fourth level.

5. *Nafs al-radiyya*. The fifth level, *al-nafs al-radiyya*, is known variously as the *contented self*, the *fulfilled nafs*, or the *self which is pleased with Allah*. This is the level of purification of the nafs where it can be said that the real Islam begins; it is complete surrender to the divine will, so much so that one is like a corpse animated by the divine life *(al-Hayy)*. One experiences oneself as a indivisible facet of the all-pervading Divine Reality and sees the perfection of the divine justice operating in the world to such an extent that one no longer desires to ask for anything in prayer. The patience *(sabr)* and contentment which is characteristic of this station is born of a deep realization that everything is from Allah, whether pleasure or pain, praise or blame, and that nothing else

exists, nor is there any goal except *"Hu"* (the divine pronoun, He/ She), the Eternal Divine Essence. In Arabic this is expressed as: *La maksude illa Hu.*

The Qur'an teaches the mystery of the inner wisdom beyond appearances of right and wrong in *Surat al-Kahf* (18:65-84). There, the prophet Moses, upon him be peace, seeks to accompany an intimate friend of Allah (traditionally identified as *Khidr)* and learn from this exalted guide some of the deeper spiritual mysteries. Khidr warns Moses that he will not be able to bear with his guide patiently, but Moses persists and is only allowed to join him after he agrees not to question anything Khidr does during their journey together.

Though obviously Moses knows better, for the sake of helping us learn, he breaks the agreement and objects on three separate occasions when he sees Hazrat Khidr behaving in ways that appear outwardly unjust, destructive and even murderous. First, the pair comes across a ship and Khidr makes a hole in it; Moses objects that this will cause its passengers to drown. Khidr reminds him that he is not to question him. Next, they encounter a young man whom Khidr slays. Moses objects strenuously to this murderous act and is warned that he must depart if he questions Khidr's actions again. Finally, they come to a city where they ask the people for food but are refused. Nearby, Khidr finds a brick wall that is about to tumble down and rebuilds it. When Moses questions Khidr as to why he did not ask wages for his labor, he is told that, because of his repeated questioning, he must now leave Khidr. Before parting, Khidr tells him, "I will now explain about those things over which you could not bear patiently in silence."

As for damaging the ship, this prevented a king who had designs on the boat from confiscating it from its owner, a poor man who made his living toiling on the sea. As for the slain child, who was destined to suffer a ruinous future as a tyrant, Allah desired to spare him that fate and, in his place, bless his devout parents with another more fortunate, loving son. As for rebuilding the crumbling wall: under it lay a treasure which was about to become exposed. Mercifully, Allah desired that it remain hidden for a time, and only be discovered later by two orphans, whose righteous father had bequeathed them the wall. Khidr concludes: "I did none of these things of my own accord."

Like Hazrat Khidr in the story, the satisfied self is absolutely contented with Allah and has complete confidence in the divine wisdom without reservations of the limited, reasoning mind (the part assumed by noble Moses), which can never adequately weigh the balance of divine justice. Also, at this level, one first begins to become aware that Allah is also satisfied with one, and is constantly pouring out divine love and mercy upon one, even though one has hitherto been little aware of it. (This realization deepens at the sixth level).

The *nafs al-radiyya* is the second station of the *awliya*, known as the "rare" saints or distinguished, beloved saints *(havas evliya)*. At this station, the lover has shed his or her very self, coming to a complete and unconditional acceptance of Allah. Those who have reached this station speak of a bewilderment, a state of surrender so thorough that they can no longer even lift a finger by themselves. They are still making their salat but, with the self and will in total submission, who is really doing it—them or Allah? As the esteemed twentieth century Jerrahi sheikh, Fahreddin Efendi observes in a mystic hymn *(Ilahi Neylesün Nitsün)*: "O Lord, no matter how this poor heart tries, no decision can it make without consulting You."

This is the second stage of *fana*, where one not only drops one's attachments but the very core of one's self disappears in Allah. This actually constitutes the beginning of the next phase, which involves *baqa*, or divine subsistence. After *fana*—losing oneself in divine reality and dying to the limited self—one experiences *baqa*, the resurrection by divine love, in which a new being, no longer separated or alienated from the One, comes to life, animated by the divine attribute of eternal life, *al-Hayy*. One is being pulled, as it were, "from above" toward unification and beyond human qualities *(beshariah)* by the power of the Spirit, and may feel very drawn to meditation, contemplation, and non-dual prayer.

The saint's face becomes relaxed at the stage of *nafs al-radiye*, since the personal will is no longer there making an effort as it was in the fourth level. (A mundane analogy would be to liken one at the fifth level to someone who has become not merely proficient, but absolutely effortless in their mastery of some skill, such as skating or bicycle riding.) We might say, "Allah has made it easy" for one at the fifth level; yet, even up to this station, there may still be a hidden shadow of polytheism or duality lingering in the psyche.

Dream subjects in this station include angelic beings, paradise, *houris*, *buraks*, the mystic waters of *Kawthar*, flying through the air, an encounter with the mystic blackness or a green light, and even being in the fire like the Prophet Abraham—i.e., not being burned, but enjoying it. All of these show that one's mind is in a mature state and that one is near to Allah, being educated by direct gnostic wisdom. The color yellow is associated with the fifth makam; its esma is *al-Hayy*.

6. *Nafs al-mardiyya.* The sixth level, *al-nafs al-mardiyya*, is known as the *fulfilling nafs* or the *pleasing self*—that is, the self which has become pleasing to Allah. It is a station of divine nearness and intimacy in which the nafs (having already completely accepted Allah) is now itself completely accepted *by* Allah, Who shows the divine pleasure and approval by taking one as Allah's own khalifa and bestowing upon the soul the divine attributes *(sifaat Allah)*. At this level, one has implicit trust in Allah *(tawakkul),* and has unrestrictive love for all beings. Such a one says *"eyvallah"* to everything, meaning one's heart is able to accept and accommodate every possible manifestation of life as a beautiful and worthy disclosure of the divine perfection. In this purified state, the eye of the heart begins to open and one is vouchsafed divine secrets and true knowledge of Allah. The *gnostic* at this level is called *arif billah.* This access to the divine intimacy results in the incorporation of the divine manner *(akhlak-i Allah)* in one's very being, and a clear realization of the eternal nature of one's soul.

This is the stage mentioned in the *hadith qudsi* where Allah bestows upon His most intimate servants and lovers His own fresh senses and faculties: one sees through Allah's sight, hears through Allah's hearing, grasps with Allah's grasping (and we might add, loves with Allah's love). In this way, the senses become so sensitive and refined that one no longer holds even the least desire for *haram* (unlawful or negative) pursuits.

Oddly enough, despite the truly beautiful traits of character that manifest, there are often times when a person at this level cannot be distinguished from a common man or woman, because they have passed through the stage of *fana* and have emerged with the capacity to behave quite naturally amongst the people. However, inwardly this being is like the alchemical red sulphur—there is nothing quite like the soul who has reached this state. Having essentially completed their own karmic purification, most of their time is spent selflessly serving others—for the sake of Allah. The saint at this level is called a "truly genuine" saint or "the cream of the cream" *(hass ul-hass)*. The color identified with the sixth level is deep purple.

The *nafs al-mardiyya* is the first of two stages of *baqa* (which began with the end of the fifth makam and ends with the seventh) and is associated with the *esma*, *al-Qayyum*, the Eternally Self-Subsisting One. The nineteenth-century Qadiri sheikh, Hajji Muharram Hilmi Efendi, offers this advice (in his *Zikir Makamlari)* for the one who wishes to progress beyond the sixth level: look down upon one's nafs (i.e., avoid spiritual inflation), grab hold of the shariat of Muhammad (i.e., don't abandon the sacred law or its moral culture), and then leap to the seventh level.

7. The seventh level is called the *pure self* or the *perfected self.* It also goes by the Arabic term, *nafs al-baqiyya;* or sometimes the name is combined as *al-nafs al-safiyya wa kamila*, reflecting the station of the perfect human being, *al-Insan-i-Kamil.* In English, it could also be called the completed self or the nafs which is totally purified of everything other than its essential divine nature. At this station of *qutbiyya* (the pole or axis), we could say that one discovers (or is "given by Allah") not just the divine attributes and awareness, but actually receives the gift of Allah's own blessed Selfhood, or *Zat* (the Divine Essence or "I am-ness"). After this, there is no longer a question of twoness or duality; there is only One.

As Hilmi Efendi says in his *Zikir Makamlari*, at this stage the *wali ul-kamil* (the highest saint):

> becomes one in the multiplicity and multiple in the One. Whoever sees this blessed person, the remembrance of Allah will spontaneously enter their heart. At this stage, one's actions are not one's own; however one responds to others, whether in gentleness or severity, one's response reflects exactly what the other's behavior has warranted. If one at this level accepts someone, it is Allah's acceptance. Such a one has no further need for surrender and no personal desire left, understanding fully that there is only One, that "All is Hu" [the genderless Divine Essence] and that "Everything is passing while only Allah's countenance remains." (Qur'an 55:26)

As for worship, Hilmi Efendi adds, "such a one cannot fall behind, since the worship is now in every part of the body, having penetrated every cell; yet this one is still full of humility." He concludes, "What more can one say? Such a soul is *Haqq* with *Haqq* (Divine Truth)."

Obviously, the seventh level is extremely rare and exalted; it has been called "a station of mystery between the Essence and the servant," a condition which is truly beyond description. It is the level of pure unity and supreme delight, which can be compared to the condition of the blessed Prophet Muhammad when, during his *miraj*, he attained to such a degree of divine nearness as to be described as "closer than two bows-lengths," or "closer to Allah than one is to oneself." The *nafs al-safiyya* is the station of messengers and prophets, the stage of *riza* (complete satisfaction); its color is pure black and its divine name is *al-Qahhar*, the All-Sovereign, Triumphant One. One of the signs of the person who has attained the seventh level is that they are capable of raising others from the dead by the divine power, as did the Beloved Jesus, upon him be peace.

We have enumerated the characteristics of the nafs through the seven major levels of purification, from the most constricted self, which is absorbed in its own ego and bodily desires, to the most free and sublime state of the Perfect Self who has totally awakened to its own divine inheritance. We should note that there are seven subdivisions of each of these levels, giving a total of forty-nine spiritual stations in all. The first level, for instance, would be the *nafs al-ammara* of the *nafs al-ammara* (or the *shariat* of the *shariat* level of the spiritual path), while the second would be the *nafs al-lawwama* of the *nafs al-ammara* (or the *tarikat* of the *shariat)*, and so on, culminating in the forty-ninth level of the *nafs as-safiya* of the *nafs as-safiya* (or the *ubudiyat* of the *ubudiyat)*. Using this method, the Halveti-Jerrahi path utilizes *esmas* associated with the seven subdivisions of the first four levels. These add up to twenty-eight divine names, esmas which were divinely revealed by special permission through the qutb of the wise, Pir Nurredin al-Jerrahi. They are unveiled to those who actually pass through these levels and repeat these names as part of their dervish practice, under the tutelage of an authentic mystic guide. Protocols such as these vary from order to order, though most of the first seven names are standard in every Islamic tarikat.

This appendix has been provided in order to furnish the reader with a better foundation in the general structure and nomenclature of the levels of the soul and the unfolding of the spiritual path leading from limitation to perfection. Some of these Qur'anic concepts are essential to the thinking and mode of expression used by Sufi masters in every age, and thus appear repeatedly in the course of this book. Many of these ideas were formulated at a very early stage of the oral and written tradition of Islamic Sufism. Muhammad Hakim al-Tirmidhi (a prodigious writer and close associate of Hazrati Khidr as well as Abu Hanifa) wrote about four levels of the nafs and the heart in the ninth century CE, at about the same time as Sari as-Saqati (who left no writings) was developing further systematic clarification of the stations in Baghdad. Otherwise, most of the earliest extant writings which mention the various levels of the soul date back no earlier than the middle ages, from the writings and sermons of such distinguished Muslim theologians and sheikhs as Imam al-Ghazali, Pir 'Abdul Qadir Gaylani and Mevlana Jalaluddin Rumi.

GLOSSARY

Note: All foreign words in the glossary are of Arabic origin, except where otherwise noted.

A

'Abbasid. The second Islamic dynasty, descended from the Prophet's uncle, al-'Abbas; they succeeded the Umayyid dynasty and reigned from ca. 749-932 CE, retaining titular control during the Buyid and Seljuk dynasties until 1258 CE.

abjad. The system of assigning number values to Arabic letters.

adab. Manners, etiquette and respectful conduct, especially between Sufis.

adhan (azan). The Islamic call to prayer.

ahadith (sing. hadith). Sayings or oral traditions of the Prophet Muhammad recorded outside the Qur'an, and based on an *isnad* (chain of transmission from one witness to another).

Ahl as-Suffa (Ashab-i Suffa). "The people of the veranda (or sofa); a group of ascetic companions of the Prophet, including Hazrat 'Ali, who could be considered the earliest Sufis of Islam.

ahwal (sing. hal). Passing spiritual states or peak experiences on the mystic way.

'alam (pl. 'alamin). World, Universe, or sphere of existence.

'alam-i arwah. The universe of souls, the timeless dimension where souls dwell before coming to earth.

Alastu bi-Rabbikum? "Am I not your Lord?" The question asked by Allah to the souls when they were still "in the loins of Adam." (Qur'an 7:166)

alif-lam bend. Dervish belt or girdle.

'aleihi salaam. "Upon him be peace." A phrase customarily said by Muslims after mentioning the name of a prophet.

alhamdulillah. "All praises are flowing to Allah." A common Arabic expression of thanks, employed frequently in Qur'an.

alif. The initial letter of the Arabic alphabet, equivalent to "A," a silent letter connoting spirit.

amr. Command (Arabic).

Ana'l-Haqq. "I am the Divine Truth (or God)." A controversial ecstatic statement made famous by the tenth century martyr, Mansur al-Hallaj.

ansar. Followers of the Prophet who were converted in Medina.

'arif. A wise person or learned Muslim scholar.

Ashab-i Suffa (Ahl as-Suffa). The mystic companions of the Prophet Muhammad.

Ashadu-an La ilaha ilallah. "I bear witness that there is no deity except the One (Allah)."

Ashk (aşk), ashik. Turkish word for passionate love, lover *(Ishq* in Arabic).

Ashki (Aşki). The Turkish Sufi name and poetical nom-de-plume of Muzaffer Efendi, meaning "the one who is always in love."

Ash'arite. An early school of Sunni Kalam (theology) founded by Abu'l Hasan al-Ash'ari.

Ashura. The tenth of the month of Muharram, the date when the anniversary of the martyrdom of Imam Husayn is commemorated.

asitane. The main seat or primary location of a Sufi tariqat, usually where the founding pir is buried.

'asr. The afternoon prayer in Islam; also the name of a *sura* of the Qur'an.

awliya (sing. waliyullah). "Friends of God" or saints (connotes mastery).

awtad (sing. watad). A saint who is one of the four spiritual "pillars" of the world.

Glossary

Aya Sofya (Hagia Sophia). Famous fourth century Byzantine Church in Sultanahmet, Istanbul, which the Ottomans converted into a great mosque; now a tourist museum.

ayat (ayah). A sign or indication; may denote a verse from a *sura* (chapter) of the Qur'an.

ayn. A letter of the Arabic alphabet.

Azim. A divine name meaning "glory" or "The Glorious One."

B

baqa (baka). "Abiding in God;" a form of resurrection which the seeker experiences after having been lost in Allah *(fana- fi'llah)*.

bala. Arabic for "yes."

Balkh. Refers to ancient Afghanistan where Ibrahim Adham once ruled as king.

baraka. The blessing or spiritual power of a holy person.

Batin. The hidden or inner reality (a divine attribute often mentioned in the Qur'an along with *Zahir*—the outer, the manifest.)

bayat (bay'a). Initiation; joining the right hand in allegiance with a Sufi sheikh to join a tarikat, after the ceremonial manner in which the Prophet received converts into Islam.

Bayt Allah. The House of God, i.e. the Ka'ba.

Bedevi (Badawi) Topu. A section of the standing *dhikr* in which the dervishes crowd in around the sheikh, while chanting powerfully; given as a gift to the Jerrahis from the practices of the Badawi tarikat.

bid'a. Innovation; (heretical) changing of what was handed down by the Prophet Muhammad.

bilocation. The ability to appear in a place other than where one is physically located.

Bismillah (ir-Rahman, ir-Rahim). "In the Name of God," (the Compassionate, the Merciful); an opening invocation found at the beginning of most suras of the Qur'an.

C

Caliph (khalif). "Successor; viceroy." A *khalif* or *khalifa* (pl. *khulafa)* is an initiating leader in a Sufi order, a deputy to the head sheikh. Caliph refers to the political and spiritual head of Islam who is a direct successor of the Prophet Muhammad. The Caliphate was discontinued after the fall of the Ottoman Empire in the 1920's.

chador. A Muslim woman's full covering garment, usually black.

chakra. A subtle spiritual center or nexus in the body. There are seven main chakras.

Chelebi. An honorific title; may also refer to the head of the Mevlevi Order.

chile. A forty-day retreat.

Coptic. Egyptian.

corban. "Sacrifice;" may refer to an offering such as a slain lamb.

D

dalli arakiye. A ribbed cap given at the fourth initiation in some Sufi orders.

Dar al-Islam. "The abode of peace;" a land where Islamic practice and government prevails.

dede. "Grandfather;" an elder, or in some cases a sheikh.

dergah. "The Sultan's court;" can refer to a main Sufi Lodge.

dhikr (zikr), dhikrullah. "Remembrance (of Allah);" can refer to the chanting of the names of God (especially *La ilaha ilallah),* often in a circle or in lines, as in a Sufi ceremony.

dhikr al-mawt. The remembrance of death (or of one's own mortality).

Dhul-Hijja. The month in the Islamic calendar when Hajj or pilgrimage is made.

Din-i-Muhammad. The religion of Muhammad.

dua. A prayer; a personal, often extemporaneous, divine supplication, frequently uttered with palms raised in prayer.

Glossary

E

Efendi. (Greek) A Turkish honorific title similar to "sir;" may also indicate a grand-sheikh.

ekstasis. The Greek root of the word ecstasy, meaning to "stand outside one's self" or "be beside oneself" (with joy, or the reconciliation of opposites).

Elohim. Biblical Hebrew for "the gods" (singular for God=*Eloha*), etymologically related to the Arabic Allah, ("The One") and the Aramaic word for God, *Alaha.*

esma. Arabic for "name;" may infer one of the 99 divine names from the Qur'an.

Esma al-Husna. The most beautiful (divine) names; a Qur'anic phrase.

Estaghfirullah. "I seek forgiveness from Allah;" a common Islamic phrase.

evrad. Plural for *wird,* an Islamic liturgy, including passages from Qur'an, recited on various occasions.

Eyvallah. Common Turkish phrase of consent meaning, "All right," or "I accept (everything, as being from Allah)."

F

fajr (prayers). The first of the five times a day Islamic prayers, made just before dawn.

falsafa. The Muslim philosophical movement of the early centuries of Islam.

fana. "Annihilation," in *tassawuf* (Sufism), it refers to being lost or effaced in the sheikh, in the Prophet, or in God, a positive spiritual state of ego transcendence which may be followed by the station of *baqa* (being found or "subsisting" in God).

fana-fi'llah. "Lost or effaced in God." (See *fana* above)

Fatih. ("Conqueror"); an area of Istanbul, named after Mehmet II the Conqueror.

Fatiha. The opening sura of the Qur'an; to recite the first sura, whose utterance—especially among Islamic mystics—is considered to contain great power of spiritual blessing.

Fatimid. Isma'ili dynasty which founded Cairo, setting up a rival Caliphate descended from the family of the Prophet (909-1171 CE).

fatwa. A ruling by an Islamic religious authority.

Ferhad. A famous lover who bore through a mountain for the sake of his lover, Shirin.

fiqh. Jurisprudence; there are four major Sunni schools of *fiqh* or observation of Islamic law, as well as Shi'ite and Kharijite schools of *fiqh.*

firdaws. Paradise; a walled garden.

fikr, fikra. Meditation; silent repetition or contemplation of the divine names, or of *dhikr.*

fu'ad. The inner heart.

fuqara. Plural of *fakir;* poor ones, dervishes.

Futuwwah. Chivalry.

G

Gabriel (Jibra'il). The angelic divine messenger who delivered the Qur'anic revelations from Allah Most High to the Prophet Muhammad.

Gaylan (Guilan). The province of Persia in which Abdul Qadir Gaylani was born.

ghalaba, ghlabat. The overwhelming quality of Allah; rapture.

ghazal (gazel). A lyric poem.

ghous (ghawth). A great saint, "helper" and protector of his community.

grand vezir (wazir or vizier). Prime minister to the ruling sultan.

gülbang. Closing prayer at end of *dhikr* ceremony; Bektashi and Janissary prayer.

H

hadith (pl. ahadith). An oral tradition or non-Qur'anic saying of the Prophet Muhammad.

hadith qudsi. A sacred hadith in which Allah speaks directly in the first person through the Prophet Muhammad.

hafiz. One who has memorized the entire Qur'an and can chant it by heart.

hajj. "Pilgrimage"; visiting Mecca during the Islamic month of Dhul-Hijja, with its rites, including circling the Ka'ba, visiting Mina, Arafat (and Medina); one of the five pillars of Islam.

hakikat (haqiqa). Ultimate Reality, the realm of highest truth, the One Source which transcends all duality or separation.

hal (pl. Ahwal), halat. A spiritual state or peak experience, especially an ecstatic one.

halal. That which is considered lawful or permissible in Islam (as opposed to *haram*, forbidden).

halvet (khalwa). A spiritual retreat; traditionally entailing forty days and nights of seclusion.

halvethane. Retreat lodge.

Halveti-Jerrahi (Order). A Turkish Sufi tarikat which was founded in Istanbul by Pir Nureddin al-Jerrahi ca.1704 CE, a branch of the older Khalwati (Halveti) Order.

Hanafi. One of the four Sunni schools of jurisprudence, or madhahib, founded by Imam Abu Hanifa (d.767 CE) of Kufa.

Hanbali, Hanbalite. One of the four Sunni schools of jurisprudence, founded by Imam Ahmad ibn Hanbal (d.855 CE); generally considered the most conservative of the four schools.

hanif. A believer in the One God (such as Abraham); the hanifs are mentioned in the Qur'an as pious monotheists in Arabia and elsewhere prior to the time of the Qur'anic revelations.

Haqq (Hak). "Truth" (Ultimate Truth or "God").

haram. That which is forbidden in Islam (can refer to certain acts or foods, such as pork).

Haram. "Restricted, set apart." May refer to the sacred areas in

Mecca, Medina and the Temple Mount in Jerusalem.

Haydar i-Karrar. A name referring to Hazrat 'Ali, the "courageous (fighting) lion" of Allah.

haydariyya. A sleeveless vest worn by dervishes after the manner of Hazrat 'Ali.

Hayy. "Life" (the divine life which never dies).

Hazrat, Hazrati. "Presence;" an honorific title placed before the name of a revered, holy person.

henotrophy. The concept that physical creation is transcendent spirit which has become "congealed" into solid matter so that the divine is now actually limited by natural laws.

Hermetic. Esoteric alchemical tradition, associated with the wisdom of Hermes Trismegistus and the ancient initiatory mystery schools of Egypt.

hidayat. "Guidance." (true or divine guidance).

Hijaz. The lands of Arabia, including Mecca and Medina.

hijra (hegira). "Flight or exodus;" generally refers to the Prophet Muhammad's departure from Mecca to Yathrib (Medina) in 622 CE, which marks the beginning of the Islamic calendar.

hikma, hikmat. "Wisdom;" also used in the Qur'an to signify the oral esoteric tradition, as in the saying: "We have given you the *kitab* ("the book", i.e. Qur'an) and the *hikma* (wisdom)."

hizmet. "Service"(duty); to serve Allah by serving and helping others.

Hiya. (Arabic) The feminine form of *Hu* ("He," the Divine Essence or Presence).

hizb. A portion of the Qur'an; also a liturgical work by Pir Ahmad Badawi.

hoja. (Turkish) A Muslim teacher.

houris. The feminine companions of paradise mentioned in the Qur'an. The male equivalent (mentioned in Qur'an 52:24) is called *gilma-nun (llahum),* (handsome) young males.

hulul, hululi. "Descent;" the idea that the divine can incarnate in the body of a mortal person (a heretical idea in Islam, whether describing Jesus, al-Hallaj, an avatar, or a Pharaoh). There is also a Hululi sect whose members believe in divine incarnation.

I

Iblis. "The adversary," the name by which the Qur'an refers to the *shaitan,* Satan, or devil. In the Qur'an, Iblis is depicted as a rebellious *jinni,* rather than a fallen angel.

Ibrahim. Arabic name for the prophet Abraham (upon him be peace).

'ilm. Knowledge.

ijazet (icazet). A diploma, usually a long scroll, which shows the lineage of a sheikh or sheikha.

ijma. Community consensus.

ijtihad. Individual reason and judgment (to be used when no relevant ruling can be found in Qur'an).

ilahi (pl. ilahiler). Divine hymn; mystic poems which are sung by dervishes.

imam. One who leads prayers, or heads a congregation; in Shi'ism, an intercessory title (such as Imam 'Ali).

iman. Faith.

insha'llah. "If God wills it." A common Arabic expression.

Insan-i kamil. The perfect human being.

Isa. The Arabic name for Jesus (upon him be peace).

isharat. A special esoteric code of the mystics which veils the meaning of their words.

ishq (ashk or aşk). Love or desire.

isnad. Chain of transmission supporting and authenticating the sayings of the Prophet.

istikhara (istihare). "Asking for the best choice;" a special two-rakat prayer (based on sunna) before sleep, asking for divine guidance or dream resolution on some matter.

i'tikaf. "To stay in a place;" the spiritual practice of secluding oneself in a mosque, especially during the last ten days of Ramadan.

ittihad. Pertaining to union, or community consensus.

J

Ja'fari. A Shi'ite school of jurisprudence.

jahannam (jehennam) Arabic for "hell" (from Aramaic, *Gehenna,* the name of the place where rubbish was burned outside old Jerusalem).

jahiliyyah, jahiliyyat. The "time of ignorance" and paganism (particularly in Arabia) prior to historical Islam.

jahri. Spoken aloud (three of the five times a day prayers are *jahri;* the other two are done silently).

jalal. The powerful qualities (including wrath and splendor).

Janissary. "New Troops" (from *Yeni çeri* in Turkish); an elite Ottoman military corp, comprised mainly of Christians, conscripted as boys and trained in the sultan's service.

janna (jennah). Arabic for "the (enclosed) garden;" paradise or heaven.

jamal. The gentle, beautiful qualities.

jami (cami), Jami. Turkish word for a "mosque;" a divine name meaning "the Collector;" also the name of a famous mystic poet.

Jerrah Pasha (Cerra Paşa). The section of Istanbul where Nureddin Jerrahi was born; also the site of a well-known hospital (thus the meaning of Jerrah, which is "Surgeon").

jihad. To struggle (in the path of righteousness). The lesser *jihad* is outward, defensive warfare against an enemy or oppressor; the greater *jihad* is the inner struggle against the negative manifestations of the *nafs* or ego.

jinn (sing. jinni). Unseen beings of the subtle world (related to "genie" and "genius"), distinct from angelic beings.

Jum'a. Friday, The day of congregational prayer and worship in Islam.

jumhar (cumhar). A collective hymn, sung by all (especially at the beginning of standing *dhikr).*

Glossary

K

Ka'ba. The central black, cublical shrine of Islamic pilgrimage, located in Mecca. It is considered to have been built by Abraham as the first temple to the One God.

Kabbala. The primarily oral Jewish mystical tradition; the *Zohar* and *Sefer Yetzirah* are part of its written corpus.

kafir. One who rejects the faith.

kalam. Islamic scholastic theology.

Karagümrük. The section of Istanbul where the main Halveti-Jerrahi *dergah* is located.

Karbala. The place in Iraq where Husayn, the grandson of the Prophet, was martyred.

kaside. A mystic ode (often sung over the chanting of the divine names during *dhikr*).

Kawthar. A blessed fountain in paradise.

khafi (hafi). Silent or hidden; also a divine name meaning "remedy."

Khajarite. An early separatist school of Muslim thought.

khalwa, Khilvat (halvet), The practice of spiritual retreat.

Khalwati (Halveti), Khalwatiyya. The Sufi order of retreatants, founded in the middle ages by Pir Umar al-Halveti and Pir Yahya-i Shirvani, one branch of which became the Turkish Halveti-Jerrahi Order.

khanqah. Persian word for a dervish lodge or convent.

khannas. The "whispering" inner urge to do evil, mentioned in Qur'an.

khilafat. The process by which a sheikh invests a dervish with rank and authority of *khalifa* (deputy or sheikh).

khirka (hirka). A woolen jacket; a dervish cloak.

khutba. Sermon.

Khwajagan. The Sufi Masters of Central Asia.

kitab. Book.

Knights Templar. A small fraternity of European Christian knights who stationed themselves at the Temple mount in Jerusalem during the crusades, protecting and acting as a bank for Christian pilgrims; they are thought to have brought certain secret mystical ideas back to the West.

L

Labbayk. "Here I am (Lord!)" The traditional cry of the *hajji* (pilgrim) during *hajj*.

lahut. divine nature (as opposed to human nature, *nasut*).

La ilaha illallah. *Tawhid;* the quintessential Islamic declaration of unity: "Nothing exists except the One (Al-Lah); there is nothing worthy of worship but God, the Only Reality."

libertinism (ibaha). Pejorative label applied to various (often secretive) sects who are thought to stray too far from normative religious practice (accusations may include: free love, dualistic or hulul doctrines, use of intoxicants, even anti-authoritarianism).

Lote Tree (of the Far Boundary). The point in the heavenly night journey of Muhammad beyond which no being or angel could pass to enter the divine presence (yet the Prophet, in complete *fana,* did pass it).

lubb. The innermost level (or kernel) of the heart.

M

madhhab (pl. madhahib). Islamic school of jurisprudence; there are four major sunni schools and several of Shi'i persuasion.

madrasa (pl. madaris). An Islamic school or university of higher study.

madzub (majdhub). One who is appears "crazy" with divine love and attraction.

Maghrib. "the place of sunset;" sunset prayers; also, the lands West of Arabia (including Western North Africa).

Magian, Magi. A wise person, astrologer or priest, associated with the ancient Persian-Zoroastrian tradition.

mahabba (muhabbet). Spiritual love *(agape);* friendship.

Glossary

Mahdi. "The Guided One;" a great being whom, according to popular Islamic belief, will appear toward the end of time, after the return of the Messiah Jesus, to restore righteousness to the world.

makam (maqam; pl. makamat). one's spiritual station or place (such as "the fourth level" of the seven levels; a musical mode (such as *hijaz* or *rast),* especially in and Arabic and Turkish music.

malamat, malami (melami), Malamatiyya, Malamiyya. The spiritual way of blame; a sect (also a *makam* on the Sufi path) in which the Malami purposely eschews outward displays of piety and religious convention so that the false ego will receive public contempt instead of praise. This cultivates humility and checks any "holier-than-thou" tendencies.

Maliki (school), Imam Maliki ibn Anas. Founder of one of the four major Sunni schools of jurisprudence.

Mamluk. Originally a military corps, the Mamluks established a brief sultanate during the late Middle Ages, associated with Egypt and other nearby territories.

Mandaean. An Iraqi sect associated with John the Baptist, which rejects Jesus as Messiah.

Manichean, Manicheism, Mani. Mani (215–276 CE) established a syncretic, gnostic-dualist Persian religion which accepted the prophets of all religions; he was imprisoned and martyred.

Maqam Ibrahim. "The standing-place of Abraham;" a stone footprint of the patriarch located in a small shrine next to the Ka'ba in Mecca.

marifat (ma'rifa). "Knowledge;" one of the four levels in Sufism, associated with higher understanding and the living embodiment of Truth *(hakikat).*

Masha'llah. "How wonderful that God has willed this!" a common Arabic expression.

masjid. A mosque, a place of Islamic worship.

maya. (Sanskrit) Illusion; associated with Indian spiritual thought; the idea that what the senses apprehend of the physical world is a misleading perception (maya), veiling a greater spiritual Reality—like a rope in the dark that appears to be a snake but is not.

mazar. (Persian) A tomb or sepulcher.

medet. Help or aid; the Sufis often call out for spiritual assistance to Allah, a saint or a *pir* (ex. *Medet ya Hazrat Pir,* meaning "Help us, O venerable Pir").

meshk (meşk). (Turkish) Musical practice; dervishes who gather for *meshk* usually sit, singing ilahis and chanting divine esmas, often with instrumental accompaniment.

meshreb. Temperment, character or natural disposition.

mevlud. A poem by Süleyman Chelebi depicting the nativity of the Prophet Muhammad, which is sung by special singers on the Prophet's birthday or during a religious service to commemorate a departed soul.

meydan. An open space or circle; often associated with the area in a *tekke* where dervishes gather to make the ceremony of *dhikr.*

mihnah. Inquisition.

mihrab. A niche in the wall of a mosque indicating the direction of prayers *(kibla).*

minbar. A pulpit in a mosque with a staircase, from which the Friday sermon is given.

mi'raj. The Night Journey of the Prophet Muhammad.

mithaq. Covenant.

Mount Hira. The mountain near Mecca where the Prophet Muhammad meditated in a cave and received the first revelation of the Qur'an (also call Jabal an-Nur).

mu'azzin (muezzin). One who makes the call to prayer in a mosque or from a *minaret.*

mubah. Neutral according to Islamic law; neither *halal* (permissible) or *haram* (forbidden).

muhabbet (mahabba). Spiritual love *(agape);* friendship.

muhib. One who loves; a sympathizer or friend of a dervish order.

muksharaf. Spiritual revelation from the unseen world.

muqarrabun. Qur'anic word meaning: "one who is very near Allah."

Glossary

murid, mureed. "One who is willing;" a student of a Sufi teacher.

murshid, murshida. "A guide" (from *rashid),* especially a Sufi spiritual teacher (male or female) or *sheikh(a).*

mushahada. Pertaining to the meditative or visionary way.

mushrik. Idolator.

muslim. One who is submitted to the divine will (in peace).

(Sahih al-) Muslim. A famous hadith collection by Abu'l Husayn Muslim (816-873 CE).

Mutu kabla anta mu'tu. A famous mystical utterance of the Prophet Muhammad meaning: "Die (to your limited ego-self) before you die."

Mu'tazilite. An early school of Islamic thought which took a position between two extremes, such as taking sides in the Muslim Civil War between 'Ali and Muawiyya, or between judging a Muslim who committed a grave sin as either a Muslim or infidel.

muwahhid. A person who is truly cognizant of the divine unity.

N

nafs. The soul, inner self, ego, life-force; associated with the breath.

nafs al-ammara. The animal soul, one's carnal nature, the "lower," less civilized, or self-centered impulses, the commanding self; the lowest of seven levels of the soul or nafs.

nafs ar-Rahman. The breath of the Merciful.

nafs as-safiya. The pure soul, the highest level of the *nafs.*

namaz, nimaz. Persian word for prayer *(salat* or *salah* in Arabic).

nasut. Human nature (as opposed to divine nature, *lahut).*

Nasruddin Hoja (or Mulla Nasruddin). An often humorous fictional character in many Sufi teaching stories.

Nefilim. Mentioned in Genesis 6:2 and Numbers 13:33 as "sons of God" or "beings of great renown" who existed before the Biblical flood and who married "the daughters of men."

Neo-Platonism. Third century mystic, philosophical school founded by Plotinus, which combined Platonic and Oriental mysticism with elements of Christianity, positing that all existence emanates from the One (to whom all souls return); a precursor to Sufism whose schools were closed in the sixth century by the Roman emperor Justinian.

Nestorian. A Christian sect, founded in the sixth century by Nestorius, the Syrian patriarch of Constantinople, which held beliefs about Jesus and Mary similar to Islam, namely that Jesus was a human (the Christ spirit being divine) and that Mary was not the "Mother of God" *(Theotakos)*, but simply the human mother of Jesus; he was exiled by the Church as a heretic.

ney. A flute of reed, often utilized to accompany the Mevlevi turning ceremony *(sama)*.

Nuri Muhammad(i). The Muhammadan Light, the first light of eternity through which creation was brought into existence, a concept first elucidated by the theologian, Tabari.

Nurun 'ala Nur. Light upon light; the divine light behind the soul's light, mentioned in Qur'an 24:35.

O

Orientalism. The study of the Oriental (Middle-Eastern) literature and religions by Western scholars; it often tends to distort Islam, viewing it unfavorably through Western biases.

orthopraxy. Right practice or action; Islam is characterized by orthopraxis, allowing Muslims to choose from several interpretations or schools *(madhab)*, rather than orthodoxy, which insists on one single "right" belief or interpretation (as promoted in Latin and Eastern Orthodox Christianity).

Ottoman. The Turkish empire, founded in the thirteenth century by Osman, which ruled most of the Islamic world until its final demise at the end of World War I.

P

padishah (padişah). Ruler or sovereign; the Turkish sultan of the

Ottoman Empire.

pantheism. "God in all," the belief that the universe is the emanation of the body of God, that God is nature, rather than a personality or force transcendent of creation.

Peshitta. The New Testament in the original Aramaic language, the language of Jesus.

postnishin (postnişin). Head of a religious order; the Sufi grand-sheikh who sits on the blue post (sheepskin).

Q

qadar (kader). Destiny or preordained fate; also the *esma (Qadir, al-Qahr)* signifying Divine Power.

qadi (kadi). A judge of Islamic canon law.

Qahhar (al-Qahr). *Esma* (divine name) signifying divine sovereignty and victory; the overwhelming, overarching) aspect of the Divine

Qalandar (Kalendar). A wandering dervish, an unconventional bohemian. A loose mystical movement out of which many of the early *turuq* developed, such as the Yasawis, Alawis, Bektashis and Bayramis. This Khorasanian stream, with its outwardly antinomian, *malami* tendencies, was more open to the participation of women and non-Muslims than traditional *turuq*.

qalbi. The heart; the innermost part.

Qarmathian. A (heretical) mystical gnostic-Shi'ite-Sevener organization founded in the ninth century CE by Hamdan Qarmat, which fostered a political peasant uprising against the Islamic authorities, removing and hiding the black stone from the Ka'ba, finally returning it years later.

Qayyum. Divine *esma* signifying the Self-Subsisting and Everlasting.

qibla. The direction faced during prayer (for Muslims: the Ka'ba in Mecca).

qiyyam (kiyyam). Standing; dhikr which is done standing in rows is called *qiyyam dhikr.*

Qur'an. The scripture of Islam, revealed by Allah, through the angel Gabriel, to the Prophet Muhammad over a course of 23 years.

Qur'an al-Karim. The Generous Qur'an.

qutb (qutub; pl. aqtab or aktab). The spiritual pole or axis, a saintly person who may be known or hidden; one who has been divinely appointed as a leader of spiritual affairs in the world during their lifetime. Such a person often spiritually intercedes to help stop wars, mitigate disasters or bring succor to other souls.

qutb'ul arifin. Qutb of the wise.

qutb'ul medar. Intercessory pole who furnishes spiritual aid and assistance to others.

R

Rabbi'l alamin. The Lord of the worlds, the Lord of countless universes.

rahmani. Having a sweet, gentle or uplifting spiritual quality, as in rahmani music.

rajil. A man (in the highest, most honorable sense), a true human being.

raji'un. Those who return *(raj'ah)* to the world after spiritual ascension. An idea associated with Shi'ite doctrine, such as the return of the twelfth imam.

rak'a (pl. raka'at). A cycle of Islamic prayer; for instance, the morning salat consists of two *raka'at* (in each *rak'a,* one recites *tekbir* and Qur'an while standing, bows *(ruku),* performs two full prostrations *(sajda),* and after repeating a second rakat, ends the prayer sitting in the kneeling position).

rakiye. A vertically ribbed dervish cap, usually white.

rasul, Rasulullah. A prophet or divine messenger; "Rasulullah" (Rasul Allah) is a commonly used Islamic title referring to the Messenger of Allah, the Prophet Muhammad.

ribat. A hospice or fort, originally connected with religious duties and Islamic military service; in time they also became meeting-places (khanaqas) for Sufis.

rishi. A sage, poet, or meditation adept associated with the Vedic (Hindu) tradition.

ruhaniat. Arabic word referring to the spirit *(ruh);* also the name of an American Sufi Order in the lineage of Hazrat Inayat Khan Chisti, founded by Murshid Samuel Lewis.

ruh. Spirit (or soul); Jesus (Isa) is known in Islam as *Ruh Allah* (the Spirit of God).

ruhu haiwani. The animal nature (animal soul), common to all living, breathing creatures.

ruhu insani. Human nature (human soul), a higher (fourth level) aspect of the soul possessed only by human beings.

ruhu madeni. The mineral soul; corresponds to the lowest level.

ruhu nafsani. The personal soul; corresponds to the third level.

ruhu nebati. Vegetable soul; corresponds to the second level.

ruhu sirr. The secret soul; a higher, eternal aspect of the human soul, corresponding to the seventh level.

ruhu sultani. The sultan soul; a higher ruling (kingly) aspect of the soul, the inner master; corresponds to the sixth level.

rukhsa. A "dispensation" or "indulgence;" a loosening of a strict rule.

ruku. Bowing, a prayerful half prostration; to stand and bend over with hands on knees.

S

sahaba. A companion of the Prophet Muhammad.

safa. Pure.

sadaqa. Alms or charity to the poor.

sadr. The breast (or heart).

sahw. The state of sobriety (as opposed to ecstacy or *wajd.)*

Safavid (or Safawid dynasty). An Iranian Shi'ite dynasty founded by Safiyyaddin (Sheikh Safi) which lasted from 1501 to 1732.

sajda (sejda). (Ritual) prostration, kneeling with forehead and palms to the ground (a part of Islamic prayers, and also found in other spiritual paths).

saki. (Turkish) Cupbearer or distributor of water; a spiritual teacher to a novice; God. (Saki or sake is also a Japanese alcoholic rice drink.)

sakr. Intoxication.

(as-)salaam(u) 'aleikum. "(May) Peace be with you;" a common Islamic greeting, to which the response is: *w'aleikum salaam,* "And with you be peace."

salallahu 'aleihi wa salaam. (abbreviated as s.a.w.s.) "Peace and blessings be upon him;" a blessing of respect traditionally uttered by pious Muslims after mentioning the Prophet Muhammad; *'aleihi salaam* is said after mentioning any other prophet, etc.

salat (salah). Prayer *(namaz in Persian)*.

salawat. A blessing on the Prophet Muhammad, one of the most common being: *Allahuma sali 'ala Sayyiddina Muhammad* ("May Allah bless our master Muhammad").

Salawat Qutbiyya. The qutb's salawat; a special blessing by Pir Nureddin Jerrahi which is recited by his dervishes, especially at the beginning of *dhikr* and in the *wird* (dervish liurgy).

sama (sema). "Listening;" a sacred ceremony involving uplifting spiritual music and dance (specifically among the Mevlevis, "the turn" or ceremony of the whirling dervishes).

Sasanian. Persian (Zoroastrian) Empire which lasted from 224 BCE to 642 CE.

Sayyid. Master or Lord; a title for a descendent of the Prophet Muhammad.

Sayyidina. "Our Master."

Seljuk. A Turkic people in military service to the 'Abbasids, who took over the empire (ca.1038 CE) and installed their leader, Toghrul Bey, as sultan of the Seljuk dynasty.

semahane. The meeting-house where *sama (sema)* takes place.

Sepher Bereshith. (Hebrew) The Book of Genesis, the first book of the Torah in the Hebrew Bible, and of the "Old Testament."

Sertarik Baba. Captain; the second-in-command sheikh in a *tekke,* who sits on the red post located to the right of the head sheikh, who occupies the central blue post of guidance.

shafa'at. Intercessory help.

Shafi'i, Shafi'iyyah. A school of Islamic jurisprudence named after Muhammad ibn Idris al-Shafi'i (767-819 CE); it emphasized the legal authority of Qur'an and Sunna over *ijma* (community consensus) and *ijtihad* (individual judgment).

shahada. Bearing witness to the divine unity and the authenticity of the prophetic message brought by Muhammad, the prerequisite declaration by which a person becomes a Muslim: *Ashadu an La ilaha illallah wa ashadu anna Muhammad ar-rasulullah.*

shaitani. Having a profane, decadent or lewd character (as in *shaitani* music).

shariat (shari'a). The sacred law; the basic religious observance and duties of Islam as revealed in Qur'an; the first of the four worlds or levels, *shariat* being the foundation of the other three *(tarikat, hakikat, and marifat).*

shath (pl.shatahat, shatiyat). An ecstatic saying, uttered in a state of spiritual intoxication.

sheikh (shaykh). An elder or "old man" and leader of a community or village *(sheikha* is the female equivalent); a murshid, spiritual guide, or leader of a Sufi Community.

Shema Yisrael. The Hebrew declaration of divine unity, as revealed in the Torah by the Prophet Moses: "Hear O Israel, the Lord *(YHVH)* our God, the Lord is one." (Deut. 6:4).

Shi'i, (pl. Shi'a) Shi'ite. The smaller branch of Islam (prevalent today in Iran and Iraq) which separated from the main (Sunni) body of Muslims, in order to follow the spiritual leadership of Imam 'Ali ibn Abi Talib and his descendants, who include the twelve imams.

Shirin. The woman of Middle-Eastern legend who inspired Ferhad to accomplish near-impossible deeds out of love for her.

shuhud. Consciousness; verbal noun of the verb *shahida,* meaning "to witness."

sidq, siddiq. Truthful, sincere; a title given to the first caliph, Abu Bakr.

Sifaat Allah. The divine qualities or attributes of Allah.

sikke. A dervish headdress; a tall, conical tombstone-like hat worn by Mevlevis.

silsila. The "chain" or lineage of succession from one Sufi master to another.

sirat al-mustaqim. The straight or direct path, as advocated in the Qur'an.

sirr. Secret, mystery.

sohbet. Conversation, spiritual discourse by a teacher.

Sophia. (Greek)Wisdom, personified as a woman in the biblical Song of Solomon and Proverbs; also the goddess of wisdom. The word Sufism may be etymologically related to the word *sophia.*

subhana Rabbil 'ala. "Glory be to my Lord, the Highest Sustainer." Arabic phrase repeated three times while making full prostration *(sajda)* during Muslim prayers.

Sufi, Sufism. The mystical path of Islam, the religion of the heart; also referenced as *tasawwuf* and *tarikat.*

sultan. Sovereign ruler or Lord (in an Islamic country).

Sultan Enbiya. Sovereign of the prophets; a sobriquet for the Prophet Muhammad.

suluk. The path, the journey to God taken by the Sufi, *salik* being a sojourner.

sunna (sunnat). The customs, words and actions of the Prophet Muhammad, which serve as a model and precedent for good Muslim behavior, in addition to the Qur'an.

Sunni, Sunnite. The main body of Muslims (as opposed to the ten percent who are Shi'ite, who don't accept some of the Sunni caliphs as legitimate); most Sufis are Sunnis.

sura. A chapter of the Qur'an (which contains 114 suras).

Glossary

T

tabi'un. The followers or believers; the first generation after the passing of the Prophet Muhammad. The *tabi'un* received the teachings of Islam from those who had received them directly from the Prophet during his lifetime.

tafsir. "To explain;" a teaching elucidating the meaning of passages from the Qur'an.

tahajjud nimaz. Night vigil; extra prayers performed during the night after Isha prayers.

takbir (tekbir). "To magnify;" to pronounce "Allahu Akbar" ("God is great"), especially at the start of prayers.

takke. A white dervish cap.

taksim. A division; an instrumental, improvised musical prelude.

talbiya. Words of Abraham found in the Qur'an which are recited by the pilgrims on *hajj: Labbayk Allahuma, labbayk!* etc. ("Here I am God!").

tarawih. Special group prayers performed in the evenings during Ramadan (instituted during the reign of Caliph 'Umar).

tarikat, tariqa (pl.turuq). "The (mystic) path" of the heart; a Sufi order; one of the four worlds or levels in Islamic Sufism.

tasawwuf. Sufism, esotericism, the science of the soul.

tatawwur. Bilocution, appearing in two places at once.

Tat twam asi. "That thou art;" a Sanskrit saying from Hindu Upanishads, identifying oneself (the immortal soul) with the Divine Source, the Only Being, God or Brahman.

tawaf. One ritual circumambulation around the Ka'ba.

tawakkul. Trust in God.

tawba. Repentance.

tawhid. To unify, to acknowledge the divine unity (from the verbal noun, *wahhada)*. The Arabic phrase of unity, *La ilaha illallah,* is known as *tawhid (tevhid* in Turkish).

tayy-i mekan. To travel through time and space, so that one appears in a distant place.

tejelli (tecelli). A manifestation or unveiling of the divine, for instance, in the human form; transfiguration.

tekke. A dervish lodge.

tesbih (tasbih). Dervish prayer beads; doing *tesbih* is repeating one's practice of *dhikr* or divine esmas; also the words *Subhan Allah* ("Glory to God") are called *tesbih*.

Topkapi. (Turkish) The name of an elaborate palace complex and haram of the Ottoman sultan in Istanbul; now a museum.

Tigris River. An ancient river in Mesopotamia which joins the Euphrates.

türbe. (Turkish) Tomb.

turuq (sing. tarikat). Sufi orders.

Twelvers. Shi'ite school of thought recognizing the twelve imams.

U

'ubudiyyat. The highest station, that of servanthood to one's Lord.

ujub. Spiritual pride or inflation.

'ulama. The body of Islamic theological scholars.

umma. A community or nation.

ummati-Muhammad. The community of people who follow the Prophet Muhammad.

Ummayad. The first dynasty of (Sunni) Islam, 661-750 CE.

'umra. The lesser pilgrimage to Mecca, made outside of the month-long period of Hajj.

uns. Intimacy.

urs. The date of passing, usually of a Sufi saint, which may be memorialized with liturgy or *dhikr.*

Üsküdar. A section of Istanbul on the Asian side of the Bosphorus.

usul. A rhythmic pattern; among Sufis, may refers to the formal group recitation of their special liturgy *(wird)* and divine names (esmas) during meetings at their lodge.

Glossary

V

Vedanta, vedantic. Referring to the Hindu spiritual teaching of Vedanta ("The End of the Vedas"); Advaita Vedanta, the non-dual branch of this tradition, has certain similarities with Sufism, especially Ibn 'Arabi's teachings on the unity of being, *wahdat al-wajud.*

vezir (Turkish, also: vizier, wazir). Minister. The grand vezir was second in power to the sultan.

W

Wahhabi (Salafi). A conservative, militant Muslim sect, established by 'Abdul Wahhab in Najd (Saudi Arabia) in the late eighteenth century, which still controls Saudi Arabia today. They set the tone for other strict, modern fundamentalist groups such as the Taliban in Afghanistan.

wahdat al-wajud. The unity of being; in simplest terms, the non-dual teaching that everything is part of the One Divine Being, and that no separate beings actually exist.

Wahid. The attribute of Divine Oneness.

wajd (wejd). Ecstasy; a state of spiritual upliftment.

waliyullah (pl. awliya). Friend of God; a spiritual master (saint).

waqfa. Pilgrim ritual done standing at Arafat during Hajj.

wazir (vezir, vizier). Political minister.

Wird as-Sattar. One of the longer litanies of the Halvet-Jerrahi Order.

Wird-i Yahya. A Halveti litany composed by Pir Yahya Shirvani.

wujud. Being or existence.

Y

Ya Rabb. "O Lord."

Yathrib. The Arabian city to which Muhammad fled from Mecca; after the *hijra* it was renamed Medina.

Yusuf. Joseph in Arabic; in the Qur'an, the name refers to the

Hebrew Prophet Joseph.

Z

Zabur. The Psalms of David.

zahid. (Turkish) Ascetic.

Zahir. A divine attribute: The Manifest, the Outward (as opposed to *Batin,* the Hidden, the Inward); *Zahir* and *Batin* also connote respectively, the exoteric and esoteric meaning.

Zahirite. An early literalist Islamic school of thought, now extinct.

zakirbashi. (zakirbaşi—Turkish) The music leader and director among the Sufis.

zam-zam. The pure water that emerges from an underground spring in Mecca.

zandaqa. Heresy or blasphemy.

zat, Zat-ullah. Essence, the Divine Essence.

Zaydi. A Shi'i school of jurisprudence.

zindiq. "Freethinker;" heretic or dualist (from Persian *zand).*

zuhr. The noon prayer.

zunnar. A sacred thread worn across the chest by Zoroastrians.

ABOUT THE AUTHOR

Photo by Nicola D'Antona.

GREGORY BLANN, also known as Sheikh Muhammad Jamal al-Jerrahi, has been an active student of Sufism and the world's religions for over four decades. He received initiation from Pir Vilayat Khan in the Inayatiyya in 1980 and served as a representative in that order for a number of years. In 1990, he received *bayat* (initiation) in the Halveti-Jerrahi Order from Sheikh Nur al-Jerrahi (Lex Hixon), and also studied with Safer Efendi. He was given the name Muhammad Jamal, and became a Jerrahi sheikh in 1994. He worked closely with Sheikh Nur for four years, translating the traditional mystic hymns of the Jerrahis from Turkish into English, to be sung by dervishes in the West.

Sheikh Muhammad Jamal received a degree in music and art from Vanderbilt University in 1974 and continued his studies at Massachusetts College of Art in Boston. He also trained for ten years in Carnatic South Indian music. In more recent years, he has worked in the graphic arts and web design field, published numerous articles on spirituality, led local Sufi groups in Nashville, Tennessee and taught Sufism in various cities throughout the United States. He has also been a frequent participant in ecumenical dialogues and panels, serving on the board of the Interfaith Alliance of Middle Tennessee. Sheikh Muhammad Jamal brings to the present work the experience of over forty years on the Sufi path, as a member of both a contemporary universalist Western Sufi Order originating in India and a traditional Islamic dervish Order with Ottoman Turkish roots. He is an advocate of universal spirituality, affirming the essential core of unity, love and compassion in all the world's great spiritual traditions, beyond narrow sectarian divisions and distortions which manifest as religious violence.

Made in the USA
Monee, IL
14 August 2023

41039148R00197